# FRENCH
# TEXTILES

FROM 1760
TO THE PRESENT

# FRENCH TEXTILES

## FROM 1760 TO THE PRESENT

Mary Schoeser
Kathleen Dejardin

LAURENCE KING

In Memory of John Richard Schoeser
and Alfred Leonard Troye

Published 1991 by Laurence King Ltd

*British Library Cataloguing in Publication Data*
Schoeser, Mary
French textiles 1760 to the present
1. France. Textiles. Manufacture, history
I. Title   II. Dejardin, Kathleen
677
ISBN 1-85669-006-7

Picture research by Susan Bolsom-Morris
Designed by Karen Stafford
Printed in Singapore by Toppan Ltd

# CONTENTS

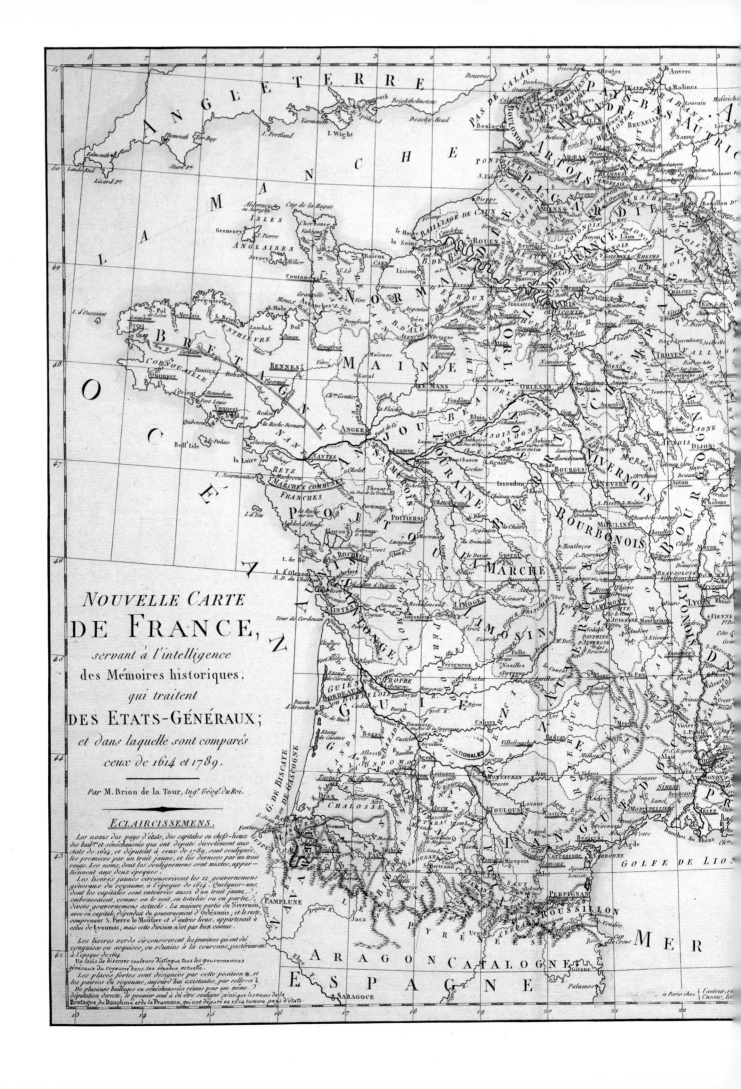

## NOUVELLE CARTE DE FRANCE,

servant à l'intelligence des Mémoires historiques, qui traitent DES ETATS-GÉNÉRAUX; et dans laquelle sont comparés ceux de 1614 et 1789.

Par M. Brion de la Tour, Ing.' Géog.' du Roi.

### ECLAIRCISSEMENS.

Les noms des pays d'états, des capitales ou chefs-lieux des bail.'' et sénéchaussées qui ont député directement aux états de 1614, et députent à ceux de 1789, sont soulignés ; les premiers par un trait jaune, et les derniers par un trait rouge. Les noms, dont les soulignemens sont mixtes, appartiennent aux deux époques.

Les liserés jaunes circonscrivent les 12 gouvernemens généraux du royaume, à l'époque de 1614. Quelques-uns, dont les capitales sont entourées aussi d'un trait jaune, embrassaient, comme on le voit, en totalité ou en partie, divers gouvernemens actuels. La majeure partie du Nivernois, avec sa capitale, dépendait du gouvernement d'Orléanois ; et le reste, comprenant S. Pierre le Montier et d'autres lieux, appartenait à celui de Lyonnois ; mais cette division n'est pas bien connue.

Les liserés verds circonscrivent les provinces qui ont été conquises ou acquises, ou réunies à la couronne, postérieurement à l'époque de 1614.

Un lavis de diverses couleurs distingue tous les gouvernemens généraux du royaume dans son étendue actuelle.

Les places fortes sont désignées par cette position ✶, et les pairies du royaume, aujourd'hui existantes, par celle-ci ⚜. De plusieurs bailliages ou sénéchaussées réunis pour une même députation directe, le premier seul a été souligné ; ainsi que les noms de la Bretagne du Dauphiné et de la Provence, qui ont député en 1614 comme pays d'états.

a Paris chez l'Auteur, re Cassac, Cassac

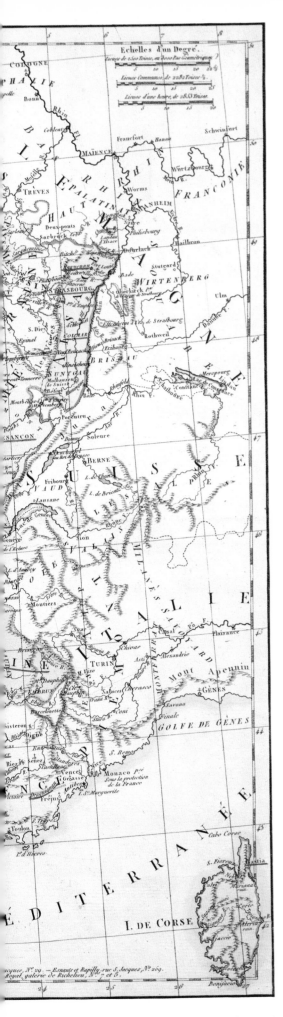

# ACKNOWLEDGEMENTS

Much of the pleasure of writing this book was due to the excellence of the team behind it at Laurence King. Just the right combination of pampering and pestering was provided by Kevin Childs, in-house editor, Sophie Collins, commissioning editor, and Ruth Müller-Wirth in Production. Eleanor van Zandt edited the text, bringing to her task both insight and invaluable attention to detail. Without the efficiency and fluent French of Sue Bolsom-Morris, the range of illustrations included would have been impossible; and they were brought alive by Karen Stafford's sensitive use of them within her design of the book. The majority of the UK photographs were the work of George Shiffner, whose patience and skill is evident and appreciated. Outside the publisher's world two other people deserve recognition. The first is Kay Staniland, who in introducing me to the subject of printed handkerchiefs also introduced me to Kathleen Dejardin; the second is Annabel Westman, who offered words of encouragement just when they were most needed.

For assistance, advice and accommodation during the research stage we would both like to thank Dilys Blum, Betty Brennan, Mme du Bellay at Prelle, Denis Boully, Hester Bury, Syd Chase, M. Chatel, Arlene Cooper, Sophie Desrosiers, Debbie Diament, Monique Drosson, Audrey Duck, Guy Evans, Brigitte Exbrayet, Lynn Felsher, Philippe de Fabry, Sarah Franklin, Ola French, Patrick Frey, Jean Marie Giraud, Monique Graf, Bernadine Gregory, Jacqueline Jacqué, Monique Jay, Jean François Keller, Susan Meller, Leslie Miller, Eddy Morris, Henri Petitjohn, Natalie Rothstein, Richard Salvin, Margaret Schoeser, Helen Smith, Eddie Squires, Judy Straeton, Murielle Théraz, L. St John Tibbits, François Verzier, Yvonne Vissouze, Judy Wentworth, and all those who generously allowed access to their collections for photography and research.

*Map of France, published in 1789 and drawn by the Royal Geographer and Cartographer M. Brion de la Tour. Alsace, on the Rhine border, is shown as part of France, and the important textile centres of Mulhouse, Lyons, Marseilles and Rouen are clearly visible.*

# PREFACE

THIS BOOK traces the history of French furnishing textiles over the past three centuries, focusing on two hundred years between 1760 and 1960. It examines the diverse trends that successively brought different types of fabrics to the fore.

The story of the French textile industry is one of both excellence and compromise – aspects that cannot be understood without reference to the world outside its borders. Never committed so wholeheartedly to exports as were the British, nor quite so inward-looking as the American manufacturers, who founded large firms and prospered entirely within the domestic market, each section of the French industry found its own way, maintaining distinctive methods and patterns, many of which survived for centuries. On the one hand French manufacturers never produced all the fabrics required by the French market, while on the other they often contributed to the finest interiors created elsewhere in Europe and in America. In design, the French reputation for excellence spurred the British on to re-examine their own methods of design; the Americans, by contrast, have always cherished the elegance of French taste, happily incorporating it into their own style. The following pages therefore also explore the ways that the British and Americans made use of, copied and, occasionally, ignored French furnishing textiles, ending with a brief glimpse of today's French textiles.

There are good reasons for concentrating on the exchange between France and these two countries. Speaking of one of the many exhibitions that punctuated the nineteenth century, a contemporary observed that 'the contest has been, and will be, mainly between those noble foes, now happily firm friends and allies – England and France. The two nations which are foremost in prowess and strongest in arms, first in knowledge and civilization, take likewise the front rank in the world's arena of arts and manufactures.'[1] Behind the self-congratulatory style of the writer lay the truth; and had this been written in 1920, instead of 1862, as it was, the United States would have been included as another formidable contestant in the arena of power, arms, arts and manufactures.

Kathleen Dejardin and I have been drawn to the subject of French textiles by our shared and complementary interests – she by her interest in cultural artefacts and I by my research in textiles. Although the labour of writing the book has been mine, the text would not have been possible without the collaboration of Kathleen, whose skill as a linguist, wide-ranging knowledge of contemporary civilization and extensive research have underpinned the structure and content of this work. We know that the topic we have chosen is enormous; noted historians have already provided many detailed studies of their specialities – whether in textile, economic, social or political history – and there is much more as yet scarcely studied. In the following pages we have tried to suggest the rich interplay between France, her textiles for interiors, and those of her Anglo-Saxon rivals.

Mary Schoeser

*The continuity of French textile patterns is exemplified by this copperplate-printed linen, depicting* Télémaque et Calypso. *First printed in Nantes in about 1790, the scene of the nymph and her suitor was derived from a painting of 1722, by Jean Raoux, itself inspired by Fénelon's* Aventures de Télémaque, *published in 1699. The plates continued to be used for a number of years and either the originals or new engravings were also used to print cloth throughout much of the twentieth century. Some stock still remains at Diament, the fabric suppliers in the Philadelphia area.*

# CHAPTER ONE

# PERSPECTIVES

THE PRESENT is distinguished from every preceding age by an universal ardour of enterprise in arts & manufacture. Nations, convinced at length that war is always a losing game, have converted their swords and muskets into factory implements, and now contend with each other in the bloodless but still formidable strife of trade. They no longer send troops to fight on distant fields, but fabrics to drive before them those of their old adversaries in arms, and to take possession of a foreign mart. To impair the resources of a rival at home, by underselling his wares abroad, is the new belligerent system, in pursuance of which every nerve and sinew of the people are put upon the strain.' (Andrew Ure, in *The Philosophy of Manufactures*.)[1]

These words can be found in the introduction to Andrew Ure's *Philosophy of Manufactures*, first published in London in 1836. They may seem an odd choice to introduce a book on French furnishing textiles, but they express the tensions that helped to shape France's textile industry and, at the same time, focused other countries' attention on the achievements of French designers and technicians. French state policies affecting the nation's textile industry were often made in response to foreign competition.

The foundations of the French textile industry, as it existed in the period between 1760 and 1960, upon which this book concentrates, were laid in the seventeenth century, during the reign of Louis XIV (1643–1715). Of foremost importance were the measures initiated in 1665 by Jean Baptiste Colbert (1619–83), Minister of Finance, regulating the weaving industry – its trade, its working practices and the quality of its cloth. The differing statutes for weavers in Tours, Lyons, Orléans and Paris were given royal approval in 1667; Marseilles followed in 1672 and Nîmes in 1682, the year before Colbert's death. Colbert's intention was to reduce the variety and improve the quality of cloth in each weaving centre, so that they would not compete with each other but, instead, with foreign imports. (He taxed heavily but did not ban foreign goods. This had already been attempted in 1599–1600, when all foreign silk, gold and silver fabrics were prohibited for about a year until it became clear that the plain silks and silk velvets that could be made in France could not satisfy tastes accustomed to the fine figured silks then produced in Italy and the Near East.) By the time Colbert's regulations were adopted, the draw-loom (which needed two people to operate and was perfected in the first decade of the seventeenth century by Claude

*This detailed view of the* chambre du roi *at Versailles (restored in the late 1960s, based on the decorations of 1679) illustrates the richness of royal interiors for which the French court became known. Heavy silks interwoven with gold and silver are edged with a deep gold fringe, the bed has added embellishments of gold braid, and the crimson satin lining the bed curtains is couched in gold and silver thread.*

Dangon, an Italian working in Lyons) allowed French weavers – principally those in Paris – to produce sumptuous gold-brocaded silks. Lyons remained known for its silk velvets and taffetas until the next century.

The weaving of woollen cloth was also well established in France. For example, Dijonval cloth, made in Sedan, had received royal patronage since 1646. Nevertheless, a large amount of fine woollen cloth was imported, from England and Holland in particular. To help free France of this dependence, Colbert established Josse Van Robais (a Flemish weaver working in Holland) in Abbeville, Picardy, in 1666. Van Robais enjoyed considerable protection, including duty-free importation of wool, tax exemption and freedom from the guild system, which otherwise prevented a weaver from dyeing his own cloth. In 1667 Elbeuf, near Rouen, was established as a centre for fine woollen cloth of a slightly lower quality than that of Abbeville. Between 1675 and 1685 many other centres were established, with fine cloths made in northern France and lesser cloths, called *londrins*, made in the far south, from where they were exported to the Levant.[2]

As the term *londrin* (meaning London) suggests, Colbert hoped not only to decrease France's imports, but also to increase their exports by making goods which imitated those of another nation, whether Italy, Holland or England.

*Below left: The document which became known as the Mocassi manuscript was compiled as an exercise in industrial espionage for Italian use by Signor Mocassi in about 1760 and contains among its samples French textiles arranged by source. Shown here are some of the cloths made in Lille, including a checked pattern of indigo-dyed and natural linen (V), intended for furnishing and made in four widths, a velours d'Utrecht which, according to Roland de la Platière, an official inspector of factories in the 1790s, had a goat's hair pile on a linen base (U), and a woollen moquette (X). The latter two have stamped patterns.*

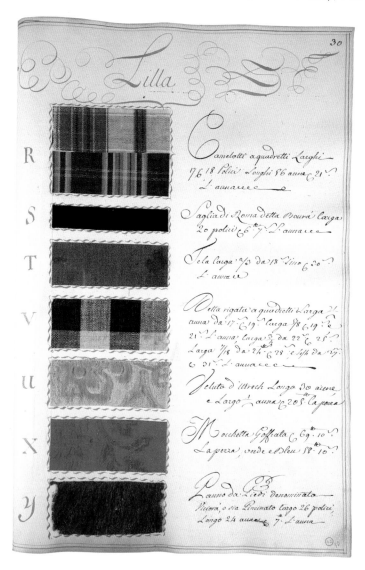

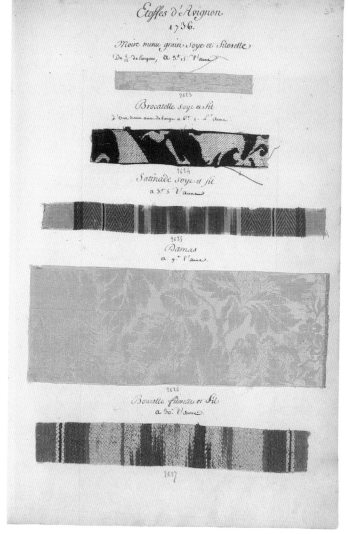

*In his engraving of 1771, Baudouin's* Indiscreet Wife *lies on a luxurious feather mattress. These were used in wealthy houses to soften the hard straw under-mattress – seen here on the right. Bedding was listed among the exports from France to England as early as the 1670s.*

*Opposite right: Cloths such as these samples of 1736 from Avignon represent the type of textile manufacture which was encouraged by Colbert's reforms and which continued throughout the eighteenth century. With the exception of the yellow-gold damask, all are mixed-fibre cloths.* Filoselle *was a soft yarn spun from silk waste and less expensive than pure silk.*

Evidence of the success of Colbert's policies can be found in *An Account of the French Usurpation upon the Trade of England*, printed in London in 1679. The author, who signed himself only by his initials, J.B., catalogued the foreign sources of Louis XIV's riches, including among his list of French exports to England items such as pins, paper, perfume and (of greatest single value) wines. Collectively, however, textile and related items were the most numerous and most valuable. The author stated that 'there is transported out of France into England great quantities of Velvets, plain and wrought, Sattins plain and wrought, Cloth of gold and silver, Armoysins [a lightweight taffeta], and other Merchandises of Silk, which are made at Lyons, and are valued to be yearly worth one hundred and fifty thousand pounds. In silks, Stuffs, Taffaties, Poadesoyes [paduasoy, a strong, corded, closely woven silk], armoysins, Cloths of gold and silver, Tabbies plain and wrought, Silk, Ribbons, and other such like Stuffs as are made at Tours, valued to be worth about three hundred thousand pounds by the year. In silk Ribbonds, Gellowns [galloons], Laces, and Buttons of silk, which are made at Paris, Rouen, Chaimon, St. Etiennes in Forrest, above a hundred and fifty thousand pounds by the year. A great quantity of Serges [a twilled cloth with worsted warp and woollen weft] which are made at Chalous, Charles, Estimines and Rhemes, and good quantities of Serges made at Amiens, Creveceour, Blicourt, and other Towns in Picardy, above one hundred and fifty thousand pounds a year. . . . In linnen Cloth that's made in Britany and Normandy, as well course as fine, there's transported into England above four hundred thousand pounds a year. In Household-stuff, consisting of Beds, Matresses, Coverlets, Hangings, Fringes of silk, and other Furnitures, above one hundred thousand pounds a year.' The writer also noted that 'France doth yearly drain out of the Northern Regions of Europe, sixty-five millions of Florens; the prodigious sum of money which he doth yearly drain out of the rest of Europe, is beyond my Arithmetick to tell you.' The author's anxiety regarding such sums stemmed from the fact that France's increased exports, even allowing for some exaggeration, enabled it 'to fight against us'. His solution was to 'enfeeble the trade of France', and he praised the English Parliament for the measures it had taken to reduce imports from France.[3]

At this time printed and painted fabrics were only just becoming an important part of inter-European trade, although they had been imported from India throughout the seventeenth century. First supplied to Europe on a haphazard basis by an overland route through Persia and the Levant (Turkey) or by the Portuguese, who opened the sea route to India in 1498, *indiennes*, or 'chintzes', were subsequently imported in large numbers by the East India companies of Holland, England and Denmark, formed between 1597 and 1616. The term *indienne* was used in Marseilles as early as 1580, and in 1648 the same city was the site of the first recorded attempt by a European to imitate printed Indian calicoes.[4] In 1664 Colbert granted a licence to the French East India Company, and five years later he assigned the status of free port to Marseilles, which by now had several calico printers who were joined by members of the newly established Armenian colony familiar with 'Persian' and 'Levantine' methods of printing and painting.

Many of the advancements made under Colbert's regime were undone by the revocation in 1685 of the Edict of Nantes, which had ensured religious tolerance. Many Huguenot textile workers left France as a result. England's silk industry benefited greatly from the influx of these craftsman, as did Utrecht, to which

French weavers brought their velvet-weaving skills. The new law also dispersed Huguenot printers who, in any case, had little future for the time being in France, for the government – in order to protect the figured silk-weaving industry – passed two laws banning the importation and the domestic production of printed and painted fabrics, known as *chittes* or *toiles peintes* (1686) and the importation and sale of white cotton cloth (1691). With some minor exceptions, printing of cotton and linen lay dormant until the 1750s.

But printed and painted textile were not forgotten. The laws against them were openly flouted – not least by the courtiers at Versailles, who, during the remainder of Louis XIV's reign and during that of his successor Louis XV (1715–74), used these fabrics for both dress and furnishings. The excitement caused by imported *indiennes* was due to their bright colours, which remained fast when washed. The key to successful reds was in the preparation of the cloth, which was first treated with an oil or fatty substance followed by an astringent, then patterned with an alum mordant and finally submerged in an alizarin (madder) dye bath. Blue was produced directly in an indigo dye bath; any areas to be left uncoloured were protected with tight binding or the application of a paste. Indian textiles were also influential for other reasons. Those of cotton were of far more finely spun yarns than European spinners could produce, and the admiration for Indian muslin, jaconet (a firm cloth woven with an all-over pattern), percale and other cotton fabrics, as well as their mixed cloths and all-silk weaves, was to remain potent until the middle of the nineteenth century.

*With its gilt details, rich red-and-yellow silk upholstery and curtains, and walls lined with a rep, or ribbed cloth, and embellished with applied braid, this Second-Empire interior was inspired by French decorative schemes of the 1730s. The boldly detailed lambrequin, however, is typical of the mid-nineteenth century.*

*Eighteenth-century furniture and draperies, above all others, came to epitomize the desired 'look' for the classic French interior, the sophisticated partner to the English country-house style. Here, they are interpreted with mid-twentieth-century panache in the grand salon of the Hon. Mrs. Reginald Fellowes in the Faubourg St-Germain. Tradition has it that it was for Daisy Fellowes, a noted Paris hostess of the 1930s, that Schiaparelli created her first, later famous, 'shocking' pink dress.*

The fascination with Eastern textiles which motivated French cloth-makers of the late seventeenth century is captured in many of the names they gave to their own cloths. *Indienne*, for example, came to have a more specific meaning to cloth printers working a century later, but even beyond that time it remained the vernacular term for any printed cotton or linen cloth. Cloths having a silk warp and cotton weft and multiple stripes or checks – the most elaborate worked with additional small floral sprigs – were called *siamoises*, having first been made in imitation of the magnificent fabrics worn by ambassadors of the king of Siam, who visited the court of Louis XIV on two occasions in the 1680s. By the 1720s they represented a large part of the manufacture of Rouen, a weaving centre known for its use of cotton yarns. Inexpensive siamoises, made of cotton and linen, rather than silk, were the furnishing fabrics for most French people during the whole of the eighteenth century. They were also made plain – that is, without their characteristic stripes or checks – and in that form provided a base cloth for printers, who continued until 1759, in isolated or protected areas, to pursue the secrets behind the making of *indiennes*.

After the court's near-bankruptcy in 1699, an uneasy half-century followed, culminating in the removal of the ban on printing in 1759. From this point onwards the continuity of the French textile tradition can be charted both by words and by surviving samples, and its story can be amplified by observing the response of England and North America to French tastes and ideas. The importance of the inheritance from Colbert's time was considerable, for his regulations also established royal and state patronage as an important part of the promotion of France's textile industry.

Colbert's inventory of crown furniture, tapestries, plate and cloth began, in 1666, a series of documents with inestimable value for historians. These form the basis of the *Journals* of the royal Garde-Meuble, which made or purchased and subsequently cared for the court's furnishings. Looking back from three centuries on, we can see how these new attitudes to manufacturing were to ensure the French a key role in the trade wars that motivated much of the European textile industry's development until after the Second World War – when the threat of Far Eastern competition served to unite old European adversaries.

# CHAPTER TWO

# ENLIGHTENMENT
## *(1760–1790)*

'THEN WE SAW astonishing things on cloth: flowers and fruit true to nature, velvety peaches, transparent grapes, rich-hued and glorious birds, charming landscapes in which the far distance created a delicious illusion. No-one before had ever produced such work with so much skill, lightness of touch and spontaneity in the draughtmanship.' *(Abbé Bertholon, in Etude sur commerce et des manufactures distinctives de la ville de Lyon.)*[1]

In the thirty years that passed between 5 September 1759, when France lifted its ban on the manufacture and use of *toiles peintes*, and the French Revolution, the French textile industry produced both weaves (that is, non-printed fabrics) and prints with patterns that were destined to remain influential up to the present day. Many of the finest were produced for the courts of Europe and in particular of Louis XV and Louis XVI (1774–93) in France; less expensive ones – though often of great charm – were made for the middle class and artisans. Each region's textiles had their own distinctive character. This diversity was maintained against a background of economic upheaval and the spread of the ideas of the Englightenment, an already established philosophical movement which sought to replace authoritarian beliefs with rational scientific enquiry.

Widespread smuggling, clandestine factories, open use of *indiennes* at court and the liberal interpretation of the law were among the factors that had contributed to the removal of the ban on printed fabrics. They all reflected a growing disenchantment with the old order, which had made the court, Paris and her merchants supremely important in the French textile industry. The merchants grouped themselves in different quarters, each known for cloths of a particular fibre and quality, but not yet divided into specialist dress or furnishing fabric firms. In the second half of the eighteenth century, the most expensive silks were to be found in the Faubourg St-Honoré. There the taste and buying power of the merchants was so influential that Joubert de l'Hiberderie (silk designer and author of *Le Dessinateur pour les fabriques d'étoffes d'or, d'argent et de soie*, published in Paris in 1764) advised designers to study the wares of these famous silk merchant-houses, citing sixteen of the most prominent among them.[2] Such merchants sold to wealthy customers throughout France, using the post to receive and dispatch their orders. Wealthy themselves, merchants of this calibre provided credit for purchases and much of the money for the creation and extension of manufacturing establishments.

*A detail from a brocaded satin designed for a wall-hanging by Philippe de Lasalle. The theme is the four seasons, showing a move towards more orderly, neoclassical tastes; the abundant fruit represents autumn.*

Merchants in regional textile centres exercised a more specific but equally significant control. The silk merchants of Lyons, for example, had a monopoly on raw silk and silk cloth imports, their customs duty and warehousing, but those of Marseilles dominated the export of silks to the Levant. Each area's merchants had a vested interest in maintaining its unique manufacture, and this they did with some success; in 1765 woollen cloths for different purses and purposes could therefore still be described by Duhamel du Monceau in *L'Art de la draperie* as unique to certain areas. For the very rich, the northern town of Julienne and the leading firms in Sedan supplied costly red- or black-dyed cloths (traditionally the colours of power and authority). Mixed colours and the finest wool yarns were still associated with Van Robais of Abbeville. The cloths of Louviers, in Normandy, were for the next most well off; those of Elbeuf, for skilled workers. Duhamel noted that woollens destined for export to the Levant were made in Carcassonne and Nîmes (the latter one of the most successful weaving centres of this period, using various fibres for a variety of cloths). Cloth described as 'very common' – meaning the product of individual, rural weavers – was used only by peasants and for shrouds.[3] Distinctions were maintained in other ways: each weaving centre invariably made its own, often unique, width of cloth, measured in relation to the aune. (The aune – or ell as it was called in England – varied throughout Europe, but in Paris it was about 1¼ yards [1.118 metres]. There were 44 pouces [inches] in an aune.)

The enormous power wielded by Parisian and regional merchants was increasingly being challenged. In Lyons, for example, the establishment of a silk design school in 1759 (ostensibly intended to give an opportunity to the poor, who otherwise could not afford the expense of private tuition) was an attempt to gain a measure of freedom from Paris, where designers had been expected to complete part of their studies. In the same city many weavers bankrupted themselves while fighting merchants' accusations of bad workmanship, doing so in tribunals whose membership was biased in favour of the very same merchants.[4] Weavers in Lyons had also violently contested the enactment of a bill of 1743, which, while continuing the regulations of their trade established by Colbert (rigidly specifying their products and working practices), was amended in favour of the merchants. By 1787, when the Abbé Bertholon published his forward-looking opinions in *Du Commerce et des manufactures distinctives de la ville de Lyon*, it was apparent that there was general frustration – even among the enlightened privileged classes – with these antiquated rules. Among the restrictions criticized by Bertholon were those controlling wages and forbidding combinations of workers (that is to say unions). He also decried the rule banning the entry of women in their own right into the ranks of employer-weavers, or 'maîtres-ouvriers'. Bemoaning the fact that 'we always show a ludicrous respect for any ridiculous practice'[5], Bertholon's impatience with such constraints typified the new liberal spirit in France.

During the 1730s and '40s, the merchants of many other established weaving centres besides Lyons had made similar attempts to suppress the weavers by petitioning the king to proclaim anew their detailed trade regulations. Such inflexible rules were, particularly after 1760, made ineffectual by the competition of printed fabrics, which were used for all types of furnishings, especially in the country. Nor did these rules take into account the impact of imported cotton yarn and cloth, which could now enter France legally on payment of a very high duty.

*Woven in Lyons in about 1755, this type of three-colour silk damask was frequently used in royal residences. In 1765 the Lyonnaise silk designer Joubert de l'Hiberderie discussed such green, red and white damasks and noted that, in their design, invention was allowed only if it remained fairly true to nature. He added that the most successful designer within this genre was M. Dacier, who had been rewarded for his talent by a pension from the city of Lyons.*

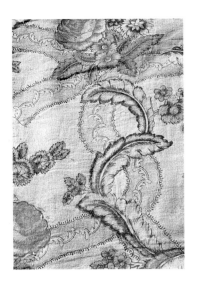

A detail of a block-printed siamoise of about 1765, showing the characteristic unevenness of the handspun cotton and linen yarns. The blue areas, coloured by the use of indigo, weld or pastel, have been added by hand, or 'pencilled'.

Some restrictions, however, continued to apply; an observer of the French–Dutch trade noted in 1783: 'What Holland sends to France are Cloths, Cambricks, Hollands, Cotton Wool [that is raw cotton] and Thread, Chints [*sic*] and Muslins (but these are by stealth, as they are contraband).'[6] Of domestically produced cloths, from the 1760s onwards, cotton yarns increasingly displaced silk, linen and wool. Rouen was now spinning eight times more cotton than it had forty years earlier, using raw cotton imported mainly from the Antilles. The increased use of cotton yarns was apparent almost everywhere; by 1770, for example, cotton and linen damask was called 'Abbeville' damask after its main source, a town previously more famous for its woollen cloths.[7]

Throughout this period the price of many fabrics was being reduced, either by the substitution of cheaper yarns or by slight changes in cloth construction. *Siamoise* typified these changes; now it contained silk less often, but cotton and linen (if made in Rouen) or linen and wool (if made in Paris).[8] This meant that skilled workers, as well as the middle class, could better afford such fabrics. Demand increased, as did the number of looms recorded by the census-takers, but during the 1770s and '80s the trend was towards simpler cloths, for which the weaver received less pay.

The new preference for simpler, lighter-weight cloths was more evident in fashion than in furnishings. This was partly because dress cloths always accounted for the greater part of production. Tastes in dress fabrics also changed more rapidly – a fact indicated by the Lyons copyright regulations of 1787, which confirmed the existing practice of assigning weavers the sole right to dress fabric designs for six years, in comparison with twenty-five years for furnishing fabric designs. Thus some styles of furnishing fabric of the 1750s, particularly those of damasks, remained current into the 1770s.

While some of the simple patterns used by weavers altered little during the latter 1700s (many of them being damasks or plain, striped or checked), their role in interiors became more prominent, and weightier, more elaborately patterned cloths fell from fashion. The classical revival, which from the late 1750s onwards gradually replaced the lighthearted, curvaceous rococo, brought with it a taste for less ostentatious furnishing fabrics among the rich. Roubo, a cabinet-maker and author of several books on joinery, commented in 1771, with regard to upholstery in coaches (which reflected the type of work carried out in house interiors), that some had, in the past, been highly decorated with 'precious stuffs' woven with gold thread or embroidered, concluding that his contemporaries had more taste than their predecessors, who could 'not leave aside their love of magnificence'.[9]

Although embroidery remained an important feature of the finest cloths for interiors – so much so that it become a recognized section of Lyons' trade – it was increasingly done on plain cloths such as satin. Gold and silver threads, however, were now only rarely included; nor were they woven into fine fabrics (save those for export to the Levant); Lyons' great designer Philippe de Lasalle (1723–1805) is thought never to have used them, preferring chenille when extra richness was wanted. Precious metal threads even began to disappear from trimmings, where their stiffness and brilliance had previously been particularly exploited. The upholsterer Bimont noted in 1770 that striped taffeta wallcoverings and curtains of taffeta or of other similar fabrics had no separate trimmings at all, but were now often bordered at the top and bottom with pieces of the main fabric (presumably with the stripe running horizontally). This trend could have been disastrous for the

*Possibly by Philippe de Lasalle, this brocade and its accompanying border were woven by Camille Pernon for Stanislas Leczsinski the exiled King of Poland, in the early 1760s and were used together at his palace at Nancy. Silk chenille and ondé (wavy twisted strands) added richness.*

trimmings industry in St-Chamond and St-Étienne, both near Lyons, had it not adopted a Swiss loom which allowed several relatively plain, striped edging tapes to be woven simultaneously. Paris, once the centre for weighty gold and silver brocades and elaborate passementerie, now became known for its lightweight gauze, while Avignon fared well since its lustrous thin silks, taffetas *Florence* and *d'Angleterre* – increasingly fashionable fabrics – were preferred to those of Lyons.[10]

Lightweight and light-reflecting fabrics were natural partners. In 1770, when Bimont described damask as the most commonly used fabric in interiors, he praised its glossy sheen and its fine colour, two features that also characterized many other elements of neoclassical interiors. He praised other light-reflecting fabrics as suitable for upholstery, especially moirés (in French called *moires*) of silk, linen and silk, wool, or linen and wool (the latter two of which he called *Camelots*), all made by a technique – introduced from England in the mid-eighteenth century – which used rollers to apply a watered finish to ribbed cloth. In use, these cloths provided a subtle glowing pattern. By contrast, only passing mention was made of two fabrics traditionally woven in elaborate or dramatic floral patterns: brocatelle with is raised repoussé-like patterns said (together with satinate, a lightweight silk or silk and cotton satin) to be suitable for 'closets' or small rooms devoted to paintings or books, and lampas (with patterns created by extra horizontal threads or wefts), described by Bimont simply as silk suitable for good furnishings of all kinds.[11]

As lighter, glossy fabrics gained in favour, the more textured cloths also lost their former status. These changes are charted by the *Journal* of the Garde-Meuble and the more specialized inventory, the *Journal du Magasin des Etoffes du Garde-Meuble*, started by Thierry de Ville d'Avray, who was installed as intendant in 1784. Tapestries, already consigned to bedchambers by mid-century were, by

*Right:  Pekins, painted silks imported from China, were already fashionable furnishing fabrics in 1760, at about the time when this example was manufactured in France. The Lyons merchant Benoit Mangeaut traded in such cloths and, according to the encyclopaedist Havard, many were made in Valance, to be sold in Paris at the Hôtel d'Aligre, which was situated among the best silk merchants on the rue St-Honoré. Until 1790 they were widely used by aristocrats to increase the opulence of their country châteaux, as well as their town houses.*

about 1770, being replaced by painted walls, wallpapers, embroideries, silks or Chinese hand-painted taffeta, known as *pekin*; velvets, also previously highly prized as winter wallcoverings, were now restricted solely to upholstery. According to Bimont, whose advice encompassed both middle- and upper-class tastes, rooms dressed *ensuite* for winter, when the fabric was a one-colour damask, no longer used damask curtains to match exactly the upholstery and wallcoverings; instead these were made of silk taffeta, which as early as 1745 was the favoured fabric for summer wall-hangings and curtains. (Alternatively, one could use *gros de Tours*, a medium-weight ribbed silk also called *quinze-seize* because it was that proportion of an aune wide.)[12] Although taffeta could be *flambé*, flowered or *chiné* (all achieved by using a pre-patterned warp), both it and *gros de Tours* were often plain, striped or checked. Checks were so closely associated with taffeta, in fact, that Bimont described a checked *siamoise* as imitating taffeta. There is no doubt that – like the more elaborately patterned taffetas – checked taffeta was fashionable, for it was available from the Parisian silk merchant Barbier, who appeared first on Joubert's list of eminent merchants, and who in 1782 sold 24 aunes of red and white checked taffeta *d'Angleterre* to the Chevalier de Jerningham.[13]

Such plain or informally patterned silks not only appeared less expensive – presenting a gentrified 'country' look, in keeping with the fashion for the bucolic led by Marie Antoinette – they *were* less expensive. With prices held (often artificially) fairly stable from about 1765 to 1789, taffeta d'*Angleterre* (at 27

*Below right: Said to be of Marie Antoinette, this portrait was painted by Lié Louis Pernin-Salbreux in about 1773–75. The chair is upholstered in a hand-painted silk pekin, a cloth known to have been used in her rooms in the palace at St-Cloud. The passementerie and the lavish folds of her sack-back robe demonstrate the popularity of buoyant, ethereal details and light, crisp satins at this period.*

pouces, or inches, wide) and *chiné* (at 22 p.) could be obtained for about 8–10 livres per aune, and all-silk *moire* (19 p.), linen and silk brocatelle (20 p.), and the much wider *gros de Tours* (40 p.) worked out at about the same price. *Pekin* and satin were only slightly more expensive. In contrast, three-colour damasks were at least twice the price, lampas was three times more, and silk *velours ciselé* (patterned with contrasting cut and uncut loops) was four to five times more. Bimont's price lists of 1766 and 1770 do not even mention silks containing precious metals, although there was still limited demand for them: a 1760 order to Barbier from the Marquis de Molinasi requested such a cloth at 100 livres per aune. Clearly, the 8–10 livre fabrics were liked as much for their price as anything else; Bimont himself described *velours d'Utrecht* (22 p. wide at 7–10 livres) as particularly esteemed for upholstery because it was so much cheaper than damask.[14]

For most people, however, even these prices were too high; a skilled worker could scarcely afford the cheapest silk, since 8 aunes of taffeta represented a good month's salary before taxes. He was far more likely to aspire to the cloths listed by Bimont at about 4 livres: wool and linen *siamoise*, moquette, serge, medium-quality printed cloth (the best cost the same as taffeta *d'Angleterre*, although it was 6–9 pouces wider) or silk and cotton checked *gros de Tours*. The inclusion of cotton made a cloth noticeably more affordable. Abbeville's cotton and linen damask cost half the 4 livres per aune of an all-linen damask from Paris (where silk and linen damask was also made). *Siamoise* made with cotton was half the price of that made with wool, and the checked variety was so popular for window curtains that it was made 1½ aunes wide especially for this purpose. The poorest of the French peasantry were excluded from the purchase of these manufactured goods, but used their own coarse linen and woollen cloths, which they made during the winter months.

The seasonal rhythm of rural life also influenced manufactured textiles. On average, about thirty-six weeks a year were occupied with both printing and cloth manufacture, for spinning and weaving were occupations that, in rural areas, complemented agriculture. Travelling through the Seine-Inférieur region near Rouen, in 1788, Arthur Young, an English writer on agriculture, recorded that he saw signs of cotton manufacturing in every farmhouse and cottage.[15] While at this time England was industrializing its textile manufacture, and therefore increasing its annual production dramatically, France remained faithful to its domestic system, in which hand spinners and weavers worked at home for distant merchants or merchant-manufacturers. Printers also worked seasonally, since linen and cotton cloth could not be bleached in the fields during the winter. With relatively small workshops, urban textile centres such as Lyons and Paris experienced less seasonal variation in available workforce, as did the royal factories such as that of Van Robais, which in 1788 had 12,000 employees, who were subject to a quasi-military discipline.

The strong agricultural basis of France's economy, together with the difficulties of long-distance selling of her yarns and finished cloths in the face of internal tariffs, high internal transportation costs and the competition of the products of Switzerland and England, in particular, meant that there was little incentive for most French textile manufacturers to invest in improvements to speed up production. This was particularly true in the cotton and linen industries, which relied almost entirely on local markets. Only the more expensive cloths could overcome these obstacles and were able to capture a national market. A handful of manufacturers also entered the international market – not, as in the case of the British, with low-priced cloths, but rather with their most fashionable fabrics. Without doubt, France's most important cloth exports (to Sweden, Portugal, Spain, Prussia, Poland and Russia) were her sumptuous weaves, now principally created in Lyons, where the weaving industry was known as La Grande Fabrique. As in the past, aristocratic patronage was vital to the survival of such manufacture, particularly in the 1780s, when royal orders went to the Lyons firms of Desfarges, Gros, Reboul or Fontebrune, or through Parisian merchants such as Nau, Michel or Le Normand. On the eve of the Revolution Maison Pernon, whose successors still operate today, made silks not only for the French nobility but also for the courts of Russia and Spain. High-quality prints, such as those made in Jouy (near Versailles) and Nantes, were sold to Switzerland, Italy and Germany. A certain number of furnishing fabrics also found their way to the diminished French possessions in the New World, including the Louisiana territory, which stretched up the length of the Mississippi River, the Caribbean colonies and Quebec (British after 1763), as well as to the new United States. Exports to the latter were aided, no doubt, by the prominent American representatives whose presence in Paris resulted from the political alliance between these two countries, formalized in 1778. Cloth was also considered by some French, including Bertholon, as satisfactory payment for American raw materials.[16]

American politics exacerbated France's uneasy relationship with Britain, with whom she was at war for much of this period. Nevertheless, once the Seven Years' War was formally concluded in 1763 by the Treaty of Paris (which ended the French dream of a North American empire), exchange between the two countries increased. Three years later, however, the British banned imports of French silk altogether, and taxes on other French goods entering England were so high that only the rich could obtain them. The British government did everything in its

L'Encyclopédie Diderot et d'Alembert, *issued volume by volume between 1751 and 1777, contains detailed illustrations of each process in textile production, as well as general views of workshops such as that shown here. The sparsely placed and simple but elegant furnishings in this spinsters' room are typical of the period.*

power to suppress French imports, and was considered most unsportsmanlike, by the French, for its vigilance against smugglers.[17] The costliness (or illegality) of French textiles seems to have increased their cachet. English taste in décor, however, was different from that of France, and as a result these textiles were used in different ways. For example, while tapestry was passing out of use either on walls or furniture in France, the wealthiest English were creating a fashion for tapestry rooms, absorbing six of the nine sets created in the Gobelins factory between 1764 and 1789.[18] In exchange, Britain gave to France her taste for simplicity, which many blamed for the hardship experienced by fancy-cloth weavers.

Long aware of the French influence on the design of their own silks, the English were at once disdainful and admiring of their competitors – a sentiment that extended to the French who had settled in British weaving centres such as Spitalfields in London. This was true in 1749, when John Gwyn's *Essay on Design* described such weavers as 'better instructed but not more ingenious'[19], and still applied in 1777, when the Frenchman François La Combe commented bitterly that 'thirty years of irreproachable conduct is neither qualification nor guarantee of obtaining the Englishman's confidence.'[20] Although the better training of the French designers and weavers remained indisputable for many decades to come, surviving English prints and weaves that post-date 1760 show relatively little French influence.

French designs for weaves did, however, influence French printed fabrics, and they were also now copied by Italian weavers, who had lost their dominant position as suppliers of furnishing fabrics to the courts of Europe (although they continued to supply England with many of her good furnishing cloths). The reputation of silks from Lyons was greatly enhanced by the formidable talents of Philippe de Lasalle, a designer of repute in his own time, and, in the true spirit of the Enlightenment, a considerable inventor. He reduced the setting-up time for a loom from two or three months to a matter of days for brocaded patterns (made on the draw-loom) by creating and manufacturing a removable grid-like structure, known as a semple, through which the pattern was determined in advance and placed on the loom when required. Having accomplished this by the mid-1770s, during the same decade he improved or invented several new looms, including one that accommodated three separate flying shuttles. (The comparable English invention, patented by John Kay in 1733, had only one.) A manufacturer and merchant of simple cloths, Lasalle also designed magnificent silks for one of Lyons' leading merchants, Camille Pernon, taking advantage of his removable semple to create patterns that were no longer restricted in practical terms to less than about 20 inches (50 cm.) in length. By 1779 he was also holding stock for Pernon, having become partner to the Paris silk merchant Le Roux. The regal silks such as those he designed for Catherine the Great of Russia and Marie Antoinette brought him lasting fame, but in his lifetime it was his contribution to new industry and commerce that brought him both financial rewards and honours.

Lasalle's career also provides an insight into how designs could easily be copied. In 1759 he had attempted to find a Paris shop that would sell silk *toiles peintes* of his design and manufacture. This venture was unsuccessful, but because Lasalle sold them instead into Italy and Germany, and circulated samples to merchants in both countries, as well as in Paris, by 1760 his methods and designs had begun to be pirated. Many other designers – and in 1760 there were

*The curving ribbon in this satin-ground lampas of about 1775 was a device frequently used in patterns of the period. Similar designs have remained popular since their introduction and have subsequently been manufactured in England and America as well as in France.*

about sixty designers registered in Lyons alone – must have met with the same consequences if they tried the same route to gain a foothold with powerful merchants. Among Paris's fine silk merchant-houses, were two shops mentioned by Joubert in 1765, whose respective proprietors, Monsieur Beagle and Madame Sule, 'copy onto varnished paper all the beautiful designs that appear'. These were useful to the designer, according to Joubert, to ensure that one was not copying another's style or repeating an old idea – or, more likely, as a source of new patterns.[21]

Designing for silks was a distinguished occupation, considered a fine art. Methods of training varied (having never been stipulated by a guild) but always included a certain amount of painting or drawing. Nature was therefore an important source of original designs, and it is no coincidence that Lyons developed an important school of flower painters. There were, however, other sources, including the King's Library on the rue de Richelieu, Paris, where in the print room (*Cabinet d'Estampes*) in 1765 were sixty volumes containing engravings of plants from all over the world, drawn by artists commissioned by the crown over the past century. These were recommended by Joubert, and were available to anyone on Tuesday and Friday mornings. There were also many publications of antiquities, such as Charles Antoine Jombert's *Repertoire des artistes*, which he published in Paris in 1765. This was the first large volume devoted exclusively to ornament. It contained plates taken from sixteenth- and seventeenth-century engravings by Jean Berain, Daniel Marot and others, as well as several after Raphael. The latter type was particularly influential in the 1780s, when Renaissance-style designs such as grotesque motifs were suited to the fashionable Italianate form of neoclassicism. For printed textiles, aside from those that imitated *pekins* or Indian prints (or woven patterns), pictorial scenes, often engravings based on paintings, proved the most influential. This was particularly true of copperplate printing on textiles, which evolved its technique from printing on paper.

Similarly influential were the activities of French furniture makers and *tapissiers*, the latter responsible not only for upholstering furniture but also for the

*Below right: Copied faithfully from Philippe de Lasalle's design of about 1773 for wall-hangings in the palace of Catherine the Great of Russia, this block-printed cotton was produced in Nantes in the 1780s.*

*Below: A brocaded wall-hanging designed by Philippe de Lasalle in about 1773 and woven by Camille Pernon for Catherine the Great's palace at Tsarskoe Selo, near St Petersburg. The design stretched across two widths of cloth, each woven on a separate loom and using silks from different dye-baths, as may be seen in the varying shades of the yellow ground.*

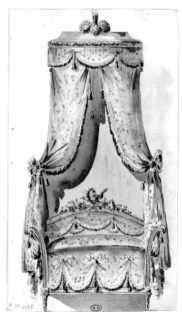

Two country scenes are here block-printed onto a loosely woven linen cloth, the texture of which can be clearly seen. The printer who produced this pattern – between 1775 and 1785 – left no selvedge for seaming, causing the edge of the design to be interrupted.

This lit à la polonaise, sketched by Richard de Lalonde in the early 1770s, shows the transitional stage during which beds facing out into the room, with their heads to the wall, became less fashionable than those placed sideways-on against the wall. At this date the intended fabric could have been printed, hand-painted, woven or embroidered.

design and creation of wallcoverings, bed-hangings and curtains. Their opinion of the quality and appropriateness of a cloth was crucial to its acceptability; for example, Lasalle's difficulty in selling silk *toiles peintes* in Paris was, he said, 'the old prejudice that these cloths split easily'. Bimont obviously preferred using weaves; he warned fellow *tapissiers* to be prepared to add extra vertical sections to joined panels of prints, since otherwise the pattern would not match properly. Christophe Philippe Oberampf (1738–1815) overcame this problem by the mid-1770s, by leaving wide blank selvedges, which later became the norm. Bimont advised that fabrics for wall-hangings should have designs that were well balanced when the pieces were joined together (particularly those that employed a pattern set into a cartouche); some needed their selvedge cut at intervals in order to stretch enough to match the lengthways repeat; and, he continued, others such as serge needed support at the edges, which were slack. *Toiles peintes* with busy patterns had to be studied in great detail, in order to decide which way was up.[22]

French cabinetmakers and *tapissiers* also created furniture and furnishing styles that were copied abroad. In 1792, for example, Thomas Sheraton illustrated a 'French state bed' which scarcely differed from the French *lit à la polonaise* of twenty-five or thirty years earlier (except that it was not so tall), having a small dome (Bimont called it a *baldequin*) held centrally above the bed by iron supports curved inwards from short posts at each corner. A *polonaise* was meant to be seen from the side, as were (most often) *romaine*, *dauphine* and *turque* beds, which

*Of a type frequently used in royal residences during the 1770s and 1780s, this damask was made in Lyons in about 1786. The brocaded floral sprays, each within its oval surround, set just over 8 inches (21 cm) apart, could be used for seat furniture or joined into panels which also repeated in a brick-like pattern. The bows at the top of two lower medallions can just be seen along the bottom edge.*

could also have their small *baldequins* halved, as it were, and fixed to the wall. (The English and, after their example, the Americans continued for many decades to use the term 'French bed' to indicate either type of *baldequin*.) All were finished in varying degrees of elaboration. The draperies alone could consume up to eight lengths of fabric, each the height of the bed. The principal difference between these beds was in their decoration. A *lit à la turque*, for example, was merely a plain, undecorated version of *la romaine*, the latter of which seems to have been distinguished by its use of printed fabrics. Certainly Bimont suggested that one use 'two different sorts of *indiennes* or other stuff, or two different designs; the inside of the bed is in one colour and the outside in the other, as are the bed curtains, which are not seamed together'.[23]

This was a period of considerable invention with regard to treatments for beds and alcoves (which were gradually to become so small that they often contained only the bed or sofa). Increasing informality was reflected by the intimacy of these alcoves, as well as the interest in more comfortable seating, which extended the already large range of chairs and sofas. Bimont describes nearly two dozen types and also instructs on the making of two types of cases, or loose covers, for preserving seating furniture. One type was fastened entirely with tacks; the other was stitched together in the manner still used today, but with the seams joined on the right side and neatened to suggest piping. Covers were especially popular in the summer because few *bourgeois* had the fashionable and expensive *double sièges* – by which he meant two sets of upholstered seat, back and arm pads which could be interchanged twice yearly. Informality was also evident in more flexible furniture, for example the *lit à l'anglaise*, which served as a sofa when necessary. (The English simply called this a sofa bed; it was, in fact, a sofa draped with a wall-mounted *baldequin*.)[24] Less formal, tightly drawn-up curtains also became fashionable, and single curtains which drew straight up were less favoured than those in two parts (crossed over in the middle) which drew up diagonally to leave tails down the sides of the upper part of the window (both types were called *à l'italienne*). Floor-length draw curtains also began to be fashionable once again. Bimont warns against placing their poles too close to the inward-opening French windows, discussing at the same time the use of cords to pull them open (useful to protect the cloth from the ravages of constant handling and an early reference to what twenty years later in the English language would be called a French rod – today called a cording set in Britain, a traverse rod in the United States). For ease of draping, bed or window curtains could be cut on the cloth's diagonal or bias grain, a point clearly illustrated by Richard de Lalonde, who depicted striped fabrics in use throughout most of his series of *Cahiers d'ameublemens*, published in Paris over a number of years beginning in the late 1760s.

With the British keeping a wary eye on France's achievements in design, her dominance of courtly silks and the elegant life-style reflected in the best French interiors, France sought out information on British inventions, particularly those relating to spinning and the cotton industry in general. The best-known example of the transfer of British technology to France is the case of John Holker, a Lancashire man who secretly took to France a document compiled around 1750 containing examples and technical details of printed chintzes, silks, calendered wools, checks, plaids and cotton velvets. Roland de la Platière, the official inspector of factories, must have been speaking of Holker in 1780 when he wrote of a man from Manchester who came to France with a calendering machine, his family and other workers, and made the largest fortune in the century. Certainly Holker was welcomed in Rouen, where he initially settled, and where his expertise improved the region's cotton velvets; and he later rose to a position of considerable power. (With the formalization of the French-American alliance in 1778, his son, John Holker, Jr., became French consul general in Philadelphia where he imported French *siamoises*, *toiles*, *picqués* and *cannelés* (a tightly woven cloth textured to resemble a brick wall), both for the United States government and for himself).[25] Others from Britain, less well known and often less well rewarded, motivated by politics as often as through hopes of gain, made similar contributions to the development of France's textile industry. Emigration by skilled labourers had been forbidden by English law since 1719, so most information and machinery was obtained by smuggling, stealth and cunning. It was economic warfare; every country did the same – fiercely protecting its own ideas while attempting to obtain the best of its competitors'.

The restless, enquiring spirit that characterized the Enlightenment ran contrary to such secrecy, so at the same time there was a movement towards sharing of information, evident in the sudden increase in publications of all kinds. Voltaire and Rousseau[26] were among the more than two hundred scholars who contributed to Diderot's great *Encyclopédie*, which appeared in twenty-eight volumes between 1751 and 1772 and five further volumes in the year from 1776 to 1777.[27] The *Encyclopédie*'s numerous illustrations and notes on textile and furniture making, the reports, surveys and publications of the period dealing with textiles, as well as books on architecture, upholstery and cabinetmaking, gave a thorough picture of the French furnishing textiles industry, its products and their use. They also indicated the importance the French gave to the dissemination of information; some years later Andrew Ure was to observe that French manufacturers had 'derived great advantage from the illustrated systems of instruction published under the auspicies of its government and patriotic

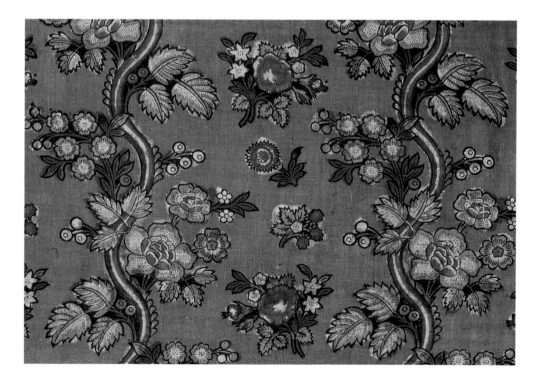

*With a resist-dyed blue ground, this block-printed linen was produced in 1760 in Mulhouse. It is an indication of the advanced state of printing in this independent republic – free from the restrictions against printing – where Schmaltzer & Moser were recorded as manufacturers of printed or painted fabrics (toiles peintes) as early as 1740.*

societies'.[28] The Royal Society of Arts, founded in London in 1754, represented the same spirit. The Society's present curator-historian has noted: 'From 1761 the Society could count Frenchmen amongst its members, and though economic nationalism remained the *leitmotif* of its policies until the middle of the next century, it never forgot its obligation to spread practical knowledge, ''for the benefit of mankind'''.[29]

Included in the category of 'practical knowledge' was chemistry, a subject in which the French were particularly advanced. This was a natural consequence of their strong understanding of dyes, which itself derived from Colbert's reforms of 1669 (published in 1671). These controlled dyes and dyers, dividing them into two groups: *grand teint* for superior fast dyes and *petit teint* for less effective dyes. In 1760 a similar division was decreed for printed fabrics, which by law had to bear a stamp (*chef de pièce*) containing the manufacturer's name and *bon teint* – in place of *grand teint* – or *petit teint*. These stringent controls contributed, in mid-eighteenth-century France, to the development of the first dye chemistry based on scientific principles – that is, on the observation and explanation of *why* certain substances made certain colours, as opposed to the traditional methods which relied on the trial-and-error refinement of ancient recipes.

The standard works on their subjects for many decades afterwards were published by French dye-chemists J. Hellot in 1750 (for wool yarn and cloths), Pierre Joseph Macquer in 1763 (for silks) and Lepileur d'Apligny in 1776 (for cottons).[30] By 1789 all three of these works – in total or in part – had been published in English.

In some cases, however, information was obtained through personal contact. This can be seen in relation to *rouge Adrianople*, or Turkey red, as it is called in English. A complex process, which produced an extremely fast orangish red on cotton, it was used for the expensive, bright red-dyed cottons imported in large quantities from Turkey through Marseilles. From the late 1740s efforts to produce *rouge Adrianople* began both near Rouen and in the Montpellier-Marseilles region, spreading up the Rhône valley to Lyons after 1756, when Turkish spinners and dyers were brought to nearby St-Chamond. Twenty years later Lyons was still known for its red cottons.[31] With government assistance, however, more Turkish dyers were imported to Darnétal, near Rouen, in 1776 by two Parisian merchants, who then saw their process pirated by neighbouring dyers, Varon Frères and Dubos. In 1779 Varon and Dubos were granted a royal patent for dyeing in all colours, owing to their skill in producing Turkey red.

With the subsequent establishment of other Turkey red dye works in this region, and because of its concentration of cotton and linen spinners and weavers, Rouen was soon to become known as a centre for this kind of dyeing. It was from Rouen that Louis and Abraham Henry Borelle took their knowledge of this dye to Manchester, in return for a grant of 2,500 pounds from the British Parliament in 1786. Two years later, another dyer from Rouen, Pierre Jacques Papillon, opened the first Turkey red dye works in Glasgow with a partner, George Mackintosh.[32] For most of the period under review, therefore, this distinctive bright red identifies French, as opposed to English, fabrics, as it continued to do in lesser degrees until the mid-nineteenth century.

The development of different styles or colour combinations in printing relied on the increasingly sophisticated understanding and use of dyes and mordants (which except for indigo blue, requiring no mordant, were the substance actually printed onto the cloth prior to immersion in a dye bath). It also relied on safe sea routes, for many of the necessary mordants (also called drugs) came from America, Africa and the Levant. Rupied, in his unpublished report of 1786 on *L'Art d'imprimer sur toile en Alsace*, was able to list ten different genres of design, many of which relied entirely on their colour content in order to be distinguished from each other. For example, *les indiennes ordinaires* used black, red, or black and red combined, while *les patenas* were superior *indiennes*, having blue and yellow added, overlapping each other to create green. *Calencas*, almost always a leafy floral design, were similar to *Indiennes ordinaires* in colour, having black outlines but up to three reds; their quality varied according to the beauty and accuracy of the printed design. *Doubles bleus*, *doubles violets* and *camayeux rouges* were cloths with designs printed in two or three shades of the same colour.[33]

*This block-printed siamoise, thought to have been produced at Jacques de Mainville's printworks (founded in Orléans in 1762), corresponds to Rupied's description of a patena, with blue and yellow added to the basic colours of black and red. The edges of the 15⅛ by 7¾-inch (38.4 by 19.7 cm)-block can be seen clearly in the zig-zag ground.*

The colour or colours of a fabric also helped to determine its price. Bimont listed a wide range of woven and printed fabrics with their widths and prices, and within each type the red was invariably the most expensive.[34] *Les calencas*, with more colours than *les indiennes ordinaires*, were twice the price. The value of a good colourist to a printworks was also demonstrated in monetary terms; a report of 1765, giving information on a printworks at Sierentz, in Upper Alsace, noted that whereas a master designer was paid 15 livres per week, the master colourist received 24 livres.[35]

Variety in the quality of dyestuffs and the skill in their application were responsible for regional variations in the final appearance of both woven and printed textiles.[36] Such discrepancies, while often occurring due to lack of control, also seem to have been purposely maintained to preserve the unique character of a textile centre. Thus in 1777 La Combe could published a list of colours which in his opinion were best dyed on silk by the Lyonnais: *cerise*, *rose*, *ponçeau* (poppy red), green and pale blue. By contrast, he stated that English silk dyers were better at lilac, violet, *gris de lin* (a bitter pale yellow made with sumac and sulphate of iron) and purple; their greens and yellows on cotton were superior to those of any other country (red cottons being acknowledged as better in France); and on wool they were most successful with brown, purple, *verd (sic) du cuve* (copper green), and two blues: *turquin* and *d'enfer* (presumably turquoise and a dark shade, evoking the underworld). He thought the Strasbourg wool dyers succeeded best in Saxe green and sky blue colourings.[37]

However much improvement was made in dyestuffs, their final effect, as La Combe noted, was influenced by the quality of the wool, silk or cotton yarn and its weaving. Rupied noted that for delicate printed work (*petites façons*) the smoothest cloth was necessary.[38] This factor was also recognized by Christophe Philippe Oberkampf, who opened his block-printing works in Jouy-en-Josas in 1760. Initially using French-made linen and cotton *siamoise* (with its hand-spun yarns of uneven diameter producing a knobbly surface and the soft texture and image characteristic of many French printed textiles of this period), Oberkampf experimented with imported all-cotton cloth in 1767. In 1773 he visited London in order to buy cotton fabric made in India. Believing that better quality cloth, though more expensive initially, was cheaper in the long run, he began, from 1776, purchasing finer cotton cloth directly through the French East India Company, finding that this was cheaper than buying cloth woven in Rouen.[39]

Today still the most widely known textile printer of his day, Oberkampf was neither the first nor immediately the most successful. This accolade must go to Rodolphe Wetter, who in 1744 established a block-printing factory outside Marseilles. Being a free port Marseilles was outside the authority that had banned textile printing (although importing them from Marseilles into the rest of France was still illegal until 1759). In 1757 nearby Orange became the site of Wetter's new printworks. His block-printed *siamoise* became so famous that for some time all French printed *siamoises* became known as *toiles d'Orange*. Early in the 1760s Wetter may also have installed the first copperplate printing machine to be used in France.[40] Of greater importance, however, was Oberkampf's acquisition of one in 1770, for the scenic copperplate printed patterns he produced on all-cotton cloth were so successful that the name *toile de Jouy* was eventually applied to all such designs. (In English this type of design is also referred to simply as a 'toile'.) This method of printing was also adopted in Nantes by about 1780.

*This copperplate-printed cotton was produced in France in the 1780s. In its manner of rendering the undulating bands of flowers the design shows the influence of English patterns – said by the encyclopaedist Havard to be a characteristic of patterns produced in Orange.*

Copperplate printing of continuous patterns on cloth, known to have been practised in Ireland as early as 1752 and in England shortly afterwards, was a technique that appears to have been initially employed almost exclusively on fabrics intended for use in interiors. This was because the copper itself was very expensive compared to the wood used for printing blocks, and too great an investment for dress fabrics, which went out of fashion more quickly. The high cost of copper was, however, offset by its long life, which was a positive asset for the relatively long-lived furnishing fabrics. Thus it was possible for many of the scenic designs, first made in the 1770s and '80s, to be produced for several decades.[41] The use of copper plates also increased French printers' need for imported fine-cotton cloths, for the thin engraved lines of the copperplate-printed pattern depended even more than did detailed block prints on a smooth surface in order to show the delicacy of the design.

Just as French printers were becoming familiar with the copperplate printing process, the British were perfecting the copper-roller printing machine, patented by Thomas Bell in 1783. Since the French internal and export markets were not able to absorb vast quantities of finished cloth, some time was to elapse before French printers became interested in acquiring this British machine, which was capable of doing the work of more than forty block printers. In Alsace, however, Rupied recorded in 1786 that such machines were in use in Colmar and Wesserling. This is not surprising, since this region on France's eastern border had become a major supplier of printed textiles in the forty years that had elapsed since one of their major firms, Koechlin Schmalzer & Cie., had been founded in Mulhouse.[42]

Like Wetter and Oberkampf, many of those who established French printworks at this time were born or trained in Switzerland. Petitpierre & Cie, founded in 1770 by two Neuchâtel brothers, was quickly to become the most prominent printworks in Nantes, where the fabric-printing industry had developed rapidly since the first such factory was established in 1758. From the same date Rouen's printworks also multiplied, and they, together with the printworks being established concurrently in nearby Bolbec, produced mainly block-printed *siamoises* with simpler designs, including naively drawn scenes. Among printers of importance in Rouen was Abraham Frey, who had come from Geneva to France in 1750 and settled in Rouen in 1758. Many of the skilled workers in these printworks – and in those of Paris, Lyons, Troyes, Bordeaux and other towns – were Swiss[43], although German, Dutch and English workers were also employed. The French kept a keen eye on the Swiss textile-printing industry, studying the products of their much longer experience with the engraving of wooden blocks and the application to these blocks of the necessary mordants. They were also mindful of the fact that they annually imported large quantities of fabrics printed in Switzerland (particularly from the workshops clustered around Neuchâtel, near their eastern border, where some firms printed to order for French merchants) and were eager to acquire Swiss expertise themselves, in order to reduce such imports.

*In 1786 a student of the Alsace textile industry named Rupied commented that the term* indienne ordinaire *referred, not to the style of a cloth, but to its colouring,* pincôtage *and hatching, all of which can be seen in this block-printed cotton and linen* siamoise. *Probably made in Bourge, near Orléans, soon after a printworks was established there in 1757, the pattern derives from that of a woven fabric. The sophistication of the* pincôtage *(small dots of colour) and reverse* pincôtage *suggests the presence of an experienced Swiss or German block cutter.*

33

French printers, too, undertook contract printing, for both French and, eventually, foreign merchants.[45] The English among the latter probably increased after 1786, when the Treaty of Eden established free trade (although not in silks) between England and France. In that year the influence of French styles in England grew noticeably. Sheringham's of Great Marlborough Street in London opened a decorating business and employed French craftsmen, as did Eckhardt's, who specialized in elaborate wallpapers; the French mercer Dominique Daguerre also opened a shop in London. The Prince of Wales had already appointed Henry Holland as his architect for Carlton House, and Holland had been to Paris in 1785 and himself employed a French draughtsman. The Prince moved in a circle of ardent Francophiles, and with the reconstruction and furnishing of Carlton House he embarked on a collection of French art which remains one of the finest outside France.[46] Thus began a vogue for Louis XVI-style decoration; it was still being adopted in grand English houses in the 1790s, and in lesser ones long afterwards. The same factors seem to have encouraged the development of furnishing silk weaving in Britain. Carlton House itself contained silks in the French style, but woven in Spitalfields.

Apart from the increased exports of luxurious textiles, for the French textile industry as a whole the Eden Treaty was disastrous. Well-made, inexpensive British cotton cloths flooded into their markets, creating a crisis that had only just been avoided in preceding years, when wage increases (and therefore buying power) lost ground against the effects of bad harvests and costly wars (notably French participation in the American War of Independence). The soaring price of bread brought severe hardship to the poor, whose anger was soon to erupt in violence. The destruction of the *ancien régime* was to bring, as one of its side effects, the end of the lavish patronage that the decorative arts, including fine textiles, had enjoyed. Furniture was to be confiscated and sold off (enriching collections abroad); interiors were stripped. Nevertheless, the reputation for excellence of pattern and colour established by French dyers and figured weavers was to remain unquestioned for many years to come.

*This detailed view of the queen's state bed at Versailles, after restoration, shows it to be a tour de force of silk weaving, embroidery and passementerie. The design of the silk, originally woven by Desfarge of Lyons, is attributed to J. F. Bony. To preserve the elaborately worked bed-curtain, green taffeta under-curtains were provided to draw closed.*

*Attributed to Jean Démosthène Dugourc, this gouache design of about 1788–89 was probably intended for a woven fabric. However, it could equally well have been embroidered, and similar wall panels were painted, or made using wallpaper.*

*In his* Recueil de décoration intérieurs *of the late 1770s, Pierre Ranson illustrated a number of variations on the* encoignure avec lit, *including this example from folio 20. Here the niche and wall panels are ornamented with Chinese motifs. At this date the panels might have been painted, made from woven or embroidered silk, or papered.*

*Inscribed 'Haury the elder 15 January 1780', this design was block-printed at the Haussmann manufactory in Logelbach, near Colmar. At this time there were six brothers in the Haussmann family, all of whom had interests in the textile industry. The Logelbach firm was run by Jean Michel Haussmann who was also a noted chemist.*

*A cotton velvet which has been printed sideways for use horizontally on walls or furniture. Its inclusion of a leopard-spot motif echoed fashionable dress fabrics of the 1780s.*

*Depicted on porcelain in about 1765 by the Sèvres painter Dodin, this bedroom is furnished* en suite, *the striped damask upholstery matching the hangings of the* lit à la duchesse *(with a cantilevered canopy or baldequin). While hangings and upholstery are undoubtedly of silk, the lace-edged counterpane and the bedding appear to be made from a fine linen cambric, a speciality of Cambrai.*

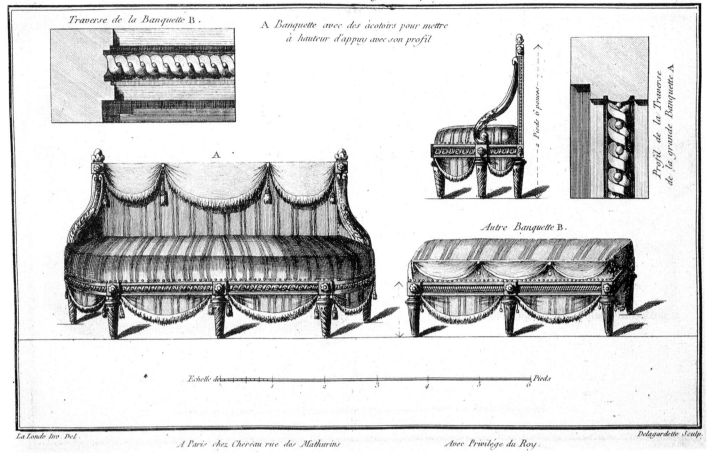

*VI.ᵉ Cahier d'Ameublemens Deßinés par La Londe .*

Traverse de la Banquette B .

A Banquette avec des acotoirs pour mettre
à hauteur d'appuy avec son profil

Profil de la Traverse
de la grande Banquette A

A .

Autre Banquette B .

Echelle de ———————— Pieds

La Londe Inv. Del .          A Paris chez Chereau rüe des Mathurins          Avec Privilége du Roy .          Delagardette Sculp.

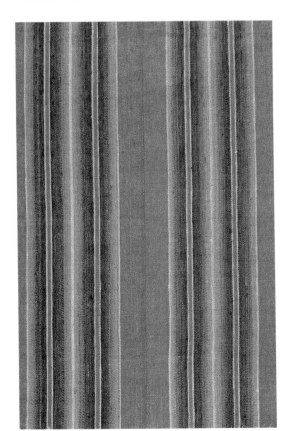

*Above: Plate 1 from the sixth volume of the* Cahier d'ameublemens *by Richard de Lalonde, of about 1780, shows two types of banquette embellished with swags of fabric in the style often called à la reine. Many of Lalonde's plates illustrate the use of striped fabrics.*

*Striped patterns of many types were widely used throughout this period. Shown below is a patterned stripe, made from cotton and waste silk, or filoselle, and block-printed at Jouy in about 1780. Both colours were produced in the same dye bath, the cloth turning red where alum had been printed and black from the printing of an iron mordant. The variegated-stripe weave, or imberline, far left, could have been made at any time during the reign of Louis XVI (1774–93). Filoselle cloths were sometimes also known as bourrettes.*

*Opposite: It was often the practice in the eighteenth century for more than one patterned cloth to be used within a single set of bed-hangings. The lambrequin and curtains of this bed à l'antique were printed in the late 1780s by Gorgerat Frères & Cie. of Nantes; so, possibly, was the second copperplate-printed cotton used for the coverlet.*

*Left: Les Petits Pêcheurs, block-printed on linen in 1775, is typical of a group of Jouy prints which show the influence of copperplate printing. The repeat is 12½ inches (31.7 cm) high.*

*Above: A return to the taste for the antique is apparent in several features of this Nantes copperplate- and block-printed cotton of 1786, known as La Toilette de Vénus after the largest scene. The figure of Venus alludes to Marie Antoinette; to the right of this scene is the temple de l'amour, which the architect Mique built to the queen's orders at Versailles in 1778. The simplicity of the contemporary costumes shown, dating from the early 1780s, also reflects the neoclassical influences of the period.*

*Left: La Draperie was copperplate-printed on cotton by Petitpierre & Cie. of Nantes between 1786 and 1795, and has been reproduced on several occasions since, including once in the 1980s by G. P. & J. Baker for the English National Trust.*

*The bedchamber of the noted Parisian hostess Madame Geoffrin, wife of a part-owner of the Royal Glassworks at St-Gobain, painted by Hubert Robert in 1772. Red damask is used en suite for the furnishings, which include protective case-curtains for the bed and what appears to be a loose cover on the caned chair. The flat-topped bed is twenty or thirty years old, but the multiple ties on the curtains were a new fashion that was to continue into the 1780s.*

The small-scale design of this cotton and silk lampasette (a modified lampas) is typical of the increasingly less imposing patterns for cloth woven in the mid-1770s and the 1780s.

During the 1780s, as printed designs became more and more popular, some woven textiles began to use patterns more familiar in block prints. The floral surround in this tissue shows a style more typically associated with Jouy fabrics.

This block-printed linen and cotton valance derives its design from a Jouy pattern of about 1775, and was printed from a single wood and metal block. The edging tapes bind both vertical edges where they meet at the corners.

Block-printed on a cotton and linen siamoise, all the colours except the pencilled blue in this pattern were created in the same madder dye bath; the olive shade resulted from an iron mordant. It was produced by an unknown French manufacturer, possibly to celebrate the birth of the Dauphin in 1781.

In the mid-1780s a number of textiles carried images inspired by French naval victories, particularly that in Ceylon in 1782. This example was block-printed in Beauvais in about 1785.

Jean Pierre François Blanchard's balloon flights of the mid-1780s inspired topical motifs and images for many decorative items, including this block-printed cotton. Ironically, in 1783 the second balloon of Pilâtre de Rozier narrowly missed the roof of the textile factory of Brenier & Cie. in the Paris suburb of St Marcel.

The French taste for chinoiserie was apparent throughout the eighteenth century, with each era interpreting oriental motifs according to its liking. This example, block-printed on cotton, incorporates a 6½-inch (16.5 cm)-wide, gently curving, lace-like ribbon, typical of prints of the mid-1770s.

Resist-dyed patterns had been produced in France before 1759; it was argued that the pattern was not printed per se but created by applying a paste which protected the design areas, leaving them white when the cloth was dyed. They continued to be popular after the ban on production was lifted, and this example, dyed in indigo, was made by Blanc of Saint-Bel near Lyons in about 1780. Its chef de pièce reads 'Blanc, dyer of cloths and indiennes in all sorts of colours, at a fair price at Sainbel' (sic).

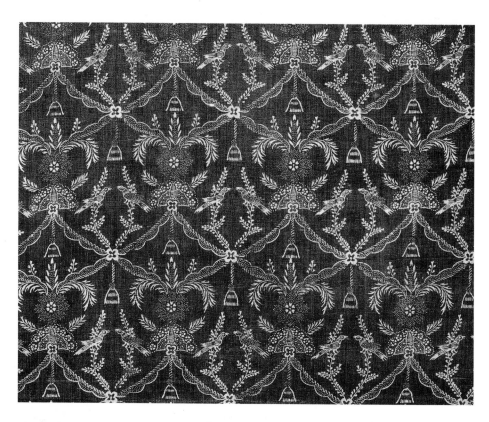

An indienne ordinaire, block-printed in black and red with large areas left plain, is shown on the right of a group of more fully coloured block prints. All represent the type of pattern which was widely used in the 1780s and which continued in production into the early nineteenth century. The border on the left-hand cloth was added when the fabric was reused in the 1830s.

Used in 1773 for winter wall-hangings in the Versailles apartments of the Comtesse d'Artois, this satin brocaded with silk and chenille was also produced for use at Fontainebleau in 1791. It was woven by Jean Charton fils who often worked to designs by Gondoin and, like his father, made numerous furnishing fabrics for royal use.

Marie Antoinette's state bedchamber at Fontainebleau retains the formality and grandeur of the previous century. Shown with its summer hangings, brocaded silks line the walls and form part of the hangings of the lit à la duchesse. The silks were rewoven between 1965 and 1986, duplicating cloths woven in 1787, their designs attributed to Gaudin.

*A block-printed linen produced in Montpellier in 1775, showing the influence of the elaborate background designs of Jouy patterns. Montpellier merchants purchased fabrics from Oberkampf, and aspects of the designs were then borrowed or copied.*

With the use of several shades of red, and with black outlines, the colours of this block-printed siamoise of about 1775 correspond to Rupied's definition of a calenca. Its flowers are inspired by those found on imported Indian printed cottons, and it has a delicate pincôtage ground made by hammering metal bristles into the block.

Even the most proficient block printers occasionally made mistakes. Here, on a block-printed linen of about 1780, one can see that the floral sprig and the swag around it in the bottom right corner have been printed in the wrong mordant, resulting in a warm yellow instead of dark pink. The three black dots across the centre show where the block-pins were placed for alignment.

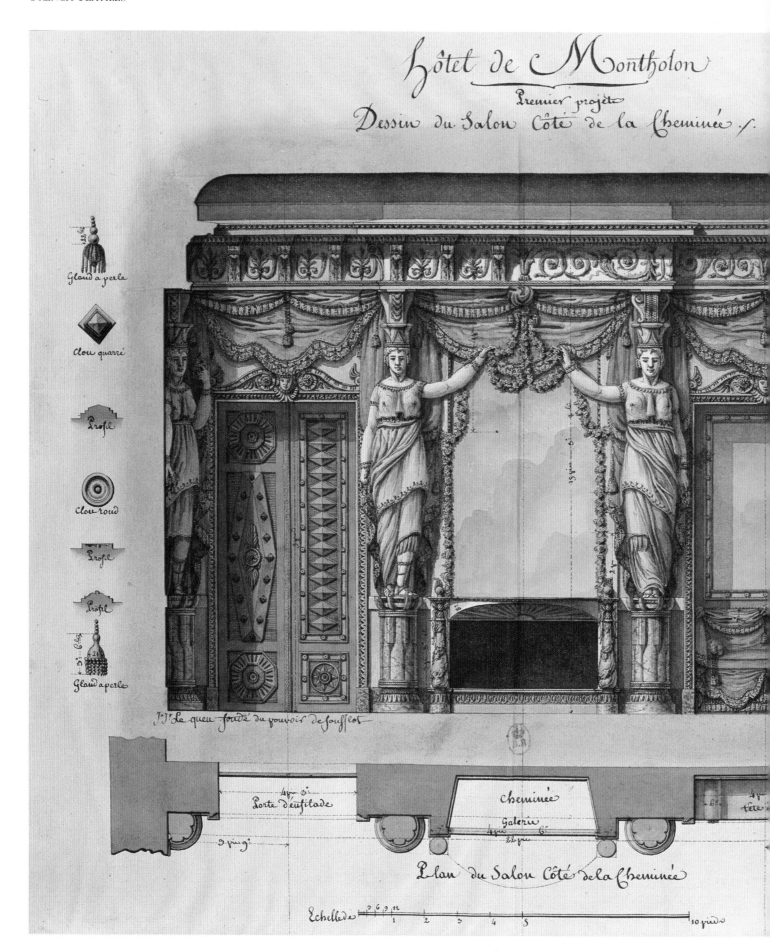

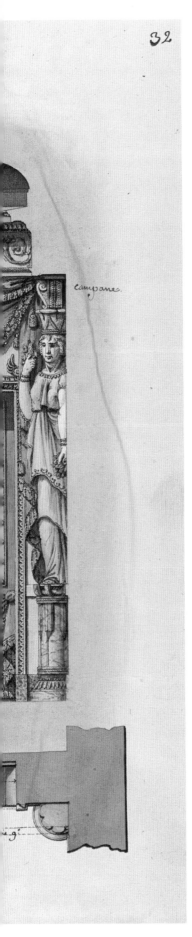

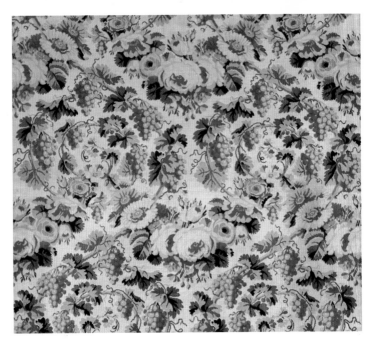

*Above:  Although the number of colours used in this block-printed cotton and linen* siamoise, *printed in the early 1770s, is limited, it nonetheless employs a sophisticated repeat in which each robust cartouche is staggered downwards to interlock with another on either side. To ensure that the sideways repeat was not interrupted the cloth has a generous selvedge.*

*Left:  To produce this* velours coupé chiné *two laborious techniques were required: the pattern was created prior to weaving by dying each warp thread with the correct vertical section of pattern, and this warp was then intermittently looped over wires and woven into a backing cloth, with the loops cut open by hand to create a pile. One of the most expensive types of cloth, this example was made in 1787 by Pernon for Madame Victoire, an aunt of Louis XVI, at Versailles. It was the only royal order given in the eighteenth century for this sort of cloth.*

*In this scheme for the decoration of the salon of the Hôtel Montholon, Paris, of about 1788, the architect Lequeu demonstrates the sculptural quality which resulted from a controlled integration of draperies, mouldings and other decorative details. The small alcove contains a* tête à tête *draped* à la reine.

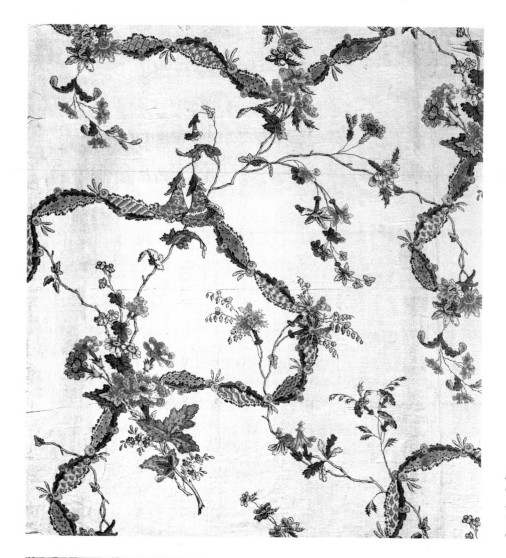

The design of this block-printed glazed cotton shows the parasol-shaped flowers associated with Jean Pillement, a French designer active in the second half of the eighteenth century who worked throughout Europe but particularly in Lyons. Between 1755 and 1760 he engraved and published a number of plates in London showing Chinese ornaments, which were drawn upon by other designers for more than fifty years. This example, of about 1775, is by the English firm Collins & Woolmer, and is being reproduced by Warner Fabrics in 1992.

Typical of the Indian-inspired block prints of the 1780s, this furnishing or dress cotton was printed near Rouen by A. Quesnel of Darnétal. Similar designs were produced at Jouy and other printing centres.

*Right: Exotic flower and foliage designs, referred to as des Indes, figured frequently in the records of the Garde-Meuble, which was responsible for all the furnishings of royal residences. This example, with its pattern derived from an additional, or tissuing, weft, was known in France as a lampas or more accurately, a lampas lancé. The term lampas indicates the use of additional weft threads and is also used to refer to a brocaded cloth, known more specifically as a lampas broché.*

*Below: Many French prints of this period carried patterns which owed much to their Indian counterparts. This example, block-printed on cotton, was produced by Oberkampf's Jouy manufactory in about 1775.*

Throughout the eighteenth century the first, and often the only, purchase of furnishing fabric a young couple would make, would be fabric for bedding. When printed cottons were used they were often quilted to provide the desired thickness. This example, block-printed by Belliard Frères in Aix-en-Provence, employs a pattern which, with slight variations, was produced by many French printers.

Block prints such as this, with what are called 'arborescent' designs, were produced in both France and England between 1775 and 1790. Since both countries typically printed this type of pattern on imported Indian cotton, often the only distinguishing features are blue threads in the selvedge, indicating that the printing was carried out in England for the export market.

Block-printed in about 1785 on an imported cotton, probably of Indian manufacture, the meandering floral stems of this pattern show the influence of woven dress silks. It is similar to a number of other block prints that have been attributed to printers in Beautiran, near Bordeaux, an important exporting centre.

Large exotic flowers set between undulating stripes were possibly the most popular sort of design in the late eighteenth century, and have been frequently revived in the last twenty years. This block-printed cotton derives its impact from the graphic exuberance of its motifs. It was manufactured by Lesourd in Angers in 1786.

# CHAPTER THREE

# UPHEAVAL
## *(1790–1830)*

'SOCIETY in France is more dispersed than in England; the luxury of the French needs therefore to be more sparkling, more frivolous, more remarkable, more agreeable than that of the English, which, in a more concentrated Society, are more striking, more amazing, and more of a piece. It is pride rather than vanity; in France it is vanity rather than pride. The luxury of the English is principally for the love of celebrity; the desire to please is the principle of the French, it is all studied refinement and delicacy: that of the English is all ostentation.' (anon: *Londres, la Cour et les Provinces d'Angleterre, d'Écosse et d'Irlande, ou Esprit, Moeurs, Coutumes . . .*)[1]

Coloured by having been written in what was one of the bitterest years of war between the French and the English, this observation contains, nevertheless, the essence of the differences in taste which divided these two countries. The unknown author has captured the style of the English *nouveaux riches*, which – both from inclination and from anti-French sentiment – was more forceful and more forthright. Many of those among the English who had once aspired to French textiles for their social cachet, now rejected them because of the war. Indeed, in the forty years that passed between the French Revolution and the collapse of the Restoration monarchy in 1830, politics played an ever more crucial role in the fate of France's textile industry. For this reason, any discussion of the furnishing fabrics of the period must begin with an indication of the upheavals suffered during these years by French dyers, spinners, weavers and printers.

Between 1789 and 1799 all French craftsmen were directly affected by the revolutionary governments, which abolished guilds in 1791 and in the following three years greatly depleted the number of patrons of fine-quality articles. All work for the Garde-Meuble – the department responsible for ordering and inventorying royal furnishings – stopped in 1792. Further difficulties ensued as roads and inland waterways were allowed to deteriorate, and inflation became severe. (Oberkampf, for example, found it necessary to increase his prices by 15 per cent in 1791, while the woollens made in Elbeuf doubled in price between 1789 and 1802.[2]) It naturally took some time for the full impact of the last two factors to be felt by all textile manufacturers, since, as in Oberkampf's experience, the increase in price did not initially harm sales. But with the introduction of conscription in 1793 (when Britain, the Netherlands and Spain joined Austria and Prussia in their war against France), labour became scarce. For trade, these problems outweighed the gains made with the abolition of internal tariffs and tolls in 1790.

*Textiles of the reign of Charles X (1824–30) are characterized by a more florid style of pattern. This silk brocade is typical. It was woven by Grand Frères for wall-hangings in the* salon de réception *of the Hôtel de Ville in Lyons.*

Measures were, however, taken to protect some sections of the French textile industry (intended, as in the past, to act also as an offensive weapon against other nations). All commercial treaties were annulled by the National Convention in 1793, and, in particular, the importation of all British-made goods (or anything similar made elsewhere) was forbidden. Protectionism was therefore beneficial for French manufacturers of cotton yarns and cloths, such as fine lightweight muslins, which the English made with greater technical expertise.[3] However, in the same year textiles were among those items that the French were forbidden to export. One effect of this prohibition was an early end to the vogue in England for French fabrics block-printed with Indian and other exotic motifs. With the internal market for fine fabrics fairly stagnant, the survival or demise of such textiles relied greatly on foreign buyers. In this respect the best of the exotic-style block printers were

*Small in scale and richly coloured,* bon herbes *patterns were in plentiful supply in the years between 1795 and 1805. Principally intended for dress fabrics, they were also used as furnishings, particularly in pieced quilts. Many were made in Jouy and much later their designs were to form the basis for the small, stylized floral prints now known as* provençales.

among the French textile manufacturers who benefited from the advance of the French army into the Low Countries, the Rhineland and northern Italy, and the imposition of a 'buy-French' policy that included a ban on British manufactured goods. In the Low Countries, which had previously imported many printed British fabrics, French prints found a ready market.[4]

Under the Directory (1795–99) and from 1799 to 1804, when Napoleon Bonaparte ruled as First Consul, the surviving French textile firms experienced a relatively stable decade, having either adjusted to the loss of their aristocratic patrons, met the needs of the now predominantly middle-class taste or benefited from France's expanding borders. This last factor was particularly important for many manufacturers, who once more gained guaranteed customers as French control was extended and consolidated. When the Treaty of Amiens was signed with Britain in 1802, France already encompassed Austria, Switzerland and Italy. Crowned Emperor in 1804, Napoleon was again at war in the following year. By 1810 he dominated all of continental Europe except the Balkan peninsula and Portugal.

Until Napoleon's first exile in 1814 his Empire provided a large protected market for French textile manufacturers; conquered states were forbidden to purchase British goods and obliged to purchase French ones. In 1807 and 1808, and from 1810 to 1812 this so-called 'Continental System' was at its most effective, preventing imports from foreign manufacturers and suppliers. But this was not without disadvantages, and the same years were the most difficult for many French spinners, weavers and printers. Whether raw fibres, yarns, plain cloths for printing or dyestuffs, most supplies became progressively more expensive and more scarce, as between 1806 and 1811 taxation and prohibitions increased. Lasting prosperity eluded even the cotton spinners, who had been encouraged to expand by the ban on English yarns; from 1806 raw cotton was heavily taxed (the rate being increased again in 1810–11), and its resulting scarcity was hardly helped by the decree of 1808 which banned the exportation of cotton yarns. The latter was particularly vexing, for spinning nearly doubled the value of cotton and had therefore previously provided a small but lucrative sale into foreign markets.[5] Also heavily taxed and banned as an export was waste silk yarn (the raw material for which was imported mainly from Switzerland and also from Germany), which was spun in France; the result was a decline in the once widespread use of striped and checked *bourrette* silks, which used this yarn, called *filoselle*, in their weft.

The resumption of the Napoleonic wars in 1805 can be seen, therefore, as a clear turning point downwards for many in the French textile industry. The great factory at Jouy began its slow decline in 1806 – a decline worsened in 1807 by the loss of Brazilian cotton while passing through Spain (which resisted French rule) from the Portuguese port of Lisbon. A compensation for this loss was the use of Oberkampf's scenic toiles as linings for the tents used by Napoleon during the Spanish campaign of 1808. (Usually of blue and white striped linen duck with a decorative outer lambrequin of poppy-coloured wool braid with black edgings, some of these tents were lined with block prints; officers' and aides' tents were also of striped linen, made impermeable by its glazed finish, but were unlined.)[6] Although the utilitarian sections of the textile industry – producers of yarns and cloths for tents, blankets and soldiers' clothing – were initially stimulated by the demands of war, makers of basic fabrics were no more assured of a market than

*In their purest forms, neoclassical motifs depended on an audience who could 'read' the images. For example, many would have recognized the figures of Venus and Minerva in this Jouy copperplate-printed cotton, designed by Huet in about 1808.*

the makers of luxury fabrics. By 1798, the coarse cloths made in Carcassonne had declined to one-quarter of their pre-Revolution production; but the number of looms working in Lyons' luxury fabric industry fell more rapidly to an even lower proportion, in part because it was the seat of the abortive counter-revolution of 1793.

Since one of the motivating forces behind the Revolution was the workers' desire to be free from merchants' tyranny, other textile centres were also highly political, among them Marseilles and Bordeaux, which joined the counter-revolution and ultimately suffered consequences worse than those of Lyons. This was because, as great centres of export trade they, along with Nantes, were consequently most harmed by the loss of overseas markets and supplies that accompanied the naval wars of this period. Marseilles, Orange and Aix-en-Provence, once centres of both imports and imitations of Turkish and Indian silks and prints, were thus already experiencing great difficulties by 1806 (when the Continental System was established) and did not survive as important textile centres.[7] Also most affected by internal transportation problems, the south and south-west of France was most damaged by the Revolution and subsequent wars.

The return of peace in 1815 did not immediately restore prosperity to the whole of France, and the nation continued for another fifteen years to struggle against economic difficulties, worsened by the severe depressions of 1816 and 1817, and 1827–30. With limited funds at the new government's disposal, roads remained poor, although water transport was improved (greatly benefiting Mulhouse, which was well served by natural and, soon, by man-made waterways). Duties on imports remained high, as did the cost of fuel. Textiles for the military were less in demand, and patronage for luxury fabrics – whether from the church or the returned, but not reinstated, aristocracy – was not abundant. (It was only after 1824, when Charles X succeeded Louis XVIII to the throne, that financial reparations to the aristocracy were considered.) Nor were exports easy to re-establish, apart from luxury goods such as silks, which only needed restored peace at sea to increase trade with the Levant (a trade that had survived by virtue of Greek traders settled in Marseilles) and with America. Makers of some high-quality cloths were unable to take advantage of the restored trade links. For example, Oberkampf's factory at Jouy was disturbed, first by 3,000 Prussian troops who occupied the village in the last stages of the 1815 war, and then in the following year by an influx of Swiss and English printed cottons, which forced the price of *toiles de Jouy* down by forty per cent. The ban on imported yarn and cloths, which came within months, did little to help Oberkampf, who by 1819 was selling his *toiles* for 3.83 francs per aune, 33 centimes below their cost. England, once a ready market for the most fashionable French cloths, even when they were contraband, only gradually overcame the wartime prejudice against French goods – a prejudice encapsulated in a Frenchman's comment, in 1813, that 'the English have no need for prohibitions against French merchandise, [since] it is public opinion that proscribes them.'[8]

In a protective climate, and without the control of the guilds, many new workshops and factories had been established on shaky ground. When a damask ordered in 1802 for the Library at St-Cloud (and finally used in 1805) was found by 1807 to have faded, its supplier, Camille Pernon, was exonerated only after a long enquiry. In 1808, an expert appointed by Napoleon concluded that the problem arose from Lyons' dyers, because 'since the Revolution many established dyers have left their profession, [and] they were replaced by young people who had little familiarity with dyeing of silks for furnishings. . . . One could also add that since the suppression of the masters anyone could obtain a licence, giving the right to manufacture, without proof of some apprenticeship, [and] there arose many workshops, of which the head lacked the capacity.'[9] Although such problems had been partly resolved by the institution of new standards for dyestuffs (and the restoration early in the Empire of a conciliation body – le Conseil des Prud'hommes – and a guild-like structure), most sections of the industry continued to operate without controls throughout the Empire period. Weavers could choose how they worked, what widths they wove and with which materials. This type of freedom to expand and experiment was good when supported by a captive market, but risky in a competitive one. As a result, the cotton industry in and around Paris, for example, which had expanded its high-quality spinning and low-quality printing works, suffered in two ways. Neither the high labour costs for good yarn nor the poor standards of cheap prints could be sustained after the loss of the Empire's large assured market; both sides of Paris's industry declined after 1815.[10] Low-priced prints soon returned to favour, but were now used – for both clothing and furnishings – by the lower classes. Fashion also turned against other cloths; no longer wanted for men's clothing, cotton velvets from Amiens were ruined. The bankruptcies that characterized the Empire period were thus also a feature of the early years of the Restoration. The remaining firms, having become more resourceful as well as more specialized, laid the foundation for the future in a spurt of machinery purchases during the 'production fever' that lasted from about 1818 until a five-year-long crisis struck in about 1827.

While the textile industry in general had a traumatic forty years, the best fabrics bore patterns that continued to show the artistry of their designers. A more classical spirit prevailed in copperplate-printed fabrics, which often featured human figures – contemporary, historical or allegorical. The master of this style was Jean Baptiste Huet (1745–1811), whose designs, commissioned by Oberkampf from 1783 until Huet's death, were copied throughout France. Jouy patterns therefore provide a guide to the changing styles of engraved designs generally.

*One of the most enduring of the Consulate patterns, this silk damask was first woven by Pernon in 1802 for the library at St-Cloud. It was copied by the English soon after 1830 and has since been handwoven in both countries. Today, curtains with this design hang in one of the Empire-style rooms of the Hôtel Beauharnais, the German Embassy in Paris. Incidently, it was fabric of this design that prompted Napoleon's complaint about fading.*

Although scenic designs prevailed, there were three fairly distinct stylistic periods. During the first period – from the outbreak of the Revolution to about 1798 – they tended to include large areas of white ground. In the second stylistic period, which lasted until about 1820 and in which neoclassicism entered its purest, Greek, phase, little ground was left plain, being crossed with foliage or with a small background pattern. After Huet's death, Oberkampf's son Emile (succeeding his father, who died in 1815) commissioned Hippolyte Le Bas for similar background-patterned engraved designs (staff designers provided patterns only for block prints). In about 1820 this style began to lose favour, and the tendency now was for the designs to be developed with little alteration from the paintings and engravings on which they were based. Due to more widespread use of roller printing, these were limited in height (the maximum circumference of a roller being about 22 inches or 55 centimetres) and so often appeared to be somewhat squashed together. Roller prints also had a more floral character, similar to those produced in England at this time.

Following a similar rhythm of change, exotic-style block prints were at their most colourful and fantastic during the 1790s. In the first two decades of the nineteenth century, block printers often imitated engraved patterns, whether by including scenes or by adopting background patterns. By the early 1820s, few block prints carried innovative designs, including those originating from Jouy. This partly reflected a change in ownership at the Jouy factory, which in 1822 became the property of Jacques Juste Barbet, a calico printer from Rouen. Block prints of this last period now had a more European aspect, in contrast to the Indian flavour of the eighteenth-century prints, although up to about 1820, Nantes firms continued to block-print Indian-style designs, a legacy of the town's long trading links with the Near East. (The beginnings of the Provençal floral print can be traced to these years.)

The long period of popularity of background-patterned fabrics was evidence of the slower pace of change which often accompanies times of war. Although fashions continued to change, if only slowly, many old designs were also used,

*Right: The medallion on this Empire brocaded silk was no doubt inspired by one of the many publications available depicting Greek, Roman, and Italian Renaissance ornament and artefacts. Cupid gestures towards a woven cloth with one hand, while the other rests on the head of a lion, suggesting that this fabric was made for a specific occasion celebrating the power and beauty of the silks of Lyons.*

*Below left: English influence was particularly noticeable in landscape design, a fact here acknowledged in a Nantes copperplate print of about 1790, depicting Le Parc Anglais.*

*Below: Three lengths of Monuments of Paris, designed by Hippolyte Lebas, were ordered in 1817 by Rose Isnard de Tarascon, one of only three orders placed by Provençal merchants for Jouy furnishing fabrics between 1790 and 1817. Several samples survive, in red, red and yellow, purple and yellow, and purple. Where a second colour is present, as in the case of the yellow here, it has been block-printed onto the plate-printed design.*

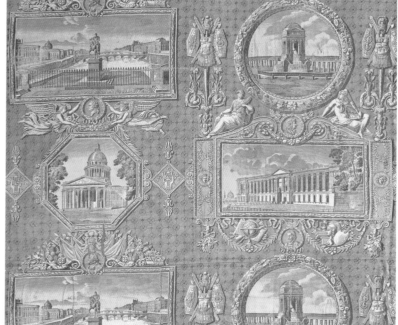

among them simpler patterns, such as the block-printed imitation plaited rush seat covers produced at Jouy throughout this period.[11] Flat copper plates in particular, were reused many times over several decades (whereas in Britain they had been largely superseded by roller printing fairly early in the nineteenth century). In Nantes, for example, Favre-Petitpierre produced, in about 1815, a list of '*Noms des dessins pour meubles*', which included several dating from 1780–95.[12] Although altogether far fewer patterns were produced by copperplate than by block printing,[13] the extended use of plates and the tendency to preserve their end result – furnishing fabrics – rather than block-printed dress fabrics, no doubt contributed to the relatively abundant survival of French fabrics produced by this method and the consequent association of scenic-printed cottons with France.

Woven designs of the first ten years of this period – particularly those by Jean Démosthène Dugourc (1749–1825) for the Spanish and Russian nobility – continued to develop the strongly vertical motifs in the arabesque/grotesque and 'Etruscan' manners which had emerged in the mid-1780s. The extreme length of patterns – in one case the repeat measured 3¾ yards (3.4 metres)[14] – and the fact that they often included human figures, sets them apart from the more formal trellis, lozenge or medallion patterns of the Napoleonic period, and the robust, florid designs that appeared as the Empire style was reinterpreted in the 1820s.

Undoubtedly, however, the woven designs that had the most continuous influence were those created in Lyons during the Empire period. Some prosperity had returned to this weaving centre by about 1800, but aside from the fine fabrics made solely for Spain, Russia, Prussia and Switzerland, plain taffetas occupied the majority of the 9,490 looms recorded as working in 1802.[15] In that year Napoleon urged the return of weavers who had emigrated (the population of Lyons was said to have decreased by 20,000 since the Revolution) and placed the first of several large orders. He also set about reinstating a new version of the Garde-Meuble, to be known as the Mobilier Impérial. Over the next eleven years Napoleon ordered numerous furnishing fabrics (by 1812 nearly 21 million francs had been spent for this purpose). Although orders were given to Oberkampf and Parisian muslin manufacturers and merchants, such as Vacher and Cartier, the silks made especially for his numerous palaces (fourteen, of which four were in Italy, one in Strasbourg and one near Brussels) came almost entirely from Lyons (a few came from Tours).

The radical change in textile design that Napoleon was able to promote during the Empire becomes evident when compared with the five years that preceded his coronation in 1804. Established in the Luxembourg Palace at the end of 1799, Napoleon immediately prepared to move to the Tuileries, having it furnished with stock from the old Garde-Meuble, existing stocks of Paris merchants and goods seized from disenfranchised aristocrats. The fabrics chosen were mainly taffetas, *gros de Tours* and *gorgorans*. All three of these were plain-weave single-colour, striped or checked silk fabrics the principal differences of which were in weight and texture (taffeta being the lightest in weight and of plain – or tabby – weave, and *gorgoran* being the heaviest, containing alternating plain and patterned stripes). Only one boldly patterned fabric, a damask in grey, green and white, was ordered. Borders provided visual interest – as, for example, in Murat's boudoir, where the furnishings of *gorgoran*, in which one stripe was a yellow check, had white and purple borders, or in Napoleon's map room, where the green taffeta had a border of 'Etruscan' scroll design. Further variety was

*This and other figured-stripe designs, known as* gorgorans *(in which frequently only one stripe was patterned), were often used in Imperial residences. They were purchased ready-woven from Parisian merchants such as Cartier.*

achieved by contrasting solid colours within a room. These could often be quite subtle: one room was in three different shades of grey; another in grey and black; and yet another in various tints of yellow, grey and rose. Other favoured colours included lilacs, light blues and bitter orange, although pure red was noticeably absent.[16]

Such simple fabrics were in keeping with the neoclassical-style draped wallcoverings, tented rooms and softly swathed bed-hangings, the artfully unstructured appearance of which was epitomized by the work of Louis Martin Berthault, who in 1798 redecorated the house of the Paris banker Récamier. This house quickly became an essential visit for anyone interested in new fashions, and during the brief period of peace between late 1801 and 1805, the visitors included many British – the most privileged among them allowed also to view the First Consul's apartments in the Tuileries. The 'Consulate' style was propagated by Pierre de la Mésangère's *Meubles et objets de goût*, which began to appear in ten-sheet *cahiers* in 1802 and continued to include neoclassical wall, window and bed draperies in plain colours and stripes until the Restoration. The taste for such schemes therefore survived in coexistence with the more luxurious, boldly patterned imperial style created for Napoleon by Charles Percier and Pierre-François-Léonard Fontaine, who became architects and interior designers to the French government in 1801.

*The dominant feature of this watercolour of about 1800 by Charles Percier, showing a design for a bedroom, is the mass of blue silk, probably a taffeta. The salmon-pink drapery is delicately fringed, its form echoed in the bed valance and the swags of the chairs which are draped à la grecque. Blue window curtains can be seen reflected in the mirror behind the bed.*

Although Napoleon had a keen sense of the importance of luxury in proclaiming his status – as First Consul and later as Emperor – he also kept a sharp eye on expenditure, making sure that decorations did not exceed their budget. This need to decorate within the allotted budget (or in a short time) ensured the survival of textiles that had been designed in the last years of the *ancien régime*. The fabrics desired in 1802 for St-Cloud (Napoleon's new official residence) were ordered solely from Camille Pernon, who used existing designs, many containing either Etruscan motifs associated with Dugourc or oak leaves and acorns. Because these were not ready in time, St-Cloud was instead decorated with paintings, Gobelins tapestries and old wall-hangings. A white satin brocaded with silk and chenille and purchased by the Garde-Meuble in March 1789 from the stock of a bankrupt manufacturer, Gaudin, was used at Fontainebleau, which was redecorated in stages between 1804 and 1812.

The need for economy in these unsettled times was apparent at all levels of society; for the strictest budget there were manufacturers who restored old fabrics, usually by dyeing or reprinting.[17] The once-affluent continued to use their remaining fine furnishings and saw little reason to follow new fashions. A visitor to France in the winter of 1815–16 described the interior of a rich widow's house in one of the best streets in Paris, finding that 'the contrast between the elegance of some parts of the establishment, and the comfortless nakedness of others, is very offensive'. He goes on to give a description of a bedchamber which corresponds to the engravings of Moreau le Jeune of some fifty years before, noting that 'the bed stood in a recess almost lined with mirrors; the hangings were of crimson-velvet bordered with rich gold lace; they were drawn up into a kind of crown at the top, fastened with an elegant coronet, and surrounded by a large plume of forty or fifty white ostrich feathers; and the coverlid [sic] was embroidered cloth.' He concludes – perhaps in justification of his belief that the French had no equivalent word for the English 'comfort' – that 'with all this profusion of expensive elegance the floor was brick, and there was not a particle of carpet in the room.'[18] He did not consider the room old-fashioned, presumably because many interiors from the period still survived in respectable residences.

As a result of these factors, the Empire style did not represent a complete break with the past. In the use of textiles and the shape of furniture, in particular, 'Etruscan' or 'Grecian' neoclassicism had already been established before the Revolution. The great cabinetmaker Georges Jacob had launched the Etruscan style (employing shapes derived from furniture depicted on Greek vases, then thought to be Etruscan) in 1780. On the eve of the Revolution he made a couch and chairs in this style for use as models in paintings by David. The sleigh-back curves of furniture and the wall-hangings of cloth slightly swagged between raised gathered points – characteristics of the Empire style – can be seen in David's painting *The Lictors Bring to Brutus the Bodies of His Sons* of 1789.[19] Similarly, tented rooms, which can be traced back to the bedroom at the Bagatelle, decorated in 1777 by the architect François Bélanger (an ardent neoclassicist and brother-in-law to Dugourc) for the Comte d'Artois (the future Charles X), were very fashionable in neoclassical interiors. These might be of appropriately tent-like blue and white striped twill, as in the vestibule and Council Chamber at Malmaison (decorated by Percier and Fontaine in 1800) or gold-trimmed blue silk, as in Queen Hortense's boudoir in the Paris home she occupied between 1810 and 1814.[20]

By contrast, the *design* of textiles for imperial palaces reflected a new taste. The orders placed by Napoleon were recorded in detail, and many samples of the silks from Lyons survive.[21] Plain silk fabrics were not extensively used, except for curtains, for which white 15/16 *gros de Tours* was most often ordered, followed by occasional requests for green *gros de Tours*, white *pou de soie* (the cross-ribbed silk also known as *peau de soie* and *paduasoy*) and other similar horizontally ribbed fabrics such as *gros de Florence* and *gros d'Holland*. The silks for upholstery, portières, wall-hangings, and bed and window drapery (meaning the decorative cloth fixed at window tops and sometimes cascading part-way down the sides) instead bore dense motifs evenly dotted over their surface or, alternatively, combined with or replaced by patterns organized into wreaths, lozenges, triangles, elongated hexagons or – less often than in the past – stripes. These geometric arrangements bore a close relationship to the motifs developed by Percier and Fontaine and published in *Recueil de décorations intérieurs* (1801, enlarged and reprinted in 1812), particularly those for low-relief plasterwork ceilings. Borders, which continued to serve as important elements of furnishings, also echoed the painted plasterwork details that surrounded alcoves, doors and windows. All designs had to be approved by the Mobilier Impérial, and even accomplished designers such as Pierre Toussaint Déchazelle and Jean François Bony (who was a designer of silks and embroideries, professor of flower-painting at Lyons' Ecole de Dessin and partner in Bissardon and Cousin's weaving firm) had to correct patterns that were thought to be unsuitable for the intended destination.

Sets of different but related patterns were often combined, so that the total interior was actually a delicate, subtly controlled architectural ensemble, even when rich with colour. The furniture itself was often set on plinths, causing Napoleon himself to remark that the architects sometimes sacrificed comfort and utility to decoration.[22]

The most expensive materials were once again used for these imperial silks – having been out of fashion for nearly thirty years. Brocades contained gold and silver threads, and muslins, such as that used for the window and interior bed curtains and bed 'throw' for Josèphine's petite chambre à coucher at Fontainebleau, were embroidered in gold. The embellished brocades cost, typically, between 150 and 200 francs per metre (although the 1806 Throne Room brocade cost 275 francs).[23] These were referred to as brocarts. Borders with a high concentration of metal threads were no less costly, being as much as 200 francs per metre.[24] The only other imperial fabrics that approached these in cost were the embroidered satins and ciselé and chiné velvets.[25]

The richest fabrics were designed for use only in the most important chambers, such as those for the emperor and empress, and even in some of these, more economical fabrics might also be used. For example, in Josèphine's bedroom at Fontainebleau, referred to above, and for which fabric was purchased from Vacher in 1806, both the white upholstery (28¾ yards [26.3 metres]) of velours ciselé worked with gold and the vermicelli-patterned silk (41¾ yards [38.3 metres]) for the bed and window drapery, brocaded with poppy-coloured silk and gold, cost 45 francs per metre (the small scale of their pattern made them less expensive than most embellished brocades), while the white gros de Tours (57¾ yards [53 metres]) for the principal curtains was 12.50 francs, the poppy-red satin (41¾ yards [38.3 metres]) for the bed-hangings was 8 francs and the white taffeta for lining, 6 francs. The satin embroidered with gold was also used as borders.[26] With its contrasting, plain-coloured cloths, this interior (which still exists today) was typical of the decorative schemes adopted by the fashionable world, although embossed velours d'Utrecht rather than ciselé, would have been the more likely velvet for upholstery.

Napoleon's insistence on strict adherence to his budgets caused him to delay the planned redecoration of the Empress's apartment in the Tuileries from 1805 to 1808, due to the architects' desire to change one room, at a cost of 25,000 francs, to suit the richness of the proposed cloth, a blue and silver brocade.[27] Because of the large number of rooms to be furnished, less expensive fabrics also had to be used in many of them. The vast majority of those ordered were damasks, which between 1804 and 1811 ranged in price between 15.50 francs and 30 francs. There was even a damas économique, in which Pernon specialized; he declined to reveal its composition because 'It's a secret which has always made it my best-selling item.'[28] Such damasks cost between 11 and 12 francs. Damasks were the only patterned silks used in place of plain fabrics as window curtains in imperial palaces. The use in relatively simple fabrics of red silk yarns dyed with cochineal – now expensive due to its scarcity – was also avoided.[29]

The inclusion of economical fabrics was also necessary if the imperial orders were to benefit the industry as a whole, rather than just the few Lyons firms that were capable of making the richest brocarts and silks to Napoleon's standards. There were therefore many more modestly priced fabrics in the large order of 1810 for furnishing Versailles (a project that had been aborted in 1806). Up until that date Pernon, or his successor in 1808, Grand, had a monopoly on the provision of imperial silks, save for a 2 million-franc grant to Lyons in 1807 (intended to help the city's weavers and not destined for specific rooms) and four orders in 1808, which went to Bissardon & Bony, Boulard, and Lacostat & Trollier, all also in Lyons. By contrast the work for Versailles (which continued until 1813) went to more than a dozen merchant-weavers, who further dispersed these orders among the several master weavers allied to each merchant in Lyons.[30]

Many of the fabrics ordered for Versailles after 1811 showed a softened version of the earlier geometric/architectural style – one that reflected the increased publication of coloured botanical studies, such as Prevost's *Collection des fleurs et des fruits* (published in 1805 with an introduction which expressed the hope that the forty-eight plates would provide patterns and inspiration to designers and manufacturers of china, *toiles*, chintzes and other fabrics)[31] and Bonpland's 1813 publication, *Plantes rares cultivées à Malmaison et à Navarre*. The latter contained stipple-engraved magnolias and peonies by Redouté, which, together with his *Les Roses* of 1817–24, were greatly to influence textile designers.

*Joséphine Bonaparte, here depicted at Malmaison by Francois Gérard in 1807 when she was Empress of France, sits on a banquette in the Turkish style, embellished with a very restrained design and a deep fringe. Decorated by about 1804, Malmaison became Joséphine's retreat, after her divorce from Napoleon in 1809 until her death in 1814. The freshly picked roses are probably a reference to her famous English garden.*

*Patterns such as this were made in most textile printing centres in France in the 1820s. There were a variety of techniques involved, whereby the red block might have been printed onto a yellow-dyed cloth, as here, or red pigment discharged (removed) from a dyed ground, while in the same process a mordant was deposited to which a yellow dye would adhere.*

In his active support of Lyons' silk industry, Napoleon revived the concept of royal patronage, transforming it into a principle of state – one that survives in present-day France. He also set out to establish a style for the imperial fabrics that would transcend fashion and last for a century.[32] In this he nearly succeeded; for every apartment decorated by the Mobilier Impérial during the Empire, *two* were decorated with imperial silks by its successor, the Garde Meuble, between 1815 and 1830, and two more were decorated in the following forty years, up to 1870. Thus the imperial style for textile designs survived, and with it the Empire style of furnishing. Both were gradually transformed over the following decade or so, with the controlled architectural quality of upper draperies giving way to a more casual interpretation, in which they often appeared to be thrown over fixtures that stood above the windows.

Printed versions of imperial silks, including borders and ready-printed motifs designed especially for chairs, could be obtained both before and after the Restoration. They were copied directly from the original silks, as in the past, or from illustrations of interiors and ornament, whether those of Percier and Fontaine or La Mésangère, or lesser works such as Joseph Beunat's *Recueil des dessins d'ornements d'architecture*, of about 1813. Wallpapers that imitated wall-drapery were also available during and after the Empire period, and, like the textile designs, a handful are still reproduced today. Of all the uses of textiles, however, it was the tent-like rooms that continued to hold the greatest fascination, remaining a hallmark of French style.

The survival and continuing influence of the large stock of imperial silks in the Mobilier Impérial was due in large measure to Napoleon's concern for their quality, particularly with regard to the dyestuffs used. In 1808 and again two years later, he intervened directly: on the first occasion to establish a chair in industrial chemistry and dyes at Lyons and on the second to offer a prize of 25,000 francs for a method of dyeing wool and silk with Prussian blue instead of indigo, which had become extremely expensive due to the loss of India as the main source of this dye. Jean Michel Raymond claimed both the chair and part of the prize, for succeeding in dyeing Prussian blue silk, but not wool, in 1811. During the same years, Roard, director of the dye works at the Manufacture Impériale des Gobelins, perfected a blue equal to indigo but made from *pastel*, a plant grown in the Languedoc, Provence and Normandy. Thereafter it was the Gobelins that produced the master samples used to judge dye quality for imperial silks.[33]

Napoleon was not alone in seeing dyestuffs as part of France's wealth; in this he was assisted by the continuing expertise of French chemist-dyers, who brought into practice new theories which were applied to all manner of textiles. Most notable among them was Claude Louis Berthollet (1748–1822), who published two major works in 1791, one on bleaching and the other on the art of dyeing.[34] Although it was Widmer, an associate of Oberkampf's, who in 1808 perfected the first fast single green for cotton (it remained for some time a difficult colour to obtain on silk, which still had to be immersed in both blue and yellow dyestuffs), the main achievements in cotton dyes occurred in Alsace.[35] The Alsation dyers paid particular attention to the difficulties of producing colours on a Turkey red ground – which they accomplished towards the end of the Empire. In the decade between 1815 and 1825 a number of important discoveries were made in France – both by working dyers and by pure chemists – which laid the foundation for the modern dyestuffs industry.[36] Among these was the introduction in about 1820, by

Nicolas Koechlin & Frères, of a deep, vivid yellow, the first of the chrome dyes. Such progress was disseminated widely, through publications and institutions such as the Société Industrielle de Mulhouse, founded in 1827; fashions in printed textiles of the Restoration were thus often more marked by new colours than by new designs.

Just as the learned societies and the journal, *Annales de Chimie*, were a means of sharing information about new developments in dyestuffs, so the national exhibitions allowed competitors to view and learn from each others' work – as well as promoting sales. Although two earlier exhibitions are documented, only those of 1798, 1801, 1806, 1819, 1823 and 1827 have left substantial records. They demonstrate two important features of this period: the domination of textiles among the decorative arts shown (in most cases about 40 per cent of the exhibits were textiles), and the increasing variety of fabrics, whether in terms of composition, method of manufacture or design. This was particularly true after 1819, when the effects of the relaxation of the guild system during the early years of the Revolution and the progress in manufacturing can be seen to have borne fruit. There were tapestries made by a new method from Rheims, printed *flanelles* (woollen serge) from Strasbourg – a revival of a fabric previously used only for clothing, but now also for furnishing – as well as woollen cloths 'dyed by a new process' in the Ardennes. Mixed silk and wool cloths came from Lyons, and lithographically printed silks, merinos and cottons from Alsace.[37] If the brilliance of design (for textiles if not in interior decoration) diminished during the Restoration, the essentially middle-class, conservative attitudes of the new regime served to encourage the production of both soundly made and economical fabrics.

The relative lack of innovation in design during the Restoration was not difficult to explain. Under the Consulate and Empire, French stylistic influences had spread throughout the conquered lands. These influences remained after the Restoration, during which time the cult of Napoleon also emerged in France, and much of Europe continued to develop the Empire style throughout the reigns of Louis XVIII (1814–24) and Charles X (1824–30), and even later.[38] Dugourc had provided a direct link between Lyons and Spain, where he resided from 1800 to 1814, acting for part of this time as architect to the king of Spain Charles IV (1748–1808), and sending designs to Pernon for silks for palaces including the Escorial, Aranjuez and the Prado (many are still in place today). Spain and Russia remained important customers after 1815; many of Mulhouse's scenic prints went to the former, while Lyons silks were made for both.

With the break-up of the Empire, those former French possessions that had their own textile industries, such as Italy, Switzerland and Germany, erected tariff barriers which made imports from France expensive. Even so they remained highly prized. For example, in a report from the annual Frankfurt textile fair of 1819 (the most important in Europe and still the largest) Mulhouse prints were listed as 40 per cent more costly than those of England, but were preferred for the beauty of their designs. Silks were once again made for the Levant, and printed textiles were designed and made especially for the Ottoman Empire.[39]

France's stylistic influence in the United States also increased considerably after the Revolution – due as much to the heightened awareness of the two countries' shared republican ideals as to America's increased acquisition of French goods, craftsmen and publications, all aided further by the relative safety

*Many textile designers of this period were also accomplished in other spheres. Here, for example, is Jean Démosthéne Dugourc's design for a* table de toilette. *It is draped with a lightly flowered cloth, similar to those he designed for the master weaver Pernon in 1797 as part of the furnishings of the Queen of Spain's dressing room.*

*Bertrand Fils sketched this window treatment as part of the* Projets de décoration intérieure of *1811. Mantle-like over-draperies, rendered as though of velvet, are fixed over crossed curtains, each arranged to complete the symmetry of the whole wall. The second fabric appears to be a figured silk satin.*

of sea passage after 1814. Overall, however, French imports never approached in quantity those from Britain, which on average sent one-third of its manufactured exports to the United States in these years. However, French furnishing fabrics could be obtained in ports such as Philadelphia and New York throughout much of this period. Their manner of use could be seen first-hand, if belatedly, as a result of the return from Paris of American diplomats, including Thomas Jefferson, who brought home with him in 1789 the curtains and furniture he had purchased in France. Some of these he used in decorating the President's House in Washington, which he occupied in 1801. He clearly kept abreast of changing fashions in interiors: back at his Virginia estate, Monticello, in 1808, he had some of his French fabric made into 'drapery for the tops of 4 windows (no curtains being desired)' in French style – the fabric sagging between pleats at the centre and either side.[40] (These were generally known as 'Roman' draperies in England and America.)

Others in the United States also had first-hand knowledge of French interiors, since the country gave shelter to many emgirés, both from France and from Haiti, where the native population had launched their own (unsuccessful) revolution. Among these were Josephine and Victor du Pont, who in 1795 arrived in Charleston, South Carolina, a thriving city and the principal southern port. Other French communities were established in New York, Philadelphia and nearby Wilmington, Delaware, cities that the du Ponts were to come to know well, for in 1799 Victor and his father established a New York commissioning firm, Du Pont de Nemours, Père et Fils & Cie., which eventually formed the basis of the great textile firm and fortune. The du Pont wealth financed a Wilmington mansion, now Winterthur Museum, with its outstanding collection of decorative art. Correspondence between Margaret Manigault and Josephine du Pont (which covers 1796–1824) illustrates the importance of letters in communicating new fashions, such as the 'truly delightful' Greek beds Josephine saw in Paris during a brief visit in 1799. While there, she was tempted to purchase such a mahogany bed for Margaret, to be covered in a green material embroidered in brown and finished with an 'Etruscan' fringe. Back in New York, however, early in 1800, she admitted that the danger of seizure of French goods by the British Navy had been too great. In New York she purchased a painted bedstead and some printed calico curtains for herself, although she found the stores in New York as ill-stocked as those in Charleston – except for India muslins, which she described as good bargains. Ultimately Margaret received a shipment including dimity, percale and cotton batiste from England.[41] It was not until after 1815 that French-style interiors in America could more easily include French fabrics; even then, the references to 'French' curtains or 'French' drapery found in some American documents of the period more often refer to their appearance – having upper draperies – than to their origins.[42]

Liberals and intellectuals in both Britain and North America were particularly interested in French neoclassical trends, and were fascinated by the wit and grace apparent at the salons of French emigrés, which in Britain included such assorted persons as Louis XVIII, the Comte d'Artois, the Duc de Berri, the painter Elisabeth Vigée le Brun and Marie Antoinette's former *marchande de modes*, Rose Bertin.[43] But because of the war between France and Britain for most of the years between 1793 and 1815, British textile manufacturers had less easy access to French patterns, and they also gave but grudging acceptance to the increasingly formal imperial style which dominated French textiles for much of this period. Instead, they sought to exploit France's preoccupation with empire building by further increasing their lead in mass production, which they did with great success: while French output remained at best static, the British were printing ten times more cottons in 1830 than in 1800. With the end of the war and the return of the Bourbon monarchy in 1814, the British antipathy towards France abated. However, despite a shared interest in neoclassical artefacts and designs for interior fittings and furniture – and the indisputable French influence in the style of fashionable décor (spread through publications such as Thomas Hope's 1807 *Household Furniture and Interior Decoration* and Rudolph Ackermann's *Repository of Arts* of 1809–1828) – patterned English textiles showed little French influence (being for a less exclusive market and advancing along different lines). This situation began to change after 1826, when the British legalized the importation of French fabrics. Some English weaves began to reflect the imperial style – influenced, no doubt, both by the orders for silks made in France from pre-1814 patterns (such as those placed with Grand by the Marquess of Bath, the Marquess of Londonderry, the Marquess of Tilbury and the Duchess of Hamilton in 1814, 1823, 1824 and 1829 respectively) and the interest in French *mise en cartes* (design diagrams) for Jacquard's new patterning mechanism for figured weaves, which was acquired by stealth by Stephen Wilson in 1820. (Jacquard had exhibited this improved loom in Paris in 1801, but it was not widely adopted in France until the 1820s.[44])

*Produced by Dollfus-Mieg & Cie. of Mulhouse in about 1830, this engraved roller- and block-printed fine cotton, or percale, employs a design typical of those originally developed by English designers and engravers in Manchester. The roller-printing process was well established there, and many engraved rollers were exported to France.*

Equally, French manufacturers took little or no notice of English textile designs until the 1820s, being more occupied with their own survival and finding it difficult to forgive their old adversaries. The Marquis de Vermont and Sir Charles Darnley captured the last moments of this hatred in their 1823 publication *London and Paris, or Comparative Sketches* with the observation that whereas in the past 'a foreigner no sooner appeared in London than he was followed and abused, and ''French dog'' and other offensive terms applied to him . . . this is now happily changed. . . . France [today] presents a very different picture, . . . at no time was her antipathy against the English more violent than at this moment.'[45]

Although not interested in British design, France *was* interested in British technology, just as she had been before the Revolution. The adoption of machines to aid production became, for many manufacturers, the only means of survival, since it saved labour costs and reduced the price of the finished product. For example, the increased use, during the Restoration, of wool for high-quality men's clothing – rather than cotton, which had been fashionable in revolutionary times – spurred on the woollen industries of Rheims, Elbeuf, Louviers and Sedan during the 1820s to introduce mechanical spinning (or, in the case of Rheims, to increase it). However, mechanization was most noticeable in the cotton industry, where it had begun before 1800. The initial improvements came in cotton printing: Oberkampf installed the first of France's roller printing machines in 1797; within seven years one was operating in Mulhouse; and in Nantes the first was introduced by Ferdinand Favre & Cie. (successors in 1818 to Favre, Petitpierre & Cie.). Hand-operated multiple-spindle machines (mules) were by this time to be found in Rouen, Lille, Roubaix and Alsace (although all but the latter had a high number of inefficient set-ups). Protected after 1816 by laws that banned imported yarns and cloths but not raw materials, French cotton cloth at last became abundant; by 1826 consumption was 170 per cent greater than it had been ten years earlier, and printed cottons that had cost 2.50 francs per metre in 1816 cost only 1.65 francs by 1822. The low price of the finished cloth was made possible both by the low wages of the less-skilled labour required to operate the machinery and by the increased output. For example, the mule spinner who replaced the woman hand spinner was paid only about 12 francs a week, a fraction of her wages as a skilled worker; he was also twenty times more productive. The first steam engine at work in the whole of the Seine-Inférieure (now Seine-Maritime) was introduced by Jacques Lécallier in 1817, and by about 1830 all mule spinning was power assisted. Much of this work was still done in the old way, with merchants putting out work to small enterprises; and cottage weaving also remained the norm.[46]

Of these mechanical innovations, roller printing had the most profound influence on design. It created a fashion in the early 1800s for short vertical repeats and, as we have noted, for background patterns of incised lines, which were ideally suited to engraved cylinders. Both of these were imitated by some block and plate printers despite the difficulties of disguising the joins in all-over fancy grounds. By the 1820s roller-printed scenic designs in England and France

*Illustrating scenes from Sir Walter Scott's* The Lady of the Lake, *published in 1810, this copperplate-printed cotton typifies the Gothic-revival style associated with the reign of Louis XVIII (1814–1824). It can be distinguished from a roller print by the length of its repeat (31 inches, or 86 cm) and is signed on the sarcophogus, 'G. Merkien, Mulhouse'.*

became similar, perhaps because the engraving techniques were so often dependent on Englishmen. Included in their design were 'gothic' scenes, a glimmer of the corresponding French 'troubadour' style, which was to provide the first break with the Empire style. These cloths were the first scenic prints made for the common man, and their designs reflect this, moving away from erudite classical allergories, so apparent in Huet's Empire designs for Jouy, for example,[47] and instead more often showing historical and genre scenes.

Amid this emerging industrialization, France's tradition of specialized centres of production remained; in the use of mule spinning, for example, Rouen went coarser, and Alsace finer. Thus the Alsatian looms (which increased in number from 10,000 to 50,000 between about 1815 and 1825) could produce calicoes, muslins and percales, the last-named being the smoothest cloth for printing. Machine spinning of cotton yarns gradually removed the soft, almost fluffy, *siamoises* from use as a printing base, as well as satisfying the preference for a crisper appearance in the folds of drapery. It also increased the provision of fine plain white cottons and muslins, both of which had become a speciality of St-Quentin, once a centre for Picardy linen weaving. Fine muslin had been fashionable for secondary curtains at the beginning of the nineteenth century, but had been found only in the wealthiest households because the high-quality cotton they required (from Georgia and Louisiana) had been virtually unobtainable during the wars. Now that trade was eased, the French middle class could join the British and Americans, who had already followed this Empire fashion in interiors because of their far greater access to these fine cotton fabrics.

The influence of the British on the industrialization of the Alsatian textile industry was particularly marked, and is well documented.[48] When Mulhouse became part of France in 1798 it was already a thriving cotton-printing centre, and its independent spirit and entrepreneurial flair were not dampened by the Napoleonic decrees which, through taxation or bans on importation, hampered so many textile printers elsewhere. By 1807 there were said to be 2,000 smugglers in the Haut-Rhin, mostly small farmers, whose activities were organized by mayors, magistrates, doctors and even priests, some of whom worked in concert with the customs officers. The prefect of Strasbourg, discussing Brer Magnier (a member of the most active smuggling family there) believed that 'in this city of merchants it is accepted that one can be both a smuggler and a good citizen at the same time'.[49] The ingenuity of these smugglers is worthy of dramatization; English muslins were brought through customs as cotton *toiles* from other countries; bales were concealed under chalk and potash, or hidden in the under-belly of a carriage; and forged documents, false seals and fast legs all played their part. Alsace was not, of course, the only site of smuggling; even at the height of the war with Britain, many muslins used in Paris came from Lancashire.[50]

The prudent Alsatians saw, however, that smuggling was an unreliable source of the necessities of their trade. They extended their businesses to include spinning, weaving, machine building and dyestuffs manufacture, creating enormous family-run firms, which, under the economic pressures of the Restoration, were separated into the independent operations, but still linked by family ties. By the 1820s Alsace was the most self-sufficient textile area of France, making machines that nearly equalled those of the British. The way of the future was already clear at the National Exhibition of Industries held in Paris in 1819; Oberkampf received a gold medal, but so did seven manufacturers from Alsace.

Allegories à l'Amour, roller-printed on cotton, was produced after 1810. An example of the rapid dispersal of designs and the reuse of rollers, the same medallions, but with a different surround, appear on a cotton printed by Petitpierre & Cie. of Nantes.

The design of this block-printed cotton of about 1820 shows a short vertical repeat made fashionable by roller printing. The deep-red background and the simplicity of the drawing suggests that it was made in or near Rouen.

*Above:* The diminutive scale of the pattern on this early nineteenth-century cotton, which has a vertical repeat of 10⅜ inches (26.3 cm), suggests that it has been roller-printed. Although the horizontal line, visible just above the centre, often indicates the use of a flat copper plate, in this case it is more probably caused by the welt formed when the roller was made. This print is thought to have been produced at Jouy.

*Right:* La Danse Savoyarde, a copperplate-printed cotton produced in about 1790 by Leclerc & Fils of Pont-de-la-Maye, has motifs inspired by the works of Greuze.

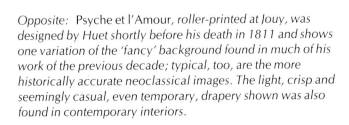

*Opposite:* Psyche et l'Amour, roller-printed at Jouy, was designed by Huet shortly before his death in 1811 and shows one variation of the 'fancy' background found in much of his work of the previous decade; typical, too, are the more historically accurate neoclassical images. The light, crisp and seemingly casual, even temporary, drapery shown was also found in contemporary interiors.

Louis XVI: Restaurateur de la Liberté *was designed for Oberkampf by Jean Baptiste Huet in 1789. The Bastille, which figured so significantly in revolutionary mythology, is depicted in the small central roundel, having been added to Huet's original design to make it more appropriate to the mood of the 1790s.*

*Above: This block-printed cotton, produced in about 1810 in Bolbec, employs delicate, leafy swags more typical of the previous century. These traditional patterns were common in printing centres that catered to a more localized market. The small pattern has a repeat of just over 12 inches (31 cm).*

*Above right: Printed in Bolbec, near Rouen, in about 1811, this design typifies the densely patterned pastoral scenes that were to become increasingly popular. The cotton was block-printed in imitation of a copperplate print, using a bistre, or brownish-yellow, colour made from manganese, one of the new mineral dyes of the period.*

*Right: Part of a set of quilted bed-hangings, this cotton was roller-printed in Alsace in or shortly after 1829. It commemorates the four-hundredth anniversary of Joan of Arc's triumph in relieving the besieged city of Orléans, which in turn led to the coronation of Charles VII. The image of her statue is set against a shaded stripe, characteristic of many prints of the 1830s and '40s.*

*Far left:* Neoclassical 'arabesque' or 'grotesque' patterns typical of the 1780s continued to be made in the 1790s. Here a tissue of 1790–92 by an unknown Lyons manufacturer, also incorporates a Roman-style cameo.

*Above left:* In the brief period of peace that marked the early years of the nineteenth century, Napoleon, by then First Consul, began his ambitious programme of refurbishment of the civil list properties. This brocart (brocaded with gold and silver) was intended for the Tuileries, but was used instead for wall-hangings in the grand salon at St-Cloud. Like most other fine silk cloths of the period, it was woven by Pernon's weavers in Lyons.

*Below left:* In the 1803 scheme for the decoration of the music room in the Tuileries, the dominant pattern was provided by the silver-brocaded borders. Behind is the moiré silk intended as wall-hangings. Both were made by J. Pernon & Cie.

*Right:* Woven in 1797 by Pernon after a design by Jean Démosthène Dugourc, this brocaded silk was destined for the walls of the dressing room of Maria Luisa, queen of Spain, in the Prado in Madrid. The trompe l'oeil lace ground was a device previously used by Dugourc, who worked extensively for the Spanish court and left France for Spain in 1800.

Ordered together in 1809, the three silks, left, below and right, were destined for ministers' offices and bedrooms at Fontainebleau. Each is a damas économique, a speciality of Grand Frères. Their silk and cotton composition contributed to their low price of between eleven and twelve livres, and the use of any colour requiring the expensive red pigment made from cochineal was also avoided. Each fabric was used for all of a particular room's furnishings, including the window curtains.

*Right: This silk damask in the Egyptian style was supplied to the Mobilier Impérial in 1813 by the tapissier François Louis Castelneaux Darrac. The fabric was intended for wall-hangings in the first salon of the grand apartment of the Monte Cavallo Palace in Rome, but was actually used in the Orléans Palace in 1814.*

*Below: Woven as part of the scheme of 1802 for Joséphine Bonaparte's chamber at St-Cloud, this gold-brocaded satin, or brocart, was among the fabrics borrowed by Pernon to exhibit at the National Exhibition, held in Paris in 1806. Designed as an upholstery fabric, it was eventually used at Compiègne in 1808.*

*Individual motifs for chair seats, backs and arms could be ready-made by printing as well as by weaving. Shown here is a Jouy resist-printed cotton of about 1818 which was intended for chair upholstery; the larger medallion would cover the seat. The design is thought to be by Lagrenée.*

*Small all-over patterns, such as are incorporated in this design for a woven furnishing fabric, were illustrated in use on sofas by la Mesangère in the mid-1820s.*

This anonymous watercolour design for a bedroom, although thought to date from about 1825, shows the influence of Percier and Fontaine, with its deeply swagged, mantle-like wall-hangings of blue silk, its unadorned window tops and the crossed curtains, one of gold-embroidered muslin. The swans holding the wall draperies and above the coronet on the bed are a further reference to the early Empire period; the swan was the emblem of the Empress Joséphine.

Left: Collection de meubles et objets de goût, published by Pierre de la Mesangère between 1802 and 1831, was influential in disseminating the Empire style. In this plate, a Grecian-style sofa of about 1805 is shown upholstered in five different patterns of cloth, including the border. Such fabrics could have been printed, woven or embroidered.

Right: One of a pair of giltwood fauteuils made in about 1790 and stamped with the mark of the master furniture-maker, Georges Jacob. The upholstery is of velours ciselé (cut and uncut velvet) typical of the fabrics supplied by Parisian merchants such as Nau.

*Above: Because the surviving records from Jouy are widely dispersed, this early nineteenth-century block print has only recently been identified as a product of Oberkampf's print works. Both the fabric and the original design are in English collections, the former in the Warner Archive and the latter in the Courtauld Archive.*

*Left: The silk and wool brocaded bands contained in this sample book, thought to have been made in Lyons between 1810 and 1830, were intended primarily as edgings for shawls, but they were equally appropriate as borders for furnishings. Similar patterns and colour schemes can also be found on printed fabrics of this period.*

*Bottom: Block-printed with a small, exotic pattern, this cotton also retains its chef de pièce naming Oberkampf as the printer. Its form indicates that it was manufactured between 1787 and 1792; it carries a royal cypher, which was granted when Jouy was made a royal manufactory in 1783.*

In this aquarelle of the Tuileries chambre of the Duchesse de Berry (wife of the son of Charles X), painted in about 1825, the artist, Garneray, shows the abundant use of muslin, now in plentiful supply, and the impact of the borders on otherwise plain wall-hangings, curtains and upholstery. After the death of Charles X, the duchess attempted to secure the throne for her son Henri, who is shown here aged about five.

Originally woven for Versailles by J. P. Seguin of Lyons in 1811, this brocaded silk gros de Tours upholstery cloth was actually used in 1819 in the first salon of the Duchesse d'Angoulême at St-Cloud. The lilac and anemone motifs decorated chair back and seats respectively. The design, however, was not thought to marry well with that of the wall-hangings, which had the lilac lozenge set within a boldly drawn trellis-work. The border shown was intended for the wall-hangings and portières, but the dark outer border was also provided singly for the seat furniture.

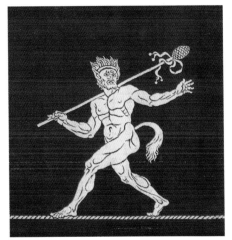

*These satyrs in the Etruscan style (above) were woven in 1797 by Pernon, after a design by Dugourc. They were intended to be cut out and applied to a wall-hanging for use in the ballroom of the Casita del Labrador in Aranjuez. In the same year Pernon made the fabrics for the set of chairs, firescreen and wall-hangings in the Escorial, near Madrid (below). Also after designs by Dugourc, the figures, inspired by Pompeiian frescoes, were cut-outs, like the satyrs, and were applied to the finished pieces.*

Taking its brilliant colour scheme from Indian textiles and its imagery from China, this Alsatian design for a block-printed fabric illustrates the taste for chrome yellow, first used in Alsace in 1819. It has recently been selected from the MISE (Musée de l'Impression sur Etoffes) for production by Warner Fabrics.

The energetic, nervous outlines of this design are typical of the block prints produced at Jouy after 1822, when the Oberkampf factory became the property of Barbet. Despite the fact that a true green had been introduced to Jouy in 1808 by its dye chemist Samuel Widmar, the green ground here was produced by dyeing in two stages – indigo blue and yellow.

Three brocaded satin bands in the
Egyptian style have here been
joined together to create a frieze.
Made in the early 1820s, they
demonstrate the continued taste
for juxtaposed patterns.

*Left and opposite: By 1790 there were over 300 printworks in France. In that year it was the products of Oberkampf's Jouy factory which were given the highest praise by Roland de la Platière, in his* Encyclopédie méthodique: manufactures, arts et métiers *(1785–90). Of the two Jouy samples shown here, the yellow-ground cotton of 1790 employs fantastic, imaginary flowers and foliage, while the other, of about 1795, derives its images from the new and exotic plants brought to Europe in the eighteenth century and illustrated in Jean Lemarck's* Encyclopédie méthodique et botanique *(1782–1823).*

*New designs with exotic blooms continued to appear on block prints from Nantes long after other printing centres had ceased to innovate in this style. Made in about 1815, the chef de pièce of Dubey & Cie. can be clearly seen. The letters to its right are the initials of the block printer.*

Although this painting by Hubert Robert shows the prison cell of the revolutionary orator and writer Camille Desmoulins, the simple furnishings of the room are typical of the 1790s. The rush-bottomed chair in particular remained a feature of rural French interiors for at least another hundred years. The bed is covered with a striped cloth, probably a siamoise of the type associated with Rouen.

Below: This late eighteenth-century block-printed siamoise juxtaposes a naive country scene with giant Indian-inspired flowers, in a manner characteristic of the designs associated with the Seine-Inférieur region. This example is thought to have been produced in Bolbec.

Left: Two block prints of about 1800 show the varying tones of red which characterized different printing centres. The cotton and linen siamoise on the right retains part of its chef de pièce, which reads 'Manufacture de LeLièvre Heutte' (near Rouen). The cotton on the left may have been printed in Jouy.

A quilted bedcover made from a cotton printed especially for the purpose. Dating from the first decade of the nineteenth century, the yellow and red pattern derives from an early to mid-eighteenth-century design. The borders were also fashionable for dress and shawl patterns. Because of their dark colouring they were called ramoneur or 'chimney-sweep'.

# CHAPTER FOUR

# INDUSTRIALIZATION

## *(1830–1870)*

'THE INDUSTRY of printing cloth, that source of so many colossal fortunes, of the prosperity of the countries where it has taken root, has made in the last century, thanks to the development of physics, mechanics and chemistry, enormous progress. . . .' (Jean François Persoz, in *Traité Théorique et Pratique de l'impression des Tissus*.)[1]

If one section of the French textile industry had to be chosen to represent the forty years that encompassed the reign of Louis Philippe (1830–48), the short-lived Second Republic and the Second Empire of Napoleon III (1852–70), it would most certainly have to be the cotton industry of Alsace. Its continued technical improvements, chemical experimentation and domination of the provision of high-quality printed cottons epitomized the spirit of the predominantly bourgeoise French nation: vigorous, prosperous and, above all, confident.

These characteristics were also expressed in Paris, which, between 1830 and 1870, was transformed both economically and visually – a transformation punctuated by several political upheavals. First came the July Revolution, the three days of rioting in Paris in July 1830 which brought Louis Philippe to the throne at the age of fifty-seven. Dubbed the 'Citizen King', he drew his support from the middle classes and his ministers from the new élite of bankers and industrialists. Despite the unrest – in both Paris and the provinces – of the first few years of the 1830s, both industrialists and liberal idealists saw industry as an agent of social reconciliation. Along with the idealism and euphoria, however, came the grim realities of the Industrial Revolution: poverty, overcrowding and disease. A cholera epidemic in 1832 killed 20,000 Parisians. Nevertheless, by the late 1840s Paris was the world's largest manufacturing city,[2] employing some 400,000 workers. The same decade saw the arrival of the first railway line, supplementing the existing canal system. (The railway's growth was supported to a large extent by private investors, including textile manufacturers, who recognized its importance to their trade.) Money seemed to abound in Paris, where the Bourse had opened in 1826.

The belief in industrial progress was sustained even through the middle years of the century, when an agricultural and industrial depression led to support for parliamentary reform. Attempts to suppress anti-government speeches led to yet another revolution in 1848 and Louis Philippe's exile to England. Thereafter in quick succession came the Provisional Government, (which gave the vote to all

*This block-printed and glazed percale was produced in about 1845, probably by Schwartz & Huguenin. Its rich colour palette includes a bluish green, produced from mineral dyes but imitating the old form of green, made from overprinted blue and yellow, as it appeared when faded.*

adult men and set up 'national workshops' to aid the unemployed); the elected government, or Assembly (which closed the workshops); the resulting 'June Days' (during which the Parisian craftsmen and workers revolted); and finally, in December 1848, the election of Louis Napoleon as president. Not wishing to face re-election in 1852, he successfully mounted a *coup d'état* and had himself declared Emperor Napoleon III. The Second Empire lasted until 1870, during which time most French people prospered, apart from the urban proletariat. In Paris, many new banks were founded, establishing local branches and agencies which accumulated vast sums. The overall income of French industry rose twice as fast as that of England.[3] Thus, in 1853, when the rebuilding of Paris began under the direction of Baron George Eugène Haussmann, the 'creative basic assumption made by Napoleon and his ministers was that, in a city as rich and on the up as Paris, work on the enormous scale which they envisaged would pay for itself in the end.'[4] Over the next sixteen years much of medieval Paris was destroyed, as new boulevards and roads, public squares and parks, and buildings for both public and private use were created.

With so many new buildings in Paris one would have expected that interiors might reflect the dominant theme of their architecture – a rich form of classicism known as the Beaux Arts style – but on the whole they did not. No single style was followed, but rather what one contemporary proposed to call 'neo-Greco-Gothico-Pompadour-Pompeiian'.[5] So it was a romantic, quasi-historical and slightly escapist vision that continued from Louis Philippe's reign to prevail over interiors of the Second Empire. This trend began with the late Empire style's excess of plain fabric and was transformed by the end of the 1830s into a mania for *patterned* excess which at its most extravagant clothed the entire room. Tent-like interiors continued to be constructed, and 'Turkish' décor (which also often included fabric that covered the ceiling) became fashionable for smoking rooms – themselves a new feature in stylish houses, more so after the Crimean War of 1853–56, from which the fashion for cigarette smoking was said to have originated.

Rooms designated for specific purposes – a departure from the *salon* of earlier times which was used for various social functions – acquired distinctive characters which they retained throughout this period. Dining rooms, for example, once so sparsely furnished that they were said by a visitor to Paris in 1815 to be 'considered merely as a lumber-room', were now made comfortable yet dignified by the more generous use of furnishings. In 1850 a Parisian ladies' magazine announced with some relief that the new-style dining room 'no longer resembles the ancient bare room with no decoration, accorded only from necessity some percale curtains and horsehair chairs'.[6] The style that by the 1840s had become firmly associated with this room was derived from the Renaissance, although so loosely that when Louis Philippe's château at Pau was refurnished in this style in 1840–45, the furniture ordered was actually seventeenth-century in style. (These interiors, which still survive, made use of imperial textiles and old tapestries.) However incorrect historically, this 'Free Renaissance' style, as it is sometimes called, had a robust, sturdy elegance thought suitable for dining rooms, as well as for studies and libraries. The first fully formed post-Empire style, 'Free-Renaissance' remained paramount in French interiors for many decades, lending a solidity and stateliness to the other pirated styles – whether eighteenth century, Pompeiian, Grecian or Oriental in derivation. Deep buttoning, heavy

*During the 1840s and '50s rococo themes were generally reinterpreted with a boldness derived from the prevailing neo-renaissance taste. This example, a brocaded silk brocatelle – with a second warp to give the cloth its raised, repoussé effect – was woven by Lemire Père et Fils.*

*This* Interior of a Salon in the rue de Gramont, *painted in 1858, epitomizes the comfortable bourgeois interior of the period. There is a variety of textiles and patterns, including a table cover, a draped mantle and two sets of curtains, the red set possibly concealing doors.*

draperies and rich colours were therefore grafted onto interior styles originally characterized by light and clarity, resulting in a style unique to the mid-nineteenth century. Vividly printed cottons, even when not used in abundance, made what today would be called a 'strong statement' – one entirely in keeping with the age.

As the effects of industrialization and increased income were felt, there were more people among the middle and artisan classes who aspired to interiors such as only the upper classes could previously afford. An American visiting Paris in 1857 observed, 'The old frugality of the French has been banished by the present regime, and luxury and extravagance are now the prevailing habits.'[7] This was a boon to textile manufacturers, particularly those who produced printed cottons that simulated the opulence of patterned silk weaves at a relatively low cost.

The Alsatian textile industry responded to this opportunity with spirit. They turned wholeheartedly towards machines; not only did they install more of them, but, more importantly, they used them to produce a more sophisticated product. Improved roller printing machines were introduced – able by 1860 to print up to eight colours simultaneously; from the late 1830s these were supplemented by perrotine machines, which used wooden surfaces with metal inserted for the design, and which, reported Persoz, 'enabled the manufacturer to print the most complex designs with maximum precision and economy'.[8] Hand-block printing was maintained for the most elaborate designs, and the variety of cloths printed was also extended to encompass the products of the better spinning and weaving facilities which were also being created in the region. The workers learned to print on different surfaces, such as satin, or on fibres traditionally associated with other areas of France. One such fibre was silk, of which it was said, by Sébastian le Normand, in a text on printing fabrics and wallpapers, that taffeta, *lévantine* (a soft silk serge), *tricot* (woven with a simulated knitted rib) and velvet are the silk fabrics used for this kind of printing'. The author also noted that these could not be machine printed.[9]

From 1830 to 1860, the Alsace industry progressed from being known for 'the green and blue prints of Mulhausen', and 'the ginghams from the department of the Upper Rhine' (described in the British *Foreign Quarterly Review* of 1829 as 'stout and well-dyed') to one that in 1862 produced 'rich goods intended for consumption by the leisured classes'.[10] These included piqués, jaconet and lightweight cloths of all kinds – all printed in large quantities, side by side with *l'indienne* proper, that is a fabric Indian in both its style and composition (block-printed smooth cotton). Such quality was expensive; to support this, the spinning, dyeing and weaving operations were extended even more rapidly, much of it just west into the Vosges, where labour was cheaper. The number of printing firms was reduced from forty in 1839 to eighteen in 1861, as many of the small printworks were absorbed into the remaining companies. A handful of firms dominated: Dollfus-Mieg, Gros Roman and Hofer-Grosjean (by virtue of their size) and Thierry-Mieg (as a result of its excellent designs). Their products were well known in Paris, winning medals at the national exhibitions which continued more-or-less regularly through this period.[11]

More efficient spinning meant cheaper yarns, helping to reduce the price of fabrics still further. Cotton velvets, sold by Adéodat Lefebvre in 1836, cost between 3 and 7.50 francs.[12] In the late 1850s a full-colour glazed percale from Schwartz & Huguenin sold for only 2.15 francs. Another of the successful mid-century Alsatian printers, Schwartz & Huguenin kept an eye on prices, commenting on a competitor's fabric that 'There is no doubt that it is a nice stripe, but it's not worth 21 francs' (presumably for a piece of about 9–11 yards [8–10 metres]).[13]

Although the perrotine had been invented in Rouen, the cotton printers clustered around Rouen did not advance at the same rate as those of Alsace, and as a consequence found it more difficult to meet the demand for high-quality furnishing fabrics. They continued, however, to supply the provincial markets, despite competition from Alsatian textile printers, who did not neglect their production of lower-priced fabrics. Against the onslaught of this range of products, many firms found it difficult to hold their place in the market, and it was during the 1840s that Oberkampf's successors at Jouy and Petitpierre & Cie. in Nantes both closed their doors.

For those firms, however, that survived the difficulties of the mid-nineteenth century, there were new sources of inspiration. The Musée Historique des Tissues in Lyons, the Musée des Arts Décoratifs in Paris and the Musée de l'Impression sur Etoffes in Mulhouse (to use the names by which they are all known today) benefited the industry by providing inspiration to many designers. All were founded between 1856 and 1863.

Of particular importance to the style of printed textiles in this period were the many independent design studios that blossomed in Alsace, supplying French manufacturers with patterns for wallpapers and weaves as well as prints. Some also sent their work to other European textile manufacturers, including those in Russia, Austria, Germany and Britain. Lancashire, the centre of England's cotton-printing trade, had particularly close links with Alsace, and as early as 1828 Jean Baptiste Romain Lebert had set up an atelier that worked especially for MacNaughton & Thon of Manchester. Adolphe Braun, a highly respected designer who was in charge of the design studio at Dollfus-Mieg from 1831 to 1848, also subsequently set up independently, specializing in supplying designs to England. There Braun's customers included Butterworth & Brooks (which was described in 1840 as a 'general dealer', meaning that its prints were produced by others) and the printer James Black. This studio had forty to fifty designers; even

*In the style of Jean Ulrich Tournier, this large-scale pattern, with a repeat 35½ inches (90 cm) high, was block-printed in three colours on a dyed ground. The 'fancy' stripe was then applied by roller, the main pattern areas having first been protected by a paste. Dating from about 1850, it may have been produced by Schwartz & Huguenin.*

*Printed about 1850 in Mulhouse by Dollfus-Mieg & Cie., the design of this roller-printed cotton is typical of a number by George Zipélius that were engraved by Koechling-Ziegler and produced primarily for export to Spain. The scene shows children enacting events from the time of Napoleon I. The reverse side of this quilted bedcover is a cotton, woven with an indigo-dyed chiné warp and alternating stripes of indigo and white wefts.*

*This selection from a sample book of about 1850, now in the Musée de l'Impression sur Etoffes, shows a range of percales, roller-printed with designs typical of the period. All are in limited colour-ranges, which would have made them more economical to produce and therefore less expensive.*

larger was the one established by one of Braun's apprentices, Edouard Schultz. Schultz opened his Paris atelier in 1841; half a century later it was described in a comprehensive history of Mulhouse as 'one of the largest design studios working for the whole world'.[14] In 1865 he formed an association with Edmund Potter of Dinting Vale, a printer who, twenty-five years earlier, had played an active role in obtaining extended copyright for designs in England.

In 1840 Potter had claimed that there was little copying of English designs on the Continent, but evidence suggests that, strictly speaking, this was not true. The extensive collection of pattern books at the Musée de l'Impression sur Etoffe shows that Alsatian designers and manufacturers kept a keen eye on the products of English printers. Among the English samples present are many marked simply 'anglais', while others state their maker's name: Stead McAlpin of Carlisle or Nelson, Knowles & Co. of Manchester, for example.[15] Of course, these may have been collected simply to examine English printing techniques; the sample from Manchester, acquired for Dollfus-Mieg, was labelled (in English) 'specimen of 14 colour copper cylinder printing in one operation, one piece 25 yards printed in two minutes'. But they also may well have been collected in order to compete with the English, for at least one anonymous French manufacturer was determined to capture business across the Channel. On one occasion this caused quite a stir between the printer Stead McAlpin, its customer the weaver and wholesaler Daniel Walters & Sons (based in Braintree, Essex) and Stead McAlpin's representative, who reported in 1862 that Walters had been approached by a French printer who was attempting to win their orders.[16]

Further links were established as a result of the continued interest in British technology. In the case of Charles Steiner, whose printworks in Ribeauvillé (Haut-Rhin) was founded in 1839 and known for its *rouge Adrianople*, the link was with his uncle, Frédéric Steiner, who had established himself in Lancashire during the Restoration. Having practised the necessary techniques in his uncle's printworks, Charles Steiner became his major competitor, at least in the eyes of the author of a report on the International Exhibition in London in 1851, who noted, that 'Frédéric Steiner has achieved a perfect mastery of his products, which are only rivalled by those of Charles Steiner of Ribeauvillé, who uses his uncle's techniques'.[17] Alsatian designers also occasionally honed their techniques in England; Charles Scheidecker worked for Walter Crum & Co. in Manchester at the end of the 1850s, and at the beginning of the same decade, Walfred Boquet had worked for MacNaughton's before joining Claude Dardel's Mulhouse atelier, which sold designs to Germany, Rouen and England. Dardel ran his studio in partnership with Isidore Jobert from 1840 to 1843, and thereafter on his own until Boquet's arrival in 1855. One of Dardel's apprentices, Jean Laurent Rock, had a studio in Paris from 1853 to 1872, which also specialized in designs for England.[18]

However much British and French designers may have copied or been inspired by each other, the British designers certainly must have envied their French counterparts, who were regarded as gentlemen rather than mere employees, and whose pay reflected their status. A report of 1840 put a French designer's salary at 8–10,000 francs per year (£320–400), roughly twice what was paid in England. At the same time it was said that there were ten times more freelance designers in Paris than in Manchester or London.[19] The difference between the two country's designers remained the strong training in painting and drawing which the French received. This was particularly important during the mid-1800s, for many of the most fashionable designs featured an almost three-dimensional realism, difficult to achieve without considerable facility as an artist. For this reason, many French designers continued to spend some time in a painter's studio, often in Paris, and some were recognized as accomplished in both the fine and decorative arts. Jean Ulric Tournier was one such designer; in mid-century known for his *meubles perses* (large-scale furnishing designs on glazed percale) for the Mulhouse firm Schwartz & Huguenin, he had exhibited a painting at the Paris Salon of 1824 which was purchased by Charles X.[20]

Many designers, whether in Paris, Alsace or Lyons (which had 50 freelance designers listed in its 1849–50 *Annuaire*), also continued to list themselves as flower painters, and the Lyons school of flower painting remained a major training ground for designers. Flowers themselves were also an inspiration to designers, whether seen locally in the greenhouses and hothouses which became popular in this period, in one of the many important botanical books printed in London, St Petersburg and Paris, or in the yearly flower shows held in Paris from 1827 and in Lyons from 1837. The rebuilding of Paris also directly inspired textile designs, as a result of the flowers planted in the newly created gardens – particularly those along the Champs-Elysées – which included fuchsias, begonias, petunias, canna lilies and several varieties of geranium and pelargonium.[21] Because the floral style of printed textiles in the 1840s and '50s, while botanically precise, preferred to depict the flower just as it reached its last, fullest and most sumptuous hours, lithographic studies that showed blooms in this state, such as those by Gérard van Spaendonck (who had died in 1822) were particularly favoured as source material. Such plates offered only one view, however – a view that did not always suit the needs of a designer. To solve this problem, Braun made early use (beginning in 1850) of photography to capture single flowers and bouquets arranged as required, which could then be consulted at any time of the year. The use of such photographs, which increased in the 1860s, also ensured that the

*Unusual colour combinations were made fashionable by the development of new dyes during the Second Empire. Here, fuchsias in unnatural shades combine with lilacs and are set against a delicately engraved background, which was often found on glazed percales of the 1850s and '60s.*

*With its well-defined, 'plump' leaves, ripe pods and fully opened blooms, the design of this brocatelle, woven by Lemire Père et Fils in 1851, typifies the new style of the mid-nineteenth century. It is in harmony with the ample forms of the deep-buttoned furniture of the period.*

*A brocaded damask, woven by Tassinari & Chatel and first made for the Duke of Devonshire in 1840, for the refurbishment of his house, Chatsworth. The order was placed through Claxet, a Parisian architect. In 1865 the same design was ordered by Séard, who at that time was refurnishing the Hôtel Païva in free renaissance style.*

flowers depicted on a given textile were all from the same season, lending an internal harmony to floral designs which was part of their distinctive appearance.[22]

As in Alsace, the trend in Lyons was also towards fewer, larger firms. The trend towards more diversity among their products also intensified, and far more cloths were now made with a mixture of silk and another fibre. Even the mayor of Paris ordered such mixtures – as, for example, in an order to Lamy & Giraud for a silk and cotton mix, to cost 22–23 francs per metre.[23] Although many designs for weaves were in revival styles, by about 1840 there was also a new style, which employed naturalistically represented flowers and fruit amid curling branches and *rocaille*, the latter taken from rococo carving and plasterwork, but new to the textile designs (it had not been used in mid-eighteenth-century fabrics). Such patterns remained popular throughout the Second Empire; one, designed by Guetant for Ringuet-Leprince in 1841, continued to be ordered until 1867, with 14,596 (13,391 metres) woven in all.[24]

It was the fine silks for furnishing that continued to demand attention both at home and abroad. Many, according to a British visitor to the United States in 1854, were used in American hotels – the public palaces of that republic. The St Nicholas Hotel in New York, for example, purchased a silk brocaded with gold (and described as half an inch thick) from Stewart's of Broadway.[25] She described the French silks as displayed alongside Persian and Indian fabrics and, at 9 pounds per yard, as two-thirds more expensive than English silks. It was this type of silk for which the Lyons firm Maison Grand received a gold medal at the 1849 exhibition in Paris. Not all exported silks were so elaborate, of course, nor were the majority for interiors, but plain silks, such as the 'very beautiful plain satins in black, white or other colours' which gained Heckel of Lyons a gold medal in 1844, were important, for 'His products have greatly contributed to retaining the lead enjoyed by Lyons manufacturers in articles which, in spite of competition, have a very important share of our export figures.'[26] Overall, exports of silks increased fourfold during this period, with England and the United States sharing more or less equally between them about half of the total, which at its highest point, in 1859, was valued at 500 million francs. American sales did slump with the outbreak of the Civil War in 1861, and at the same time a high protective tariff was also introduced by the United States. Even this depressed consumption remained greater in any one year than that taken by Italy, Belgium, Spain, or Switzerland (individually), and during the 1860s only Germany occasionally imported slightly greater amounts.[27] By 1870 the American purchases of French silks had returned to their pre-Civil War level. However, at this date, when about 80 per cent of Americans still lived a rural life away from the cities, the only opportunity they had to see the finest French furnishing silks was when making a rare visit to a fine hotel or travelling on the Mississippi in one of the elegant steamboats aptly known as 'floating palaces'.

In the mid-nineteenth century, three-fifths of Lyons' production was exported. Intermixed with the French orders in records, still preserved in the archives of Tassinari & Chatel (successors to Maison Grand) and Prelle (successors to Lamy & Giraud), are orders from Russia (which continued to favour Lyons' silks) and all the major European courts and cities. Because many orders now came through decorators or *tapissiers* such as Laflèche, Verdellet and Poncet, rather than from private customers, less is known about their eventual destination, but in

1864, when a Mr. Hutchinson ordered 100–101 yards (92 metres) of *velours coupé ponceau* in Empire style, he noted that it was for Queen Victoria.[28] Commissions from London firms, such as Wright and Mansfield, Charles Anoot and Morant, became more numerous after 1860 (when duties paid on fabrics entering Britain were significantly reduced), and Morant, in particular, was to remain an important customer for several Lyons' manufacturers.

But La Grande Fabrique remembered that overseas markets could not always be relied on, so in the 1830s and '40s the Lyons silk firms invested in new machinery with a view to producing more economical cloths for the domestic market. They copied the cotton industry's new technique for weaving waste yarns and fibres (including those swept up from the floor), increased the number of power looms and concentrated on plain silk and mixed cloths, which, due to their lower price, could be purchased by many more among the French population. This produced many new jobs, but these were often located outside Lyons. At the same time, the amount of work put out to weavers in the city declined. For most workers in Lyons (apart from those employed in weaving the luxurious cloths, which still provided a tolerable income) this meant either leaving the city or working longer hours in order to earn a decent wage. For most, life was increasingly difficult. Twice between 1830 and 1835, the *canuts* (as the male weavers were called) had revolted – unsuccessfully – and had emerged with less will to improve their circumstances. During the mid-1840s the weavers were powerless to prevent a reduction in their wages, which, for example, took a velvet weaver's daily wage from 7 francs per day in 1842 to 3 in 1844.[29] The financial and employment crisis that led to the Revolution of 1848 was felt keenly everywhere. In Mulhouse it led to a bread strike; in Lyons it affected workers and silk merchants alike. Of the 750 merchants in business in 1830, only 450 remained in 1850, representing 300 firms; the *Indicateur Annuaire*, which listed the names and addresses of those involved in Lyons' weaving trade, noted in the 1849–50 edition: 'It is remarkable that never, in such a short period as that between our first publication and this one, has change been so great', also noting that a large number of merchants had changed the nature of their product or formed new associations.[30] Fifty firms were able, more or less, to monopolize the silk trade in Lyons, and were even better able to dictate wages.

Already employed at the new looms and in associated tasks, women weavers (*canutes*) were given an increased share of the work in and around Lyons, and for less money than their male counterparts. Wages dropped dramatically; in 1831–32 a *canut* received between 2.25 francs for a satin *liséré* (Jacquard woven with the pattern made from the warp) for wall-hangings to 4.50 francs for a three-colour damask, but twenty years later the many *canutes* worked for no more than one franc a day. In the convents where workshops had been established in the surrounding districts, women who did ancillary work, such as spinning, received food and shelter and only a few centimes a year.[31] The master craftsman remained only in numbers large enough to keep alive the skills needed for making luxury fabrics, but by 1870 the days when Lyons teemed with proud artisans were over.

Elsewhere the position of weavers was no better. For example, weavers in the Caux, on the coast of Normandy, whose numbers had increased in response to more efficient spinning, were also being pushed to the bottom of the economic ladder. Like their equivalents in Lyons, these female weavers worked for

*Painted in 1837 by Michel Genod, the setting of* Great-Grandfather's Birthday *is the best room of an artisan's house. The central figure may well be a weaver, for the elderly woman – presumably his wife – holds a distaff and bobbin and it is known that the wives of weavers were often spinners. The stairs lead to a well-lit room that would have contained his loom. Although his lap rug is worn, the once luxurious eighteenth-century wing chair and bed are well preserved. The curtains are of red and white checked cotton, a material which even today is considered to be intrinsically French.*

merchants – in this case in Rouen – and could not themselves afford to buy a new loom, which cost between 100 and 150 francs. Often earning less than one franc a day, they could not even purchase an old loom (15 to 50 francs). Yet in mid-century this region had 110,000 female cottage weavers, who, together with other poorly paid Normandy weavers, produced half of all the cotton cloth consumed in France.[32] Because labour was so cheap, power weaving was introduced only very slowly. Even so, in Normandy the production of weaves gradually took over from printed fabrics. This was partly because printers in this region could not compete with those of Alsace. A few large printing firms with enough capital introduced perrotines and multiple-colour roller printing machines alongside their block-printing tables. However, some Rouen manufacturers – ever eager to economize – used brass instead of copper for their rollers; it did not print so well, but it was cheaper.[33] The introduction of machines into the Normandy woollen industry was even slower than in the cotton industry of that region, and the 'putting out' system dominated until the 1860s.

Some weavers managed to emigrate – to the benefit, certainly, of England. (It is not known how many of the 16,000 expelled for their participation in the 1848 revolution and the uprising of 1851–52 were in the textile trade.) In his record of a visit to England in the following decade, a traveller named Francis Wey noted his meeting with a Frenchman who 'had brought off several clever commercial coups during our revolution of '48 by capturing some of the Lyons' silk export market and established rival looms in England with French weavers'.[34] Disaffection with their situation also led a handful of silk workers to Paterson, New Jersey, which opened its first silk factory in 1840 and which, by 1870, had at least sixty French dyers, weavers, finishers and merchants.[35]

Overshadowed by the silk industry, with its long tradition of excellence in design, was the French woollen industry. Nevertheless, during the middle of the nineteenth century France was the centre of European woollen yarn and cloth production, surpassing all other nations in its output. The enlargement of its Algerian colony during the Second Empire played an important part in France's woollen industry, for by about 1860 there were eight million sheep in Algeria whose fleece went mainly to Roubaix and Rheims, the latter the centre of the hand-weaving of merinos (a pure worsted cloth which a British visitor to the 1855 Paris exhibition considered 'far superior to English fabrics' of a similar nature).[36] Many of the woollen cloths formed a base for printing, and the finished products (the *flanelles* described as new in 1819) were widely used as a furnishing fabric. Their method of manufacture was described by Le Normand in his *Manuel du fabricant* of 1830. Crediting a M. Ternaux with their reintroduction for furnishings, he describes their early form as dyed yellow, red, blue or green and then 'printed in black with suitable designs for armchairs, bergères, sofas, chairs, etc.', adding that 'in all circumstances we substitute cloths printed in this way for Utrecht velvet and they wear well'.[37] Later printed with a range of deep, stained-glass-like colours which became fashionable in the middle of the century (partly as a result of the development from 1856 of new chemical, or aniline, dyes), these were particularly striking cloths, with a pliability that made them well suited not only to the heavy folds of neo-rococo and neo-Renaissance draperies, but – perhaps more importantly – to the tortures of deep-buttoning. The cotton centre, St-Quentin, began making half-wools and all-wools for printing. Ribbed (rep) and heavily felted wools were also printed with designs especially made for table covers, the manufacture of which was an Alsatian speciality.

There were also other types of fabric, containing wool, which found great popularity in this period. For example, the magazine *Abeilles Parisiennes* noted in 1850 that 'furnishings should preferably be dark or mottled'. In this regard they thought that moquette, a wool velvet with its pile often left in loops, 'is very good for both curtains and furniture'.[38] Tapestry, also, was fashionable for upholstery – this was the period during which many pieces of furniture from the second half of the eighteenth century were covered for the first time in this manner (very few – perhaps about 5 per cent – were covered with tapestry when they were new). Interest in these textiles was such that les Gobelins was now open to the public; so too, was the Savonnerie carpets factory. Tapestries were not limited to use with eighteenth-century-style furniture; they were also hung on the walls in 'Louis XIII' drawing rooms. Although reproduction furniture was no less sought-after than the originals, old Beauvais tapestries, according to one reporter, seem to have been more prized than newly woven pieces.[39] This may be partly attributable to the Empress Eugénie's interest in Marie Antoinette, who was associated with the arcadian and pastoral – precisely the themes in which Beauvais had excelled.

The size of the woollen industry, the diversity of silk weavers and the adaptability of the cotton industry were crucial in the 1860s, when the American

*Block-printed by Thierry-Mieg, the pattern on this woollen twill, although similar to those shown by the firm at the Paris Exposition of 1855, employs aniline colours more typical of the company's products of the years 1863 to 1867. Wool was particularly receptive to the new aniline dyes.*

*The relatively coarse cotton and diagonally ribbed bourette (or cotton and filoselle twill) shown here were printed in about 1870, employing Indian-style patterns. Both became typical printing surfaces as a result of the cotton shortage in the aftermath of the American Civil War. The large leafy pattern, block-printed on a white ground by Thierry-Mieg, was also produced with an extra colour – bright yellow – added to the white areas of the leaves in this example.*

Civil War (1861–65) cut off America's exports of their fine-grade cottons. The Rouen cotton spinners coped by spinning even coarser cotton yarns, but thirteen printworks closed, and two other *indienne* printers switched to printing on wool. The main Alsatian firms survived because they had large stocks of cotton, and were able to use it judiciously in cloths containing more waste-yarns, in cotton and wool mixtures, or in all-cotton, but paper-thin fabrics. Even they, however, barely made a profit on their printed cloths, and would not have done so at all, had not the exports of this type of fabric already increased by 50 per cent between 1837 and 1859, creating additional external markets which – representing the luxury end of the textile industry – would more readily bear the necessary increase in prices. (By 1870 the cost of prints from Mulhouse – still graduated according to the number of colours – ranged from 1.10 francs for one or two colours on white to 2.50 francs for a full-colour block print on a 'fancy' or coloured ground, the latter being a 15 per cent increase on prices some dozen years before.[40]) With America's increased tariffs on imports, the French recognized the need to pursue other markets, and they began to investigate ways of increasing their existing trade with the Gold Coast, China and Japan (where, in the last named, silk-wool mixes from Roubaix or Amiens, as well as Turkey-red cottons were sold). At the same time, however, they recognized one advantage which would help maintain their exports to established customers: the French reputation for selecting good designs and marrying colours effectively.[41]

Perhaps most important in disseminating French fashions, both within France and abroad, were the publications of Désiré Guilmard, foremost of which was *Le Garde-meuble, ancien et moderne, journal d'ameublement*, which first appeared in 1839 and survived until 1935. Two companion journals, also by Guilmard, were *Le Garde-meuble riche* and *Le Garde-meuble simple*, the latter including furniture that could be easily made, and also indicating the extent to which more French people now aspired to decorate lavishly. Comparatively recent studies have shown that Guilmard's publications were influential in the United States.[42] Guilmard also published illustrations of the furniture shown at the national exhibitions of 1844 and 1849, followed by those at the international *Exposition Universelle* held in Paris in 1855. There were four national exhibitions during this period (the others were in 1834 and 1839). The universal exhibitions – the first of which was held in London in 1851 – quickly became more influential than the national ones, even though they soon came to exhibit only goods made for show, rather than for normal production.

These exhibitions generated volumes of documentation, which provide a wealth of information on the French textile industry and its relationship with those of other countries, particularly Britain. The difference between these two nations' approach can be seen, for example, in the exhibits of machinery at the 1855 Paris exhibition; France showed many hand looms and the English none, whereas England displayed its power looms and France showed only a few, made in Alsace. The same difference can be found in the application of technology, such as the Jacquard mechanism. The English had adapted the Jacquard loom to power, exploiting its rapidity when a change of pattern was required; the French used the system on hand looms, to provide colourful fabrics in which the elaborate pattern was obtained with greater ease for the handweaver. Indeed, this period represents France's apex in its exploration of the capabilities of the Jacquard loom (which was improved several times as a consequence). By the 1860s there was no country

*Jacquard machines, improved and used only by the largest firms in Lyons in this period, made the manufacture of very long patterns much more économical. Here, a damask curtain has been woven complete with integral borders. Several panels were ordered by Roudillon from Tassinari & Chatel in 1863 and again in 1868; each panel was 4½ yards (4.20 metres) high and 1½ yards (1.40 metres) wide, and cost 210 francs.*

that could compete with her hand-woven velvets patterned by the use of plain and pile areas, or the contrast between cut (*coupé*) and uncut (*frisé*) pile. Such velvets represented the *tour de force* of Jacquard technology; they were expensive and were naturally made only for 'the most luxurious residences'.[43] So the two countries, although competing in small measure on each others' ground, continued in many respects to invest most in their traditional strengths – the French in the most expensive fabrics, and the English in mass production.

It was on this basis that many on both sides of the Channel argued for free trade, believing – for example with regard to silks – that, in the words of M. Arlès Dufour, Secretary of the French Imperial Commission of 1855, 'it would be profitable to both countries. England would cease to copy our rich fancy silks, and would devote its whole energy to the production of the low and middle qualities, while France, on the contrary, would apply itself with increased attention to the production of the former.'[44] However the Chevalier-Cobden Treaty, signed in 1860, did not have quite this outcome. For one thing, not all French manufacturers were prepared to conform to this policy. The British silk manufacturers, of which there were more than 250, did suffer from the resulting open competition, but those British and Alsatian printers who had enlarged their production, and at each stage introduced – not radically new machinery, but methods that allowed a higher quality of cloth to be produced – were already offering machine-printed fabrics that rivalled those printed by hand. Thus the envisaged quantity-quality division between the two nations never materialized.

The lack of differentiation in the technical quality of some comparable British and French products now meant that design played a more distinctive role. Britain had started to examine its standards of design in the late 1830s; some design schools had been founded, some theories espoused. But with the Great Exhibition

*Glazed percales printed with full, lush bouquets, such as this one, were characteristic of the widely acclaimed work of Jean Ulrich Tournier. Many similar patterns were also produced in England, and it was this type of design which was regarded by English design reformers as too imitative of nature.*

in 1851 – which served only to confirm France's long-acknowledged superiority in artistic quality and ornamental effect – Britain was forced into action. The action, taken by a group of men associated with the Great Exhibition itself, was to promote usefulness above ornament, comfort above luxury.[45] This point of view then allowed the British to say that a Parisian of the middle or lower class 'cannot be content in his own home with the simple furniture suitable to his rank. His small apartments are fitted up for show rather than for comfort, a word not in his language . . . and if he cannot afford realities he will obtain the appearance of them by gaudy finery and over-decoration.'

These censorious remarks were delivered by Richard Redgrave, an official British observer at the 1855 Paris *Exposition Universelle*. He did acknowledge the superiority of the French silks exhibited there: 'Nothing can exceed the beauty of the dyes, the evident insight of the designer or putter-on into the capabilities of the material and the manufacturing means, or the skill of the weaver . . . in these respects they are real lessons to us.' But the total effect was too rich for his taste – inappropriate, he felt, for the average person's home – and he found it 'impossible to approve of the great majority of the works displayed'.[46]

In England, meanwhile, a number of silk manufacturers were developing large and prosperous mills, geared to producing precisely the sort of splendid cloths of which Redgrave disapproved. One of these was the complex in Braintree, Essex, which belonged to Daniel Walters & Sons. Many of the patterns that Walters and other furnishing silk manufacturers wove were of French design, both old and new. There can be little doubt that most members of the Anglo-American colony in Lyons – said to include some eighty British in 1853 – were there because of their interest in silk and, more than likely, in acquiring designs for their colleagues and friends elsewhere. (There is some evidence that British silk-weaving firms also occasionally ordered silks from their Lyons competitors.[47])

In the making of linen cloths, particularly fine cambrics, France had already lost its lead. Instead, it was Ireland that now occupied first place, having increased its number of linen-workers by more than five times during the reign of Louis Philippe, and placed them in a position, reported Andrew Ure, to 'command the most exclusive sale, having struggled against the produce of the German and French looms, until they have gained the upper hand in almost all cases'. To illustrate this point, the author noted that for every 10 pieces of cambric made in France in 1829 Ireland had made one. But for every 10 French pieces in 1846 there were 160 of Irish make.[48]

The universal exhibitions were a vital arena for the textile industry; in 1855 the English acknowledged French improvements in technology, in 1862 the French conceded that they now had, in Britain, a rival in the field of design.[49] These events were also occasions for celebration and international diplomacy, the latter highlighted at the 1855 Paris exhibition by the visit of Queen Victoria. This followed only months after the state visit of Napoleon III and the Empress Eugénie to Windsor, and established 1855 as the high point of *rapprochement* between these two countries. (This had built up over a number of years, for both French monarchs of this period had spent considerable time in England.)

While British and French rivalry continued on friendly terms, the United States was experiencing a new burst of francophilia. Although a distinctively American style was now emerging in furniture making (based on the gradual

improvements in mass production), the patterns on which this furniture was based tended to be French. Of textile manufacturers in the United States it was said, in 1840, that 'all superior articles [were] copied from the French.'[50] The copying of French designs was facilitated by 'pattern services', which supplied designs in several forms, including drawings, engraved plates and fabrics, collected from various French merchants, grouped into themes by design type or material, and sold to American manufacturers. Some originated out of design studios. One such, active in Paris from 1830 to 1856, was Claude Frères, from which evolved J. Claude Frères (which became one of the most respected pattern services and survived well into this century). By the middle of the century designs were also being purchased from the ateliers in Alsace. Some designers there seem to have specialized in such work, for early in the 1850s a sample from the Globe Printwork in Fall River, Massachusetts, was in the possession of the Mulhouse firm Dollfus-Mieg & Cie.; its label bore the name Fallon, described as a colourist for the U.S.A.[51] It was considered a matter of pride, by Americans, that so many fabrics made in the United States carried French designs.

For the connoisseur, fabrics actually made in France were also becoming more widely available. A. T. Stewart's (opened in 1823 as a small New York store and eventually to become America's first department store) was already known for its provision of French silks by 1840, the same year in which America's now-great foreign debt was blamed in part on purchases from France. In that year, an article in the widely read monthly magazine *Godey's Lady's Book* pointed out that a small piece of French lace to trim a dress cost 40 dollars – an amount that would have provided a week's hotel board for two adults, two children and a servant. Ironically, the same sum could have purchased enough French fabric to make one of the sets of curtains frequently illustrated in the magazine. From its inception, in July 1830, it was clear that *Godey's* considered acquaintance with anything

French to be a certain sign of good breeding; in one of its short stories, for example, the highest praise heaped on the heroine was that 'she was an excellent French scholar'.[52] Ownership of something French was infinitely better, and the magazine consistently promoted the Philadelphia store W. H. Carryl's, which specialized in French imports. (Carryl's was taken over by Walraven's in about 1865.) Trade was so brisk that Mr. Person of A. Person, Harriman & Co., an importing house founded in 1858, was said, by the author of his obituary, to have been 'largely instrumental in effecting the establishment of the direct rapid mail connection between France and America'. *Harper's Weekly*, like many other American magazines, carried regular reports on French interiors and fashions, and was particularly delighted when it could combine this with news of one of the several young American women who had married French aristocrats. In 1857, for example, it reported that 'The Countess of Morny has met with great success in Parisian society, and the happy couple have now departed for their country seat in Auvergne. In his travels on railways M. [*sic*] Morny uses a special and magnificent wagon, furnished like an elegant drawing-room. Other lucky financiers have imitated his example, and possess private "saloon carriages", in order to be always amidst the accustomed luxury.'[53]

In fact, the example was set, not by the Count but by the Emperor and Empress, who had been presented with an imperial train in 1856. Made by the Compagnie du Chemin de fer d'Orléans, it had decorations designed by Viollet-le-Duc (the architect responsible during this period for many restorations of medieval buildings, including Notre Dame). These consisted of bright green silk damask wallcoverings and upholstery in the *wagon d'honneur*, which had a ceiling of gilded and painted star-shaped casings. The ceiling in the bedroom, however, was bright blue velvet; this shone above deep red velvet-covered walls

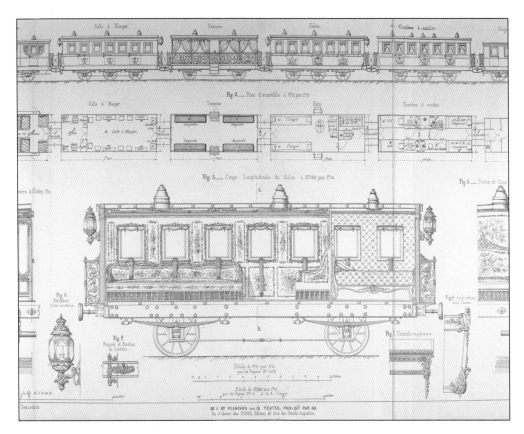

*Decorated with rich, deeply coloured fabrics, Napoleon III's private train set a standard for luxury which was followed by those rich enough to do so. This illustration of the interior, which was completed in 1862, was published in the* Album practique de l'art industriel et des beaux arts.

and door curtains, lined with white *gros de Naples* (a plain silk with a pronounced horizontal grain) and fringed with gold.[54] The luxurious decoration of railway carriages was of no small importance, since railway lines were rapidly extended throughout this period. Interiors for these carriages were often illustrated, showing the use of the latest Parisian-style curtains, wallcoverings and upholstery – the latter two often deeply buttoned. The richest of fabrics, echoing those used in mansions and hotels in Paris, were also used in private and first-class railway carriages across Europe and in the United States; scarcely less elaborate were those used in horse-drawn carriages. In 1857 Americans were also informed by *Harper's Weekly* that 'in Paris the immense increase of handsome equipages must strike every eye and the other signs of enlarged expenditure are abundant'.[55]

The ostentatious display of the age had its critics – in France, as elsewhere. The writer Gustave Claudin, who published his observations on Paris in 1867, thought that the nineteenth century had created railways instead of artists.[56] The painter Eugène Delacroix also deplored the artistic standards of his age – including architecture, interior decoration and textiles – and similarly placed the blame on France's exuberant commercialism.[57] Both associated this tendency with Americans, who had, in large numbers, begun flocking to Paris. But, as always, the local inhabitants were keen to exploit the visitors' spending power; Mark Twain, in his account of his travels through Europe, greatly enjoyed describing the persistence of his Paris cab driver, who, despite Twain's protestations, managed to find a silk merchants's shop on the way to every destination, certain that all Americans came to Paris only to buy silks.

Since the 1840s, shopping had been one of the pleasures of Paris, where *magasins de nouveautés* began to expand, to group their products into departments[58] and to fix the price of their goods. The last-named practice made purchasing fabrics easier for shoppers, as did the adoption of the metric system of measurement in 1840.[59] Among the many large Paris shops of the 1850s were the Bon Marché, the ambitiously named Louvre and the Bazar de l'Hôtel de Ville. These were joined in 1865 by Au Printemps and grew to become the luxurious department stores which over the next decades were to be influential in the design and use of textiles and interiors. Up until 1870 they operated in the shadow of the Empress Eugénie, whose intense admiration for Marie Antoinette resulted in interiors in the so-called 'Louis XVI – *Imperatrice*' style, created by her favoured cabinetmakers (such as Georges Grobé) and numerous *tapissier-décorateurs* who worked for the court and its admirers. After 1870 such shops no longer had to defer to royal preferences; for in the aftermath of the Franco-Prussian War, the French people abolished their monarchy once more.

*The bedchamber of the Empress Eugénie, created in about 1855 at the Château de Compiègne, shows the return of the four-poster bed decorated in the manner of eighteenth-century state beds. It is nevertheless tempered by a restrained colour palette and the relatively small-patterned silk on the walls. This style was known as l'imperatrice.*

*Jungle themes were interpreted by textile designers during the Second Empire both as all-over patterns and as entire scenes. Typifying the international nature of textile manufacture today – and the long-established links between France and Britain in particular – this block-printed glazed percale of between 1868 and 1870 is held in the Musée de l'Impression sur Etoffes, Mulhouse, and has recently been selected for production by Warner Fabrics in London.*

*Block-printed percales, with designs of vines carrying a mixture of blossoms, were produced by a number of Alsatian firms in the 1840s and early 1850s. This example dates from about 1842.*

*This plate, from a lithographed series of* Dessins inédits de Pierre Berjon, *published by the Société des Amis des Arts de Lyon in 1847, illustrates contemporary taste for wild forest plants arranged, as here, to form a frame around a distant view.*

*The designer George Zipélius was responsible for a distinctive series of patterns, produced between 1827 and 1860 by Alsatian roller printers. This example, from Koechling-Ziegler, may have been produced in the 1850s, during his period of collaboration with Joseph Fuchs, who was known for his bird designs. It was still in manufacture in about 1870.*

Printed wools were often used in interiors of this period, although very few survive today. This example was block-printed by Claude Frères in 1856. The vertical repeat is 16 inches (40.6 cm) high, suggesting that it was printed by machine, probably the 'Ebinger', with rotating wooden blocks.

Printed and glazed percales were used in abundance in the mid-nineteenth century, as is illustrated by this aquarelle, attributed to Kollmann. The masses of cloth were used to divide the room up for different functions. This interior was in the home of Eveline Hanska – mistress, and later wife, of the novelist Honoré de Balzac – who lived in Wierzchownia, in the Ukraine.

By about 1866, when this plate was published in Le Magasin de meubles, fringing was still used as a decorative device but no longer hid the legs of seat-furniture completely. Shown here are two alternatives for bedroom chairs and a chaise longue Mexicaine, the latter term referring to the striped pattern. The legs on this piece appear to be of cast iron.

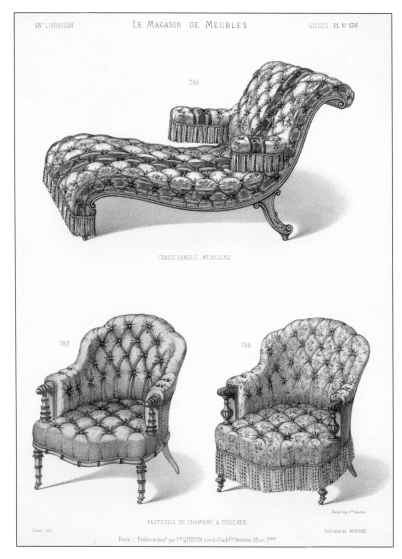

The colour scheme seen in this Alsatian copper- and wooden-roller-printed cotton was derived from two yellows and one brown, the brilliant green occurring where chrome yellow and brown overlapped. Although this example dates from the 1830s, the same colour combination was also used until the early 1850s.

*Left: Engraved by François Hipployte Lalasse, this* Interior of a Chalet in Haute-Savoie *was published in Nantes in the 1840s or '50s. The curtains, in late Empire style, that close off the alcove beds, thereby affording a measure of privacy, were a feature common to hostelries of the period. The bare floor was typical of all rural residences at this date, as was the straight-hanging, floor-length curtain at the window on the left. The fabrics would undoubtedly have been of washable linen and cotton.*

*Opposite above: The Château Lafite, north of Bordeaux, was bought in 1868 by the Baron and Baroness James de Rothschild, and furnished by the Baroness in neo-renaissance style. Here, in the library, brilliantly coloured silk damask wallcoverings and embroidered borders offset the seventeenth-century-style ebony and ivory cabinets. The colouring and boldness of execution, and not the furniture or fabrics per se, make this a 'free' renaissance interior.*

*Right: Manufactured by Grand Frères in 1812 and 1813 for Napoleon's third salon at Versailles, this velours ciselé was intended to be used for wall-hangings, portières and cantonnières. Instead, it was eventually used in 1855 by the Garde-Meuble at Fontainebleau, replacing fabrics installed in 1785. In the new scheme the walls were covered with a white damask woven in 1812 and the bed and seat-furniture upholstered with this velvet. Fabric from the same original order was also used at Compiègne in 1858.*

*Below: Wreaths reminiscent of the late Empire style are incorporated into this glazed cotton percale, printed by Thierry-Mieg in 1857–58. It is inscribed: 'It's an original enough design but does not please us, [although] Alexandre has a very high opinion of it.'*

*Above: In this photograph of about 1858, Napoleon III sits with his son on a sofa, deep-buttoned and with long fringing in a manner fashionable since the 1840s. The pattern of the silk has been entirely distorted by the upholstery technique.*

*Below: Typical of the period's disregard for geography, this richly coloured cotton, roller-printed by Frères Reber in 1863 or '64, combines motifs inspired by Chinese and Indian ornament. The label reads, '3.15 francs; we find this design rich and beautiful, it should sell well'.*

*Above right: First woven in 1848 by Tassinari & Chatel, this exotic lampas was made exclusively for their customer Despréaux. A further 835 yards (771 metres) were woven for a total of six more orders placed between 1850 and 1860.*

The use of Indian motifs continued throughout this period. Here, in a printed cotton made between 1855 and 1869, the vividly coloured, exotic motifs are set against a partially discharged red ground, in imitation of the 'damask' patterns used as a background in many tapestries of some hundred years earlier.

Indian-style patterns were associated with informal, comfortable furniture, as in this chaise longue, illustrated in about 1865 in Le Magasin de meubles, published by V. Quentin in Paris. The decline of the taste for fully upholstered furniture is signalled by the depiction of the second piece, a borne de salon with balustrades.

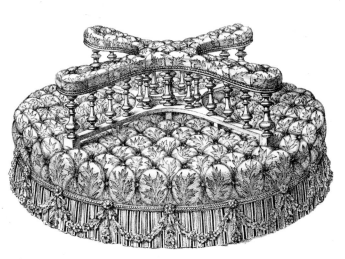

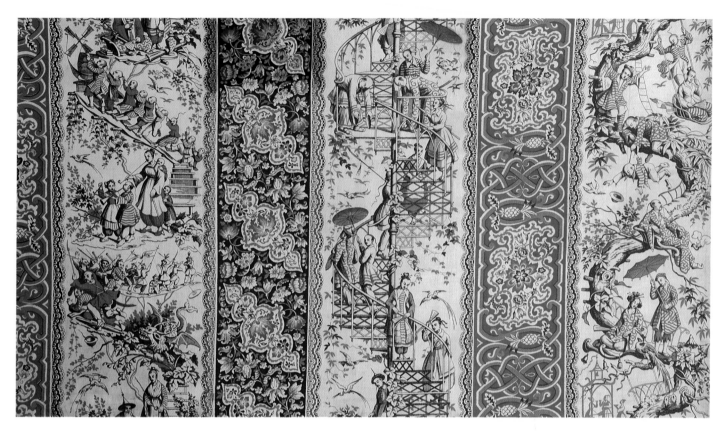

Although the pattern of this block-printed cotton was used by Frères Koechlin of Mulhouse as early as 1831, this example dates from about 1840 and employs a manganese bronze, first used in Alsace in 1834.

Block-printed by Liebach Hartmann & Cie. of Mulhouse in 1832, this chinoiserie pattern has a tobacco-coloured ground typical of the period, perhaps in anticipation of concealing smoke stains, since Chinese patterns were thought to be masculine, and were used in smoking and billiard rooms. In this example the green is made by the old method of overprinting blue and yellow.

One hundred and thirty-seven yards (127 metres) of this silk lampas mexicain *were woven by Lamy & Giraud, to the order of Brolemann & Cie. placed on 17 August 1866. To ensure that the ground was the correct colour, the customer attached a sample of the desired shade of garnet.*

*Taken from* Le Magasin de meubles *of about 1865, this illustration of an oriental-style smoking room shows entirely European upholstery and curtain treatments combined with furniture* à la chinoise.

*Right: The Manuel geometrique du tapissier was published in Paris by Jules Verdellet in 1851, when the upholsterer's art was dominant in interior decoration. This plate illustrates the making of lambrequins with widely spaced pleats.*

*Below left: Medieval- or gothic-inspired styles and designs were given impetus by the many restoration projects undertaken between 1840 and 1870. The French architect Viollet-le-Duc was particularly active in this sphere, and also encouraged a revival of stained-glass making. Both influences can be seen in the style and colouring of this brocaded brocatelle, produced in Lyons, probably in the early 1840s.*

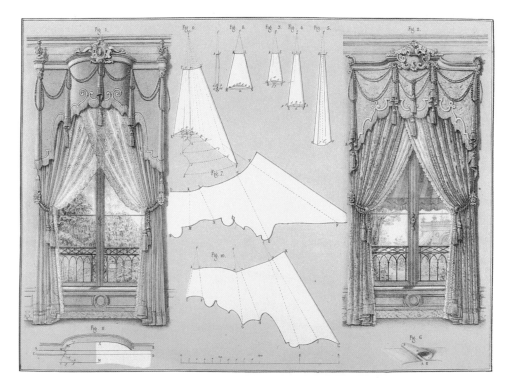

Opposite right: In the neo-
renaissance style, this patterned
silk brocatelle was created by
Lemire Père & Fils in 1845. The
vivid colouring of the main
pattern is supplemented by that of
the hand-brocaded floral bunches.

A tour de force of engraving, this
single-colour roller print was
produced by Koechling-Ziegler
from a design by or after Zipéleus,
in about 1845. Its style owes
much to the development of
ornamental low-relief metalwork.

Above: A design from Thierry-Mieg of about 1860, the detail shows one corner of a printed table cover, a product for which a number of Mulhouse manufacturers were well known. Patterns such as this were printed on a variety of cloths, but most typically on felted wool.

Left: Block-printed in the mid-1830s, the large rose and scrolling cartouche of this cotton echo elements of patterns from some fifty years earlier. By contrast, the even spacing of the vase and floral spray, each about 11½ inches (29 cm) high, are characteristic of many designs produced in the first half of the reign of Louis Philippe (1830–1848). The pattern is still available in reproduction from Simon Playle, London, who owns the original shown here.

*Right and below: Two glazed cottons with co-ordinating patterns, produced in France in 1857–58, either by or for Claye. Each has a comment affixed: the stripe is noted 'pretty and rich effect', and its partner, 'good design, new effect'.*

*Right: These nine schemes for interior decoration – all created by Leger in about 1844 – show the period's predilection for combinations of several elaborately patterned fabrics, especially prints, in private rooms. In contrast, the reception rooms (seen across the top row and bottom right), rely principally on plainer fabrics, which would have been more luxurious either in their fibre content, as with silk, or their construction, as with velvet. The room shown at the top left is similar to those illustrated in conjunction with the Paris Exposition of 1844. Note also the return of pre-Empire-style beds, with their heads once more to the walls.*

*Opposite above: Containing small scenic medallions, this cotton was produced on a wooden roller-printing machine, invented in 1800 by the Frenchman Ebinger and named after him in France, but known in England as a 'surface' machine. Initially capable of one-colour printing only, by about 1830, when this example was printed, subsequent improvements allowed several colours to be printed at once.*

*Opposite below: This picture appeared in* Le Diable à Paris *on 1 January 1846. Drawn by the illustrator Bertall, it depicts social stations in life by analogy with the floors of a house. The comfortable, prosperous and fashionable room on the first floor is in complete contrast to those of the upper two, in which one inhabitant is reduced to sleeping on the floor, with an umbrella for protection against the leaking roof. Similarly vivid contrasts between the rich and the poor were the subject of many of the novels of Emile Zola.*

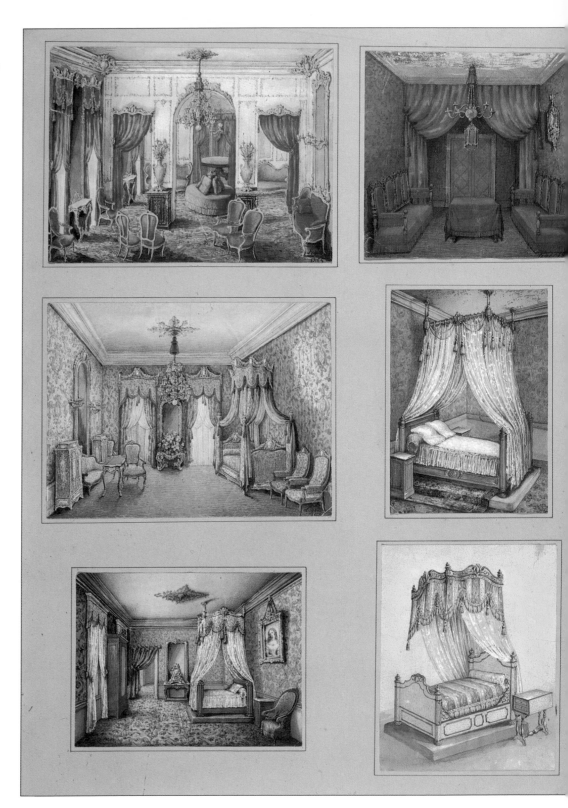

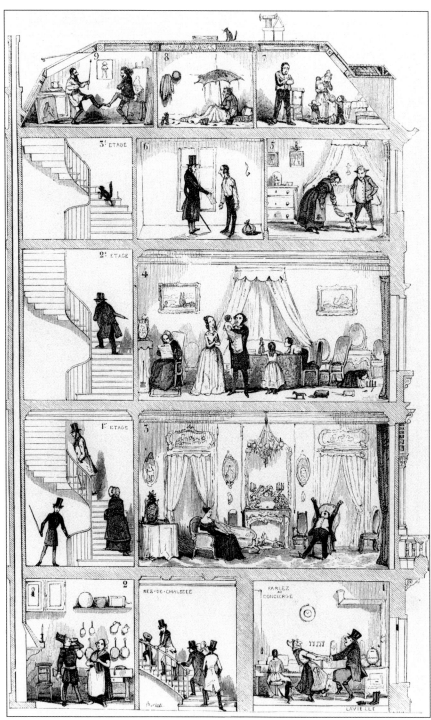

*Above:* In contrast to the mixed colours and patterns typical of middle-class interiors, the Interior of the Salon of MP, painted by Sébastien Charles Giraud in the 1860s, shows the en suite style preferred by the wealthy. The room beyond is also furnished in the same colour. The effect of the masses of silk is, as a result, one of restrained splendour. The piece of furniture in the centre of the room, known as an indiscret, is typical of the conversational seating fashionable during the Second Empire.

*Left:* This tissue, woven with a rep (ribbed) ground, has a design of beribboned flowers which shows a return to the freer, more naturalistic style that gradually appeared during the 1840s. The combination of lime green and garnet is typical of the taste of the period, influenced as it was by the development of new pigments and dyes. This type of pattern was also used by textile printers in the early 1850s.

The Paris Exposition of 1867 included a number of fabrics that indicated the growing taste for the lighter, more delicate mid- to late eighteenth-century style. Among them was this example of a silk taffeta by R. Ronza. The pattern was created from a woven rib, or rep, which was overprinted after the cloth had been taken from the loom.

The robust neo-renaissance style survived throughout the Second Empire. Here, in a velours ciselé of 1870, Mathevon & Bouvard of Lyons employed a pattern indebted to the many contemporary publications that depicted the work of Raphael. The apparent variation in the tones of red is created solely by the juxtaposition of different woven textures.

*Above: Although incorporating rococo features (such as the trompe-l'oeil ormolu decoration), this block-printed mohair of about 1860 shows the bold styling and brilliant colouring typical of the Second Empire. The colours used were probably produced by a combination of mineral and synthetic dyes, the latter having become available in the late 1850s.*

*Below: Flower painting continued to exert an influence on textile design, particularly compositions such as this, painted in 1866 by Marc Bruyas, who studied at the Ecole des Beaux-Arts in Lyons and was himself a textile designer. The artist has included fuchsias, which were made fashionable by their use in the new gardens on the Champs Elysées in the late 1850s.*

This design of the 1860s for
tapesty-woven upholstery to cover a
two-seat, wood-frame sofa, known as a
canapé, would have been produced at
the Beauvais or Gobelins workshops.
Although inspired by late
eighteenth-century decorative motifs, the
robust laurel wreath and grey-gold colour
palette are a feature of the
neo-renaissance, Second Empire taste.

Backgrounds printed in imitation of a
moiré effect were used by several
Alsatian manufacturers throughout the
1850s and the early 1860s. This example,
produced by Thierry-Mieg in 1857 or '58,
was sold for 1.20 franc, and was
described at the time as having a
'magnificent and rich design, [the] rollers
remarkably well engraved'.

# CHAPTER FIVE

# RETRENCHMENT

## *(1870–1915)*

'THE WAR, the invasion and the insurrection in Paris had impoverished our country; luxury had disappeared, everyone was in mourning, domestic consumption had greatly decreased. In such conditions, with the high cost of capital, silk and labour, with the unrest and disorganization inseparable from ten months of public misfortune and private misery . . . it seemed as though the *fabriques* of Lyons must falter. On the contrary, it was as vigorous as ever.' (Natalis Rondot, in *Moniteur des Fils, des Tissus, des Apprêts, de la Teinture*.)[1]

With these defiant words, a writer for a Paris trade journal assessed France's silk industry in 1873. Not all was well, however, behind the brave front. Although the Franco-Prussian War was relatively short, lasting only ten months from July 1870, its effect on France was harsh. In response to the surrender of Napoleon III two months later at the Battle of Sedan, Paris declared him abdicated, and a new republic, led by the Government of National Defence, continued to fight the Prussians who surrounded their city. Fighting also continued in the Loire valley. By January Paris was forced to surrender for lack of food; this defeat was followed, in March to May, by the Paris Commune's resistance to Adolphe Thiers, who then represented the French government. In May the worst week of the war occurred, with vicious factional street fighting and the murder of prisoners on both sides (representing the extreme republicans and Thiers' government, suspected by the former of wishing to restore a monarchy). Twenty-five thousand French people died – including 20,000 put to death by the victorious government – more than in any of the battles during the Franco-Prussian war.

France's first obstacle after the Franco-Prussian War was debt. And as if the indemnity of 5 billion francs (and occupation by the Prussian army until France paid its war debt) were not enough, Bismarck, who had engineered the Prussian side of the war, took the provinces of Lorraine and Alsace, intending to weaken France by cutting off her main source of iron and coal. Remarkably, the debt was paid within two years (hence the optimistic tone of the opening remarks), but the loss of Alsace had repercussions which lasted until the First World War. The heart had been cut out of the industrialized French textiles manufacture. It had lost not only weavers, spinners and printers, but a concentrated source of Europe's most advanced dye works, machine builders and industrial leaders. A dramatic, sometimes traumatic adjustment had to be made, both by the French nation and by the Alsatians.

*Supplied to an American manufacturer by an unidentified French pattern service, these five cretonnes of the 1880s and early 1890s show the rich effect which texture-woven cloths provided. The bottom sample was intended to imitate crewelwork when seen from a distance.*

Perhaps the most noticeable effect was the spread of some manufacturing from Alsace to other textile centres located nearby, but within the newly drawn French borders. The site chosen was Belfort, only 20 miles (50 km.) from Mulhouse. Branch factories were established and workers transferred; the population of Belfort doubled by 1876, and continued to grow, if more slowly, until it had doubled again by the eve of the First World War.[2] Of equal importance now were the many connections that had already been established in areas that remained part of France. A large proportion of the spinning and weaving operations of firms based in Alsace had, as noted in the previous chapter, been transferred to the Vosges, and there were others already located in *la Bourgogne*, the region south-east of Paris. Other connections, too, preceded the Franco-Prussian War: Koechlin, Baumgartner & Cie. had opened a showroom in Paris in 1864 and one in Leipzig in the same year (in 1874 it opened others in London, Vienna and Milan). Other Alsatian printing firms with outlets already in Paris were Weiss-Fries (who also had one in London and in 1894, one in New York and one in Vienna, although all had closed by 1899) and Thierry-Mieg & Cie. (whose first commercial links with Paris had been established in 1820). Some had printworks within France, and in 1875 Gros, Roman, Marozeau & Cie. constructed a weaving mill not far from Paris. And the Société Alsacienne de Constructions Mécaniques continued to supply printing machinery made in their factories (which by the early twentieth century were in Belfort, Mulhouse and Grafenstaden, a suburb of Strasbourg) and sold through their office in Paris.[3]

Thus although now in German hands, the firms that had grown up in Alsace still played a part in the supply of French textiles. But it was a different role entirely; the Alsatian industry could no longer expect to sell three-quarters of its products in France (as it had done in 1869), since attempts to establish a preferential rate of customs duties for Alsace had failed. Consider also, the impact on the rest of France as the Alsatian 'power base' was splintered and its energies dispersed. Now the remaining textile centres were forced to expand. They did. By 1909 the town of Roubaix, weaving fabrics of wool and some cotton, had grown substantially to include some 380 firms, employing about 80 per cent of the town's total workforce; its products included cloth for upholstery, velvets, and plain and Jacquard-woven carpets. Roubaix had also developed a new cloth

*This small-scale pattern was printed between 1886 and 1890, and was also produced with a cream ground. Roller-printed on cotton by Thierry-Mieg, it had been in their range since at least 1874 (when it was produced with a blue ground); such longevity was typical of floral designs. It was probably designed by the firm's own studio, which in 1874 employed, among others, Constant Gaudiot, Charles Lefébure, and Gustave Forrer.*

*Both the border of textured cotton and its companion fabric were wooden (or surface) roller-printed by Scheurer-Rott Fils in about 1873. At this time the company was abandoning wooden rollers in favour of copper-roller-printing machines, of which they had twelve, each capable of printing from two to twelve colours. A matching wallpaper could be obtained from Paniset & Cie. of Lyons.*

especially for furnishing – called *articles de Roubaix* – which was made with a mixed wool and cotton warp and an Asian silk weft. Among the firms of note were Vanoutryve & Cie., founded in 1860, who had an office in the rue St-Fiacre in Paris and opened another weaving factory in 1880 in Mouscon, just across the Belgian border. Lille, nearby, with its concentration of fine cotton cloth, net- and lacemakers, made the north the largest textile-producing area in France. Rouen and the surrounding area, having languished in comparison to Alsace during the previous forty years, became the centre of the French cotton industry, mechanizing extensively (using English and Alsatian looms and spinning equipment), so that by 1904 only about seventy handweavers remained. Its products, according to an official report, were made 'almost exclusively for France and the French colonies . . . articles of common use form the staple manufacture, including coloured woven goods, printed calicos . . . curtains and furniture covers'.[4]

The first aim of mechanization was to increase spinning and weaving capacities – that is, cloth manufacturing itself. Printing took second place; and the annexation of Alsace by Germany had already deprived France of her most important makers of printed furnishing cottons. By 1889 the whole of France still had only about one hundred printing machines, a very small number compared to the 1,100 in England, 800 in Russia or even the 400 in America. (Figures from the turn of the century indicate that Alsace alone accounted for 105 of the 230 printing machines in Germany. England saw so little need to compete with the French that only three of their printing firms exhibited at the 1900 *Exposition Universelle* in Paris.[5]) The need to supply France first meant that there was a shortage of printed cottons for export; when, in the United States, J. D. Sheldon & Co.'s 'Upholstery Goods' price list of 1872 included 'English Chintz' at 18 cents per yard and 'French chintz' at 32½ cents, the latter most probably meant Alsatian chintz. It also listed German damask at 12.50–24.00 dollars per piece, which would have been about 25 yards (23 metres) long. (One franc was the equivalent of 20 American cents in 1875.[6])

The Lyons silk industry also felt the effects of the war and the need to mechanize. By the early 1900s there were three mechanical looms for every five hand looms, and although the trend towards larger numbers of mechanical looms accelerated thereafter (often simply by adding an electric motor to a hand loom), Lyons did not make an unconsidered dash for industrialization. Instead it came to appreciate its long-held reputation for fine silks and realized that 'if we only make common silks for the mass market we shall quickly lose all our natural qualities and our personality. But if we stick to luxury goods without trying to give our industry a wider base and a more regular activity we run the risk of just becoming creators of models, designers who get copied but can't sell.'[7] The middle way was therefore taken, and Lyons became known for its diversity, improving its use of cheap raw materials (such as the silk waste yarn, *filoselle* or *bourre*), exploiting entirely new fibres (such as 'art silk', a nitrocellulose form of rayon developed by Comte Hilaire de Chardonnet in 1884 and also known by his name), and dyeing *en pièces* (after weaving).

Foremost in the minds of most weavers throughout France, however, were fears for the future. They were already familiar with the strengths of the Swiss and could only guess what effects a united Germany might have on their exports. (In fact, fine silks continued to be woven in Lyons for customers now within the

German state – but often they had to be routed through London.[8]) By the mid-1880s the industry's fears had proved correct, for the French were themselves by then the main importers of Swiss silk goods (made chiefly in Zurich). Germany also proved a threat, not just commercially but politically. When German parliamentary events early in 1887 suggested that war might again be brewing, the price of raw silk (in which Lyons merchants were the principal dealers) dropped overnight by 3 francs per kilo. In the same year it was clear that Italy had meanwhile been improving its production of velvets, for they were now, reported *The American Silk Journal*, 'regarded in France as of good quality and low price'.[9]

Lyons maintained its provision of fine silks, but not without difficulties. Having agreed in 1869 to increase weavers' wages by 20–25 per cent, they were forced by the threat of a strike to make the same increase in 1870. The effect varied according to the cloth: some figured damasks, brocatelles and printed silks increased in price 60 per cent. Surviving order books of the period indicate that velvet and lampas, which in 1867 cost from 20 to 24 francs, rose to between 50 and 70 francs per metre. Exports to Britain, which had soared in 1867, fell rapidly, England having taken advantage of the war to open twenty-three new silk works. Although by 1873 English imports had begun a slow and sometimes erratic increase, thirty-five years later they had arrived at a point that was still lower than they had been prior to the Franco-Prussian War.[10] (Cloth prices declined slightly over the same period, as did raw material costs and wages – in 1909 a velvet weaver earning an average 18 francs a week was 10 francs worse off than a Lyons bricklayer.) The war, of course, could not take all the blame. Changes in fashion also took their toll (the early twentieth-century taste for cotton and wool dress fabrics caused great hardship to silk weavers, since fashion fabrics are the largest part of any cloth industry), as did fluctuations in the supply of raw silk.

Initially, exports from France to America remained high; they were valued at nearly 50 million dollars in 1874, and these were chiefly luxury goods such as lace, fine net curtains and silks. But in the latter market the German and Swiss silks were gaining ground, and by 1880 they represented over one-quarter of American silk imports. (Just over half came from France and the rest from England – the total value was about 32 million dollars, the approximate equivalent of 160 million francs). In the same year the French consul in America reported, 'About velvet from Crefeld [in the German Rhineland], I beg to remark that it has obtained a complete monopoly of the American market.' By now self-sufficient in the printing and weaving of all but the 'high novelties and fancy styles', the Americans repeated their ill-fated attempt of the 1830s to cultivate their own raw silk, this time in California, but were once again unsuccessful.[11]

French weavers were also brought to America. Claude Chaffanjon, described as 'the well-known silk manufacturer at Jersey City Heights' (New Jersey), employed 'many French weavers and helped to bring their family and friends'. In 1887, at the time of the war scare in France, he contracted twenty-four silk weavers from Lyons (eighteen men and six women), but nearly all were turned back by the American Immigration Commission. Nevertheless, the silk weaving industry continued to grow; Paterson, New Jersey, was by now twice the size it had been in 1860 and was known as 'the Lyons of America' (not without some reason – Mr. Greppo of Weidmann & Greppo, for example, was the nephew of one of the most eminent silk dyers of Lyons). In terms of innovation in machinery and the quality of its product, another important silk weaving centre was

*A brocaded tissue woven in silk by Tassinari & Chatel in 1880. The design displays both the asymmetrical placement of motifs which was found in many eighteenth-century-inspired designs of the period, and the liking for floral basket motifs, which continued well into the twentieth century. In 1906, for example, the long established Alsatian firm Charles Steiner printed a very similar design on cotton.*

*The turn of the century was not a period during which patterns changed quickly or dramatically. Loosely drawn poppies can be found on many textiles designed between about 1885 and 1905. This example, a brocaded damask, was produced by Bérand & Ferrand in 1889, probably for inclusion in the Paris Exposition of that year.*

Manchester, Connecticut, where Cheney Brothers (founded in 1837 and manufacturers of silk sewing thread until the Civil War) were rapidly becoming the foremost silk velvet weavers in America. In 1887 *The American Silk Journal* predicted that 'the quiet but steady expulsion of foreign silks from our markets by the products of American looms is rapidly but surely drawing to a close . . . with the substantial help of the protective tariff'.[12] They were incorrect, for despite the new tariff of 1882, which added 60 per cent to the cost of imported silks (including cloths mainly of silk), affluent Americans remained faithful in their preference for French silks.

Foreign support of fine French silks was crucial to their survival, a point emphasized by the commercial attaché to the French Ambassador in London on the occasion of the Franco-British Exhibition, held in White City, London, in 1908. In reference to 'Anglo-Saxons' (meaning in this case the British, Americans and Australians), he said, in essence, that the richer they were the better it was for Lyons.[13] The 'Anglo-Saxons' were important because orders for silks from the French state and new ruling class were neither frequent nor extravagant, a trend which was particularly noticeable after about 1890. The desire to impress, a legacy of the Second Empire, may have been deemed unsuitable for the Third Republic's identity, but cost was also a factor – and not only for the French. The records at the Lyons firm Prelle reveal Russians attempting to avoid paying full import duties, and, it seems, even those from among the very richest families in the world did not mind attempting this. In 1895, for example, the *Furniture and Decoration & The Furniture Gazette*, in London, reported that the New York Custom House had seized a number of cases containing the complete decorations 'for a beautiful boudoir, an almost exact copy of one in the palace of the Petit Trianon. This work was consigned to a leading New York firm of decorators, and was said to be intended for use in the new Astor mansion, but was seized on account of an alleged under-valuation.'[14]

The preference for French furnishings had, as we have seen, already been established among the wealthy in America. With the arrival in the 1880s of what has come to be known as 'The Gilded Age', it was the Americans who now ordered furnishing silks in a manner once characteristic only of princes. The taste for French style can still best be seen in Newport, Rhode Island, where there are mansions modelled after the Grand Trianon (Rosecliff), the Petit Trianon (Marble House) and the Chateau d'Asnières, near Paris (The Elms). These three house were completed between 1892 and 1901, and the last two were decorated by J. Allard & Fils, the most highly regarded Parisian *tapissier-decorateur*. Allard often worked with the American architect Richard Morris Hunt, who designed several of the Newport villas, including The Breakers, built for Cornelius Vanderbilt. An equally well known Paris decorating firm, L. Alavoine, had a hand in the furnishings at the Elms. (Thousands of Americans had a glimpse of such interiors at the Columbian Exposition held in Chicago in 1893, where there was a Marie Antoinette room, created by Alavoine.) Some of the silks used in these interiors still survive, and others can be traced, through the order books that exist at Prelle and Tassinari & Chatel. Unfortunately, since orders from private individuals had become rare by 1870 (arriving via agents, *tapissiers* or decorators) this is not an easy process. However, taking the Lamy & Giraud orders as an example (today's Prelle was run by A. Lamy and his son Édouard from 1866 to 1914), some idea of the American trade can be gained; between 1866 and 1914 there were seventy-nine orders from

*Marble House, in Newport, Rhode Island, was modelled after the Petit Trianon. Commissioned by William K. Vanderbilt from Richard Morris Hunt in 1888, it took four years to complete. Much of the internal work, including Mrs. Vanderbilt's bedroom, shown here, was carried out by J. Allard & Fils and the cabinet-maker Henri Dasson, both of Paris. The large-patterned silks and gilt white-wood furniture typify many French-inspired interiors of America's 'Gilded Age'.*

Leon Marcotte & Co., New York, who in the late 1880s also began placing orders through a Mr Altman (the Lamy & Giraud agent in Paris, who also had a branch in New York). A small number were placed by Richard Chandler of Chicago, but it is impossible to know how many of the orders from Alavoine (who also had a branch in New York), Allard and other Parisian decorators were destined for American clients.

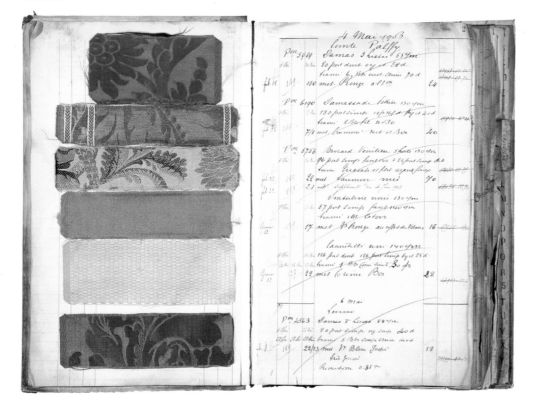

*An order book from the Prelle archive, open to show an order for hand-woven silks (the five samples at the top of the page) from Count Palffry, placed with their predecessors, Lamy & Gautier, in May 1903. Despite the fact that the Brocard Venetien (third from the top) was woven with 'false silver', its cost was still almost three times more, at 70 francs per metre, than the 24 francs charged for the damask (top). By this date few silks were being hand woven in Lyons, due to improvements made to silk-weaving power looms in the early 1890s.*

Although it is difficult to disentangle the orders from America, those from Britain are much easier, particularly after 1896, when Lamy & Giraud employed an agent in London. The decorating firm of Morant, already in the habit of buying French silks, had placed 370 orders through this agent by the beginning of World War I; these made Morant's the largest single customer, in total accounting for over 8 per cent of Lamy & Giraud's orders.

The increasing ease with which foreigners could obtain high-quality French furnishing fabrics came about partly because the Franco-Prussian War had also accelerated changes in the methods of trading. The cotton shortage in the 1860s had highlighted a new awarness that French textile firms – apart from the great Mulhouse-based companies – needed to learn to combine manufacturing and selling. This view had already been widely circulated in 1868, when the Alsatians opened a depot in Manchester for fabrics most likely to sell abroad. According to *L'Industriel Alsacien*, this agency should get useful information about foreign markets (Manchester then being the hub of European textile exports overseas) and also enable French manufacturers 'to assimilate English know-how'. With the coming of war, this lack of commercial skill was made more acute, since many of the representatives of English and American firms went home as a result. In Lyons, the Anglo-American community was halved.[15] What emerged was a complex system, in which old overlapped with new. Alavoine and Lamy & Giraud typify the new trend of establishing overseas branches among French decorators (through whom nearly all customers now purchased fabrics) and textile firms; while the remaining resident buyers from Britain and the United States continued to operate in France.

The export figures given above for 1873–74 indicate that American purchases of silks were of lesser value to the French (being at that point about 30–40 million francs lower in value than exports to Britain). But Britain was entering a period of change, in which its own designers and manufacturers were creating a new taste for what became known as the 'Arts and Crafts' style. At the same time British aristocrats – the main customers for French goods – were making an aesthetic retreat, no longer redecorating their homes periodically in the latest style, as in the past. Whether for this reason or simply the knowledge that America had so many millionaires (the *New York Tribune* listed 4,047 in 1892, and three years earlier 67 people had been identified as worth over 20 million dollars), the United States seems thereafter to have been the focus of French efforts to increase exports.[16] The strength of the French-American trade is perhaps best indicated by the founding of two wholesale furnishing fabrics firms, Brunschwig & Fils (in 1880 in France, exporting to America) and Schumacher (in 1889 in New York, importing from France), which still exist today. (Brunschwig had such success that they transferred their business to New York in 1926; Schumacher, while continuing to import French cloths, opened their first Paterson mill in 1895.) In the Philadelphia area, Albert Lightfoot Diament opened that city's first retail decorating firm in 1885; I. A. Diament, as the firm became known, specialized in French fabrics and wallpapers, becoming the major outlet for Zuber & Cie. wallpapers.[17] In 1892 new exchange rates and tariffs were introduced in France which were more favourable for the Americans than for the British, and the boom period for French goods in the United States had begun. Many Americans lived in Paris, and many others in England; it would be interesting to know how many of the British orders for French silks were destined for American-owned homes.

*Shown at the Paris Exposition of 1889, which coincided with the centenary of the Revolution, this silk has a satin ground with cut and uncut velvet motifs, loosely derived from the style of 100 years earlier. Cheaper imitations of this type of cloth were made by stamping patterns onto a plain cotton velvet.*

There were enough British and American residents in Paris in the 1880s and '90s to warrant the publication of *The Anglo-American Annual (for British subjects and citizens of the United States in Paris)*. The fourth edition, published in 1896/97, noted that while the number of British aristocrats in Paris was declining, there was an increased number of Americans, whose quarter was along the Champs-Elysées near the Arc de Triomphe. On the buying of furniture – whether for the stay in Paris or to ship home – the *Annual* offered the observation that '*meubles de style* are frequently bought in the frames and upholstered by the purchaser to suit his taste and purse', adding, with regard to price, that 'furniture, generally speaking, is higher than in England; but not so high as in the United States . . . with the exception of the "Grand Rapids" [i.e. machine-made] sort'. Although many Americans were tourists, others often took up residence for a number of years to pursue an interest, such as painting, literature or architecture. Some of these expatriates must also have been active in the many American firms whose agents and outlets were listed in the *Annual*. These, to a large extent, were established to facilitate buying in Paris, and they represented, among others, Marshall, Field & Co. of Chicago; Wanamaker's of Philadelphia; Arnold Constable & Co. and B. Altman & Co. of New York; Jordan, Marsh & Co. of Boston, and Weill, Raphael & Co. of San Francisco.[18]

*Designed and hand woven by Lamy & Gautier, this silk velours ciselé was produced in 1876 for Gillow & Co. of London (later to become Waring and Gillow).*

Some of the inhabitants of the American quarter in Paris were to have a seminal influence on American interiors in years to come. Among them, from 1907 to 1913 was Nancy McClelland, who on her return home immediately established the first known decorating department in an American department store; named 'Au Quatrième' to underscore its French connection, it was in Wanamaker's New York branch. Nancy McClelland opened her own firm in 1920. And there were others who, one way or another, were indebted to France. Among these were Ogden Codman (who worked with Allard on The Breakers), Edith Wharton (who with Codman wrote the influential *Decoration of Houses*, published in 1897) and Elsie de Wolfe (who in 1913, according to tradition, received a commission from Henry Clay Frick for counselling on the purchase of French furniture).[19]

*This early colour photograph shows the Comtesse Anna de Noailles sitting in her boudoir, which was decorated by Mercier Frères in about 1910. The countess shared the contemporary aesthetic taste for faux-Louis XVI, combined with a love of the oriental and a passion for poetry and the theatre. Mercier Frères illustrated this room in an advertisement in the* Gazette du Bon Ton *in 1913.*

The vitality of the Franco-American relationship was recognized at the time, both by references in American journals to 'our two great republics' and by the presentation of the Statue of Liberty to the United States in 1884. For France's luxury textile production, this relationship was essential to their image, for, as was acknowledged by Albert Raimon in 1909, 'The industrial strength of a nation cannot always be measured in production figures. It is also determined by the quality of its products, by the influence they have on the market and by the value of exports.'[20] The influence of France on America was nowhere more marked than in fashion – not only an important aspect of the world's perception of French taste and style, but also soon to influence the design of interiors. As André de Fouquières explained in the *Gazette du Bon Ton*, after a visit to the United States in 1913, 'Fashion is the only French industry which dominates in the United States, and it really is a source of fortune. Nowhere else are people so crazy about luxury, or show such rivalry in the fight for elegance, or such *respect* for the fantasies of fashion. An American woman never transforms last season's dress into today's fashions, she'll wear only *new* things. She watches with care the slightest transformation invented by our couturièrs, and originality frightens her so little that it is to New York that the *maitres* of the rue de la Paix send their most

audacious creations. Extraordinary sums of money are put aside every year for the feminine *toilette*, and very many French fashion houses owe much of their prosperity to the extravagance of these *faste yankees*.'[21] This last remark betrays a sense of resentment that, with regard to matters of style, French luxury industries could no longer call the tune – at least not to the extent they had before the war. Now the customer, notably the rich American, was asserting her own tastes.

Apart from the restructuring which the Franco-Prussian War forced upon the French textile industry, there was also a distinct change in the tone of French society. Even with peace restored, factionalism continued beyond the end of the nineteenth century; the government of the Third Republic and the army were accused of corruption; and financial scandals undermined the confidence that had characterized the Second Empire. In the aftermath of the Franco-Prussian War, France changed gears, slowing down social, economic and technical change. Its population stagnated, and compared to its now more powerful neighbours, Britain and a united Germany (as Prussia, its allies and acquisitions had become), France appeared to be a country of petite bourgeoisie and well-off peasants, small market towns and conservative tastes. Little wonder that furniture, interiors and their textiles were marked by a determined retrospection, and that these came to represent not public ostentation, but a more private luxury: security. Textiles played a primary role in this regard – cosseting, comforting and contriving an internal world in which it might be any century but the present. In 1889 a French reporter stressed this point, declaring, 'Without wall-hangings, rugs and upholstered furniture there would be no comfortable homes, nor would there be any charming, cosy interiors either. All our dwellings would seem cold, skimpy and bare.'[22]

Although confident formality had given way to an almost stifling abundance of furniture, the fabrics that made dwellings cosy were not dissimilar to those of the Second Empire: velvet, plush, moquette, tapestry and damasks; lightweight muslins and tulle (seldom plain, but instead having Jacquard-woven patterns or designs in appliqué or embroidery); machine-made net curtains (from Lille); and silk taffeta and *foulard* (plain- or twill-weave silk normally used for small printed patterns). The last two, according to Henry Havard, a prodigious writer and scholar of the day, were usually dyed red, to give a soft warm light when used as blinds. Because the costliest fabrics, such as *velours de Gènes* (a closely woven all-silk velvet) could cost 80–100 francs per metre, there were many imitations which mixed cotton or linen with silk to achieve the same effect.[23] Effect, after all, was of great importance – no matter that these substitutes did not feel the same and quickly lost their dusky sheen. Noticeably less fashionable were the gaily coloured *perses* for which Mulhouse had been famous. In 1887 Havard mentioned them in passing as summer covers, but by the early 1900s they became even scarcer due to the cotton crisis, when American manufacturers began to corner the supply of the finest grades of cotton, succeeding by 1904. Since texture was an important component of 'cosiness', and since it also disguised low-grade yarns, cotton fabrics for printing now typically had a ribbed, twilled or otherwise textured surface. Such prints were referred to as *cretonnes*, a term that, in this period, also included similar cloths made with a mixed fibre content.

Although a number of fashions came and went during these years, the prevailing taste was for textiles with eighteenth-century-style designs. Printed fabrics carried scenes reminiscent of Jean Honoré Fragonard's work of the late

Furnishings such as those shown in this salon of the 1890s could be purchased from Paris department stores. The eighteenth-century-style chairs typify the products of the many ateliers to be found in Paris, Nantes, Lyons and elsewhere, and the two in the foreground are appropriately covered in a silk designed in the manner of Lasalle. Popularized by French décorateurs and publications, this type of portière with swagged upper draperies was also to be found in British and American homes. The machine-made lace panels are also fixed into swags.

1760s; silks were ordered with *dessins Watteau*; and the term 'Marie Antoinette' was used in London to designate a certain style of curtaining lace. Alongside these imaginative interpretations of the Louis XV and XVI periods, relatively faithful revivals of patterns from the late eighteenth century were produced: cut velvets often had 'grotesque' designs, and prints once again sported exotic fruits and flowers. Upholstery and drapery styles (irrespective of the period to which they were ascribed) were also indebted to the eighteenth century, and, during the 1880s and '90s in particular, often incorporated swags (around the base of seat-furniture and across the top of windows, beds and doors), a style that, one hundred years earlier, had been called *à la reine*. Innumerable publications illustrated this fashion, which was widely followed. The universality of tastes was evident in the international popularity of Felix Lenoir's 1890 publication *Practical and Theoretical Treatise on Decorative Hangings, or a Guide to Upholstery*, which illustrated and explained the current French style of elaborately swagged upholstery and drapery; it was published in French, German and English. In Boston, F. A. Moreland's *Practical Decorative Upholstery* of 1889 discussed this type of rhythmically orchestrated French drapery at great length.

Interiors clad in eighteenth-century-style draperies and/or textiles could not possibly have suited everyone, however; for as an English commentator on Paris fashions recorded in 1878, the 'Bonapartists and Royalists will neither mix with each other nor with the Republicans'[24], and therefore followed distinctly different fashions. If this was the case, surely a Republican would not choose an interior so closely associated with the Empress Eugénie and her well-known interest in Marie Antoinette. It was probably only the conservative nature of the French middle classes that gave some truth to Jacob von Falke's observation (in connection with the International Exhibition held in Vienna in 1873) that 'in so far as style is concerned the modern Frenchman dwells in the eighteenth century, he sleeps in that century likewise, but he dines in the sixteenth, then on occasion he smokes his cigar and enjoys his coffee in the Orient, while he takes his bath in Pompeii, . . . .'[25] Looking back on the previous half-century, Havard penned similar lines in 1897, but was more specific, considering Louis XIV and Louis XV to have been the choice for *salons* and the neoclassical Louis XVI for bedrooms and boudoirs. Then, he continued, 'After having had a flirtation with *le japonisme*, and having borrowed a bit from China, [we] rediscovered the Empire style, which hitherto had been despised.'[26]

Textiles in Japanese, Indian and Turkish styles were abundant during the 1870s and 1880s, but by 1896 it was said that 'Oriental furniture is out of date'[27] (meaning European-style furniture with 'oriental' details). Of these, it was the taste for 'Turkish'-style textiles that survived, making sense historically of both the long tradition of French trade with Turkey and the eighteenth century's debt to Levantine design. By the 1880s, carpet and kilim style designs were often found on *cretonnes*, owing much to the Turkish, Moorish, Tunisian and Algerian dwellings and costumes which were part of the 1878 Exposition in Paris. Such patterns were intended to be used on walls, day beds, banquettes and as portières, in mimicry of the tent interiors from which they were derived. *Sultane*, *persane* and *orientale* – all low-priced fabrics woven from cotton and *bourre* – and printed *bourre* plush had, as at least the first three names implied, exotic patterns. Often associated with bohemianism, this style was given a further boost by the 1889 Exposition, in which the 'rue du Caire' – complete with Arab café, old houses, *souks* and belly dancers – was said to be one of the most powerful attractions.[28]

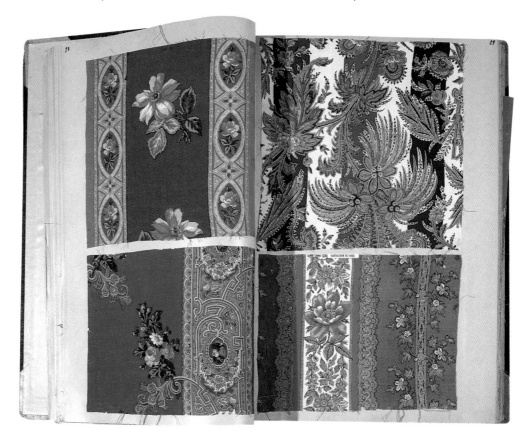

*These wooden-roller-printed wools were manufactured in Paris between 1873 and 1876. They show the rich and varied colours and complex patterns – often deployed with a strong stripe – that were used in contemporary middle-class interiors.*

Despite the changes in textile design during this period, certain elements of their use in interiors remained constant. One was the fashion for cloth on the walls. This was not reserved solely for 'Turkish' rooms, since, for example, in 1877 Thierry-Mieg was producing 'rich furnishings block-printed in fifty to sixty colours', in which its 'renaissance' composition showed '*La Danse et le Chant*, panels with 39-inch- (1-metre-) high figures'. These required a total of 700 blocks and sold for 30 francs per metre. Ten years later Havard (having acknowledged that attempts to create a fashion for moquette on the walls had failed) describes *toiles peintes* for large rooms as not the same as Oberkampf's *indiennes*, nor like *siamoises*, but of a sturdy cloth, painted or printed with designs in more or less complex arrangements.[29] Real tapestries were now made only in the French national workshops and in Belgium. In 1889 it was noted with regret in *Les Merveilles de l'Exposition* that 'these admirable panels which pass before our eyes seem to repeat the traditional [salute of gladiators about to die] ''Morituti te salutant''. The art of tapestry is indeed condemned to perish.' So although the 1889 Paris exhibition included Louis XV-style chairs covered in Beauvais tapestry, the report of this event admitted that 'the conditions of tapestry production no longer correspond to modern requirements; of all furnishing fabrics this is the only one to be made entirely by hand, and the finer the weft and the smaller the stitches, the longer it takes.'[30] Old tapestries were still sought out, but it may well have been difficult for the French to acquire any tapestries for themselves, for they seem to have been too plentiful elsewhere. Early in the twentieth century, for example, Maples, in London, advertised that they stocked 'a large variety of real Aubusson tapestry panels ranging in price from £15–350 according to size and quality, and a number of Genuine Old Tapestry Panels from £20–£1,000'. But

*Auguste de la Brely's painting of 1875,* Victorien Sardou and his Family in their Grand Salon at Marly-le-Roi *clearly shows a taste for the 'Marie Antoinette' style, apparent even in Madame Sardou's fashionable dress. Tapestry, more likely to have been machine made or printed than hand woven, adorns the walls, the firescreen and the fireplace, and has been used for upholstery.*

*Above: A room in a house in Marseilles, photographed in 1895. The picture shows a variety of imported floss-silk embroidered cloths, used as cushions, a wall-hanging and a portière or curtain. The art nouveau canapé is upholstered in a Louis XVI-style silk. 'Artistic' interiors such as this were the precursors of the 'exotic' room decoration fashionable just before the First World War.*

*Above right: This design, produced by Scheurer-Rott in 1882–3, was roller-printed onto a vertically ribbed cloth, in imitation of tapestry. Despite its deliberately faded appearance, the colour palette was guaranteed to be grand teint. The fabric itself was intended for use in a 'Marie Antoinette' room.*

painted 'tapestries' were available from suppliers in Paris, such as A. Binant, who in 1880 described his stock as 'unbleached linen for painting in imitation of tapestries and ancient stuffs'.[31] For guidance, there was Julien Goudous' 1884 publication, *La peinture sur toile et tissus divers imitant la tapisserie et son application à la décoration intérieure*. The main source of canvas in Paris was suppliers to painters and the theatre; and in fact many interiors were, in effect, sets, not meant to be taken too seriously or to be regarded as permanent. Indeed, Havard preferred moquette over tapestry (for floorcoverings as well as wallcoverings and upholstery) because its lack of large patterns made it more flexible, 'which suits our vagabond life'.[32]

Havard was only one of several writers who commented on the restlessness of the age, a mood that seemed to many people to be at odds with the lingering taste for revivals. Many despaired that any new style would arise to greet the new century, but in fact it was already there, in the mixture of historical references which (apart from avoiding any suggestion of political alliances) was a means of economizing; old furniture could be kept along with the new. What Havard had missed, the detached viewer could see. For example, an English journalist stated in 1895, as if it had been a long-known fact, that 'The French conoisseurs [*sic*] have long been cognisant of the charms of such an arrangement, and several of the best collectors of old furniture in Paris have what they call "eclectic" rooms in their hotels.'[33]

The new style – the 'eclectic' collector's interior with a touch of the bohemianism of artists' studios – had been tamed for middle-class interiors, but it was recognizable by its combination of 'exotic' textiles, be they of Indian, Turkish or Oriental origin or derivation, and eighteenth-century-style furniture, the latter mass produced in Paris's Faubourg St-Antoine and elsewhere. These were not machine made, but produced in their hundreds by artisans. Inexpensive white wood furniture, according to the *Anglo-American Annual*, was purchased without upholstery, and painted or enamelled according to taste, but there were also excellent reproductions, many of which were no doubt passed off as originals through Paris antique shops and the Hôtel Drouot's auction rooms. Much of this furniture was not even of French manufacture, but was made in Lombardy, where Milan formed the centre of a large furniture-making industry. Some of the most sophisticated furniture was made in the city itself; but in nearby Meda other craftsmen made armchairs, couches, daybeds and other 'pretty things' in 'Louis XIV, Louis XV and especially Louis XVI. Seldom in Empire style. Never in modern.' All were made for export and were 'as good as that made in Paris'. The making of this furniture was significant in terms of textiles; a local saying declared, 'Our daughters are born spinners and our sons have wood carving in their blood' – a reference to another local trade, silk weaving.[34] So Milan silk manufacturers had the perfect vehicle, its own furniture, to aid its direct competition with Lyons, where furniture-making, too, was an established craft. By about 1905, Nantes, which no longer made textiles but high-class furniture, was also suffering greatly, 'owing to the French market being flooded with cheap goods of Italian manufacture'.[35]

The long-anticipated arrival of a recognizably new style – art nouveau – was much heralded at the Paris 1900 universal exhibition but had only a small impact on the majority of interiors and the fabrics used in them. The vigorous twists and turns of petals, stems and tendrils which distinguish textile designs in this style were already present in the late 1880s. Many such designs originated in England, and they often found their way from there to France. One major source was the Silver Studio, founded by Arthur Silver in London in 1880. Art nouveau designs by Harry Napper and John Illingworth Kay (who left the Studio in 1898 and 1901 respectively) were purchased by Vanoutryve & Cie. and the weavers Leborgne, near Lille. But it was the more controlled, 'boxed-in' English designs, developed at the turn of the century, that held greater appeal for French manufacturers; in 1906, for example, Leborgne bought sixty-four such designs from the Silver Studio. Stylized patterns based on stripes also appeared, and this new, sparser style of design was evident among the prints from Alsace and fabrics from Lyons. Many of these more disciplined designs seem to have been made to suit the German taste. Not only do some of the manufacturing records in Mulhouse and Lyons suggest this, but we have the rather ungracious word of a Milanese chair-maker, who described the stark modern style of the immediate pre-war years as 'too "parvenu", too German'. In 1910, when some Munich artisans (most from the Deutscher Werkbund, founded there in 1907) were invited by the French government to include a display in the *Salon d'Automne*, their work was praised for its modernity and coherence and achieved record sales. Despite this, M. P. Verneuil spoke for many French critics when, in *Art et Décoration*, he declared the Munich style as unacceptable to the French because of the 'dissimilarity of the two races'.[36]

*This pattern was supplied to a German customer just before the outbreak of the First World War. Designed between 1905 and 1910, it probably originated from the Paris block-printing firm, Brault, who used the blocks in the 1920s and '30s. In 1938 these were sold to Warner & Sons in London, who today produce the fabric as a screen print. The block-printed version is shown here.*

If the Munich style would not do for twentieth-century France, neither, it seems, would art nouveau; for by 1909 the verdict was already in: 'In spite of a few excesses, often deliberate,' wrote Albert Raimon (spokesman for the French jurors of the silks shown at the Franco-British Exhibition, London 1908), 'art nouveau, the modern style as it is called, which has its systematic admirers and its systematic detractors, is full of pale colours which are not without charm and an honourable desire to avoid conventional ordinariness. Unfortunately this is not enough to make people forget the past. . . .'[37] Even apparent changes in interiors

only thinly disguised their continuity. By 1900, crisper cloths, plain surfaces, paler colours and less weighty fringing did much to lighten and neaten the appearance of interiors, but many window treatments nevertheless remained much the same as before, employing upper draperies, divided curtains, and secondary curtains or a blind (and sometimes both). The main concession to modernity was to replace *very* flamboyantly arranged draperies with a more modestly proportioned lambrequin, sometimes reduced to a depth sufficient only to cover the curtain rail. The shape of the lambrequin and the course taken by the applied braid or fringe (which was itself often still elaborate in style) together determined the 'style' of the window treatment – historical or art nouveau – for inevitably the curtains were straight-hanging, often made in a plain fabric, and had little in the way of extra embellishments. Even exposed curtain rods – left plain in the most modern rooms – could give a 'period' look, as can be seen in the plates published by Aubenet, Dons & Cie. in the 1880s and '90s, in which the plain curtain treatments were described as 'Henri II', 'Louis XIII' and so on through the ages, simply due to the subtle differences between the brackets or finials of the rods.

As elsewhere, such simpler arrangements were partly a reaction against overcrowded rooms, which were beginning to be seen as both unnecessary and unhygienic.[38] But the lighter, sparser style was also greatly indebted to early nineteenth-century interiors and, in its most luxurious form, to the silks of Lyons, wherever the interior may have been installed. It was most likely, for example, that when the Hotel Cecil in London was decorated by Maples, in about 1896, in Empire style, many of the furnishings came from France, for Maples then had a branch in Paris's rue Boudreau. They also expected their customers to be familiar with French terms (or used them to impress customers who were not), referring to short curtains as '*Brise-Bise*' (literally breeze-breaking) and to flat 'panel' curtains as '*Stores Bonne Femme*'.[39]

So it was not to be art nouveau that broke the hold of the past, for the past had a firm grip on the French imagination.[40] As late as 1914 the *Gazette du Bon Ton* could record that 'for the last few years the despotism of landladies has inflicted other tortures. Most modern apartments uniformly remind one of eighteenth-century *cocottes*. The walls are blinding grey, the pier-glass is pathetic, there is a profusion of Louis XVI bows, pearls, friezes, rosettes – a whole pastry of doubtful butter. Full panels with mouldings prevent our imagination from choosing the tone or design appropriate for each interior and to the objects that are to go into it.'[41] Although this was written with regard to wallpapers, textile manufacturers produced fabrics matching the same description; indeed, textile printers – including those in Alsace – had for the past decade been producing deceptively accurate reproductions of printed *siamoises* of a century or so earlier.[42]

Instead, the long-awaited new style arose out of three elements – all French – the Empire style, with its simplicity of line; the Paris fashion houses, with their reputation for daring; and the work of painters. The contribution of artists was essential; not only did they create studios (as Alphonse Mucha, for example, did) that were decorated with a deliberate eye for the effect they produced on visitors, but they also immortalized French interiors on their canvases. The pattern-on-pattern interiors of the Impressionists were perpetuated by the *pouchoir* (stencil-like) prints of Georges Lepape (who illustrated the gowns created by Paul Poiret), Charles Martin and Georges Barbier (who illustrated gowns by

couturiers such as Paquin and Redfern for the *Gazette du Bon Ton*); by the interior decorating firm Martine (set up by Paul Poiret in 1911); and even farther afield by Marcel Boulestin's shop, called Décoration Moderne, established in 1911 in London with the complete Martine range and more. The brilliant colours and naive style of the fabrics, rugs, wallpapers and other items provided by Martine owed much to the young, untrained girls Poiret employed as worker-artists. And, in truth, it also owed something to the Wiener Werkstätte (founded in 1903 in Vienna and from 1905 producing its own hand-block printed and painted textiles as well as supplying designs to local carpet and textile manufacturers such as Johann Backhausen & Sohn),[43] and to Diaghilev's Ballets Russes, whose brilliant costumes and tented stage sets provided Paris in 1909 and 1910 with a startling new interpretation of the long-established 'tented' interior.

Nevertheless, it was in Paris that this new exotic variant of eclecticism emerged, its polychromatic *cretonnes* with wallpapers to contrast presented in interiors of deceptive simplicity. It sprang from the muted, burnished polychromy of tapestries, *cretonnes* and matching wallpapers, which had reached its full strength in the 1880s and remained – moving down the social ladder, until the outbreak of the First World War. The similarity between art and the new eclecticism of interiors was seized on, at least by one French journalist, who although writing in 1914 of wallpapers, acknowledged a debt which 'naive' French textiles also owed to their painters, noting that 'there is a predilection today for sumptuous gold, burning violet, dark blues, orange and the rich combinations borrowed from the East. . . . At last our decorators dare throw upon our walls with apparent irregularity, indescribable, almost unreal flowers whose petals glow with a strange fire. The calm stripes have given way to complicated streaks so that, harmonizing with the upholstery fabric, the richness of the carpets, the daringness of the dress . . . a thousand motifs are dancing gaily as if they wanted to participate in the century in which voluptuousness, the love of speed

*The exotic informality of avant-garde interiors is captured in the ensemble displayed by L'Atelier Français at the Paris salon of autumn 1913 (above left). The folding screen is covered in a silk designed by Louis Süe and woven by Lamy & Gautier. On the silk of the same design (above right), woven with the light and dark areas reversed, the selvedge includes the name of the atelier.*

*Opposite left: Purchased in 1912 from Walther, a fashionable shop in Frankfurt, this block-printed cotton velvet was designed by Paul Poiret and was most probably made in the Atelier Martine, which he had opened in Paris in the previous year.*

*Far right: This silk tissue received a gold medal at the Paris Exposition Universelle in 1900. It was woven by Courdurier, Fructus & Descher, founded in Lyons in 1896. By 1905 they had opened a bureau in New York and some twenty years later had others in London, Toronto and Brussels.*

*Woven by Tassinari & Chatel in about 1905, this cotton and silk upholstery fabric illustrates the reserved, modern style associated with Germany. It was made for use on furniture designed by Carl Stöving, which was manufactured in 1906 by A. Wertheim of Berlin.*

and the need to surprise lead the way.' All this 'multiplicity of light and life by the entanglement of colours and lines' is, he concludes, 'as we see in the charming interiors of a Vuillard or Bonnard'.[44] He might well have added a reference to Raoul Dufy, for by 1913, Dufy not only had undertaken two textile projects for Poiret (in 1911), contributed to Martine's fabric production and signed an exclusive contract with Bianchini-Férier (established in Lyons in 1888 as Atuyer Bianchini-Férier and suppliers of silks to Poiret), but also had begun to design *toiles de Tournon*, with boldly patterned, densely packed scenes, hand block-printed onto furnishing fabrics of linen and cotton.

Dufy's homage to the *toiles de Jouy* indicate how rich a source the *belle époque* found the late eighteenth century. Others, however, had already set about creating *toiles* with a new and modern touch. With Menu & Boigegrain, the architect and painter Gustave-Louis Jaulmes had founded Toiles de Rambouillet, where fabrics and wallpapers were printed from the same blocks, all with designs that reinterpreted motifs from the neoclassical era of a century or so earlier (Jaulmes was later to become known for his tapestries). There were others experimenting with textile printing who were also artists, such as Charles Dufrèsne and Henry de Waroquier; and the decorator André Groult had, by about 1910, organized a group of craftsmen who produced wallpaper and textiles for general sale. Dufrèsne and Groult were among the contributors to La Maison Moderne, a studio that had been among the first to reject art nouveau and synthesize a new furnishing style from the controlled, elegant lines of Directoire and Consulate furniture. Among the other new decorating firms of importance was L'Atelier Français, founded in 1912 by Louis Süe, who had already decorated Poiret's houseboat and residence. Most department stores – like the Bon Marché – remained supporters of the conservative revival styles,[45] but just before the First World War there emerged the first of the ateliers that were soon to design and produce modern furniture. This was Primavera, established in 1913 by René Guilleré and run for Au Printemps by his wife, Charlotte Chauchet-Guilleré. That such energy sprang from outside the textile industry was a sign of the times. Some sections of the industry – such as the lace and curtain-net making enterprises in Lille – had scarcely recovered from the cotton crisis of 1904, while silk manufacturers in 1910 had suffered when fashion briefly turned against them.[46] For the latter, the emergence of the artist-designer was to be of great importance to their survival. The full impact of this development, however, was forestalled by the outbreak, in 1914, of the First World War.

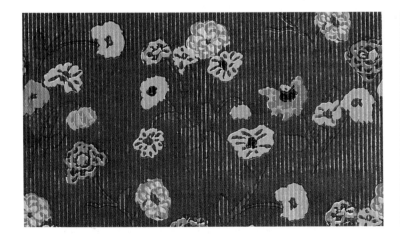

This gouache design for a textile was produced in about 1900 by the Paris design studio Forrer (which survived into the second half of this century). While realism was the forte of many such studios, they nevertheless produced designs adapted to contemporary taste, in this case the Japanese-inspired form of art nouveau. This should be compared with the illustration on page 83, top right, a more stylized interpretation of the same theme.

This roller-printed cretonne, produced by Boissière in 1892, has light, scrolling leaves that were created by printing a discharge (or bleach). The subtle shading was formed by the printing of a red stipple over yellow.

*Above left: Oriental in inspiration, this ten-colour roller-printed cotton was produced by Laveissière & Chamont in 1903. It shows a distinctive colour palette that had already enjoyed over ten years of popularity.*

*Above right: Roger Joseph Jordain painted his sitter in* A Pensive Mood, *showing her seated in a 'cosy' corner constructed around a banquette. The loose cover and cushions have three different patterns, showing the late nineteenth century's taste for informality and 'oriental' clutter.*

*A floral study in gouache, painted in about 1895 by the Wolfsperger studio in Paris. The warm, seductive shades are characteristic of the* fin de siècle, *and the flowers are rendered with the almost photographic realism that remained a principal strength of many French design studios.*

As the twentieth-century neoclassical style became lighter and more delicate, the soft, indistinct effect obtained from chiné weaving also returned to favour. Many such patterns were produced around the turn of the century, making use of the perfection of a method for pre-printing the warp mechanically. This example was made in 1906 by Gros Roman & Cie. of Wesserling, Alsace.

This roller-printed cotton of about 1870 demonstrates several technical improvements, most notably in the subtlety of the engraving and the perfect registration of the Prussian-blue ground with the delicate scrollwork. Probably printed by Thierry-Mieg, it incorporates a motif from Fragonard's The Swing, painted in 1769.

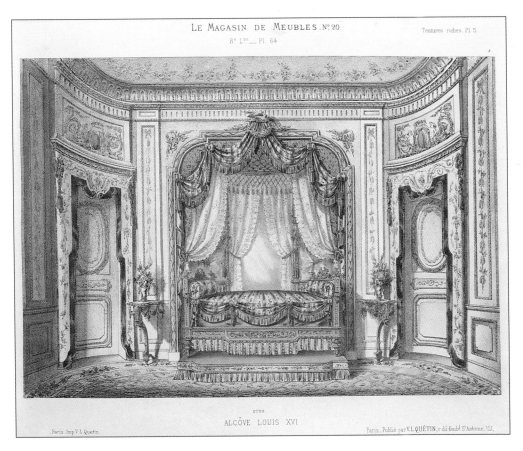

An alcove in the style of Louis XVI, published in about 1875 in the Catalogue du fabricant de meubles by V. L. Quentin, the Parisian publisher of Le Magasin de meubles. The striped and fringed fabric and the tapestry cantonières at each door are faithful to their inspiration, but the lace curtains and the deep-buttoned ceiling of the bed alcove clearly belong to the 1870s.

The fashion for lace furnishings, particularly in bedrooms, persisted until the First World War, as indicated by this page of the 1908 catalogue from Aux Trois quartiers. Illustrated is an ensemble of cotton tulle, machine-woven with large dots and constructed with inserts of machine-made Cluny lace.

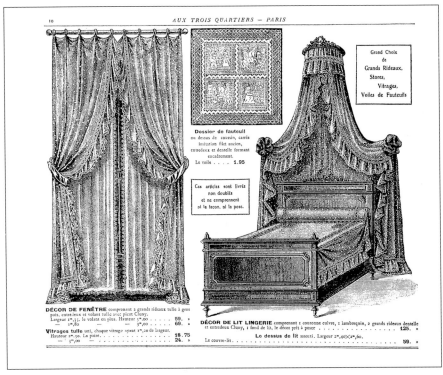

Left: Showing the bold and assured use of colour so often found in middle-class interiors of the 1870s and '80s, this fabric, block-printed in about 1874 in Alsace, probably by Gros Roman & Cie., combines a delicate rendering of late eighteenth-century motifs with a much newer fashion for boldly contrasting stripes.

During the 1880s, 'arabesque' or 'grotesque' patterns – revived from the Directoire period – echoed the heavily ornamental style of interiors themselves. This example, a gouache design, was produced in 1882 by the Atelier Arthur Martin in Paris. Martin was one of the many Paris design studios that worked closely with Alsatian printers.

These two borders (right, above and below), each about 9½ inches (24 cm) wide, were printed on a lightly ribbed cotton and linen cloth in the 1880s. Both imitate late eighteenth-century patterns, although the blue-ground border, because it is roller-printed, does so less successfully than its block-printed partner.

*Right: Roller-printed in 1899 by Boeringer, Zucher & Cie. of Cernay, in Alsace, the design of this cotton shows the way in which the taste for rococo-inspired scrollwork, fashionable in previous decades, made a contribution to the energetic curves found in art nouveau patterns.*

*Left: The use of asymmetrical cartouches characterizes many of the rococo-revival patterns of the 1870s and early 1880s. This cretonne (an unglazed inexpensive roller-printed cotton) by an unknown French manufacturer, was printed with aniline dyes.*

Both of these Japanese-style cretonnes (above left and right) were roller-printed between 1879 and 1880 by Scheurer-Rott & Cie., the company that developed from Liebach, Scheurer & Cie., originally founded in 1813 in Thann in Alsace. The dark-ground fabric has been designed so that it can also be used upside down, making it economical to cut, and avoiding wastage.

Inspired by oriental images of pond-lilies, this pattern, designed by Paul Ranson in about 1898, displays the energetic, whiplash forms characteristic of art nouveau. It was printed on a cotton velvet by Gros Roman & Cie.

*Right:* Illustrated in La Teinture moderne *in 1883, by E. Prignot & C. Remon, this* petit salon *is described as having been decorated in the* style de fantaisie, *or in Japanese fashion. Such interiors relied for effect on a multitude of patterns and objects, including, as seen here, fans. With a heavy fringe which rests on the floor, the curtains carry a pattern that in this case was probably embroidered, although many printed and woven Japanese-style patterns were also available for use in similar schemes.*

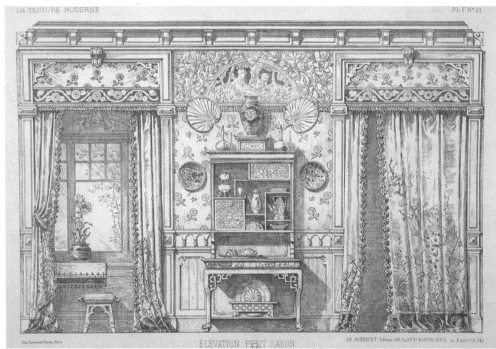

*Illustrating the continued use of
Turkish textiles in France, this
print (below) of the 1880s shows
curtains and upholstery made
from kilims. Flat-woven kilims
were by now being made in the
Near East to European
requirements. Some came to Paris
via London; the Bon Marché, for
example, purchased Turkish
carpets in the late 1880s from
George Baker, father of the
founders of the London fabric
firm, G. P. & J. Baker.*

*Above: This exotic, artistic
interior, probably decorated in
about 1890, was photographed in
1900. An informal day-bed,
covered, and piled with cushions
of Moroccan and other
North-African origins, is
separated from the rest of the
room by a pair of kilims. Imported
soft-wood furniture was a feature
of such interiors.*

In Auguste Renoir's painting, Children's Afternoon at Wargemont of 1884, a real table carpet (as the knotted fringe indicates) covers the table which is set before floor-length curtains carrying a crewelwork pattern. The simple chair is upholstered in a striped satin to match the white-wood, late eighteenth-century-style sofa. Such eclecticism, juxtaposing different styles from different periods and with a variety of textures, was to be explored further in the first decades of the twentieth century.

Although printed in Germany by Schlieper & Baum, this roller-printed cretonne of 1892 is representative of the many warm-toned carpet and kilim patterns employed by French manufacturers of the period. Similar designs were also supplied to American printers by French pattern services.

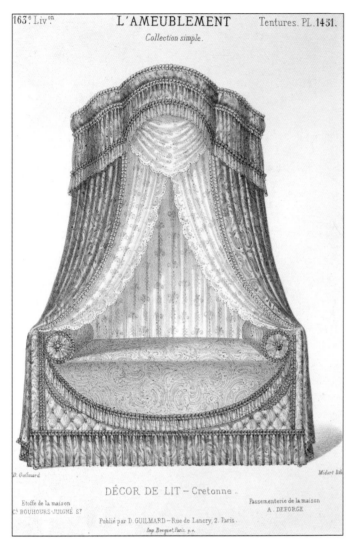

*Left:* A design for a bed of the late 1870s, showing the dense gathers typical of the period and representing a revival of the Empire style. It comes from Guimard's series of Garde Meuble publications that were intended for those of more modest means, and therefore recommended the use of a cretonne.

*Above right:* Block-printed by Groult in 1911, this cretonne was designed by André Saglio (known as Dresa), who also produced wallpaper patterns, packaging, and theatre designs and illustrations. The pattern repeat is about 14½ inches (36.7 cm) square.

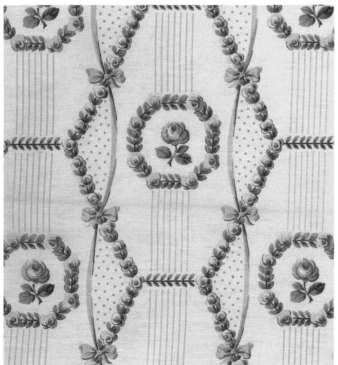

*Left:* The renewed appreciation for clear white grounds and delicate patterns – particularly those inspired by Empire motifs – seems to have come in response to orders from British distributors. Manufacturers in Britain also often used French designs for their own production of glazed chintzes. The example shown here is a 'Strathcylde Print', of 1907, a trade name of the Alexander Morton company; roller-printed on a ribbed cotton in their Rosendale works, the design was purchased for £2 from the Paris Studio, Reupp.

Chez MERCIER Frères

Tapissiers-Décorateurs

190, Rue du Faubourg Saint-Antoine, PARIS

*An advertisement in the June 1914 issue of the* Gazette du Bon Ton, *the most fashionable Paris magazine of the period. It was placed by Mercier Frères, a firm of cabinetmakers who continued a tradition begun by Claude Mercier in 1828, and shows a dining room decorated in the fashionable Empire-revival style. Mercier Frères began to specialize in producing modern furniture in 1926.*

*Looking very much like an Empire-style woven silk, this cotton is actually roller-printed. The pattern was produced on a cotton satin by Louis Besselièvre Fils, a long-established firm in Maromme, near Rouen, in about 1900.*

*Opposite: Characteristic of the work of a number of French designers in the decade before the First World War, this block-printed cotton of 1914, by an unknown French manufacturer, interprets forms of the past in a painterly manner. Rich colours and pattern-on-pattern motifs convey the contemporary taste for exoticism.*

*Right: The floral basket pattern had a long tradition in French textile design and, as seen here in a naive, stylized form, it was to become a prominent motif of the Paris Exposition of 1925. Produced by Groult, this block-printed cretonne was designed by Louis Süe in about 1912, the same year in which he opened L'Atelier Français, working in reaction against the art nouveau style with a team that included the painters Paul Véra, Charles Dufresne and Gustave Louis Jaulmes.*

*Below: In 1910 the décorateur André Groult established a block-printing workshop in which he printed his own designs and those of a number of others, including Erté, Marie Laurencin and Constance Lloyd. This cretonne, purchased from Groult's Paris atelier in 1911 and designed by Albert André, is a modern variant of the scenic toiles of the 1830s.*

*Opposite left: Designed in London by the Silver Studio, this power-woven silk and cotton was produced in about 1900 in France, probably by Vanoutryve of Roubaix. (They also had a weaving mill in Mouscron, just across the Belgian border, which was opened in 1880.)*

*This art-nouveau dining room was photographed in 1913 but was probably created some ten years earlier. The fabrics chosen for the portières are of a restrained design, and appear to be either brocaded silk velvet or printed velvet, probably of cotton. In 'pure' art-nouveau interiors such as this, textiles played a secondary role to the woodwork and wall-stencilling.*

*Alphonse Mucha, the French painter who became famous at the end of the nineteenth century for his posters of Sarah Bernhardt, produced textile designs in a similar vein for a number of manufacturers, including Hines, Stroud & Co. of London. This example, printed in France on cotton velvet, may well involve pouchoir or stencil printing, a technique that Mucha is known to have used.*

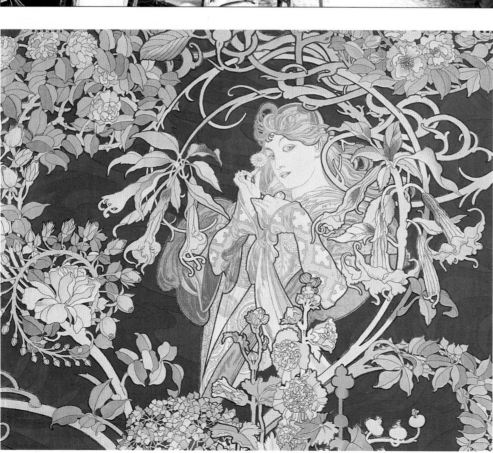

*Above right: Woven by Ombelli Frères of Lyons in about 1900, this silk velvet, brocaded with an art nouveau design, was sold in America by Schumacher.*

*Right: A power-woven French cloth made primarily of cotton, with the addition of some silk, with an early twentieth-century English-style design. It is similar to a number which were manufactured by Leborgne at their factory near Lille. The damask-patterned ground employs a subtly shaded warp.*

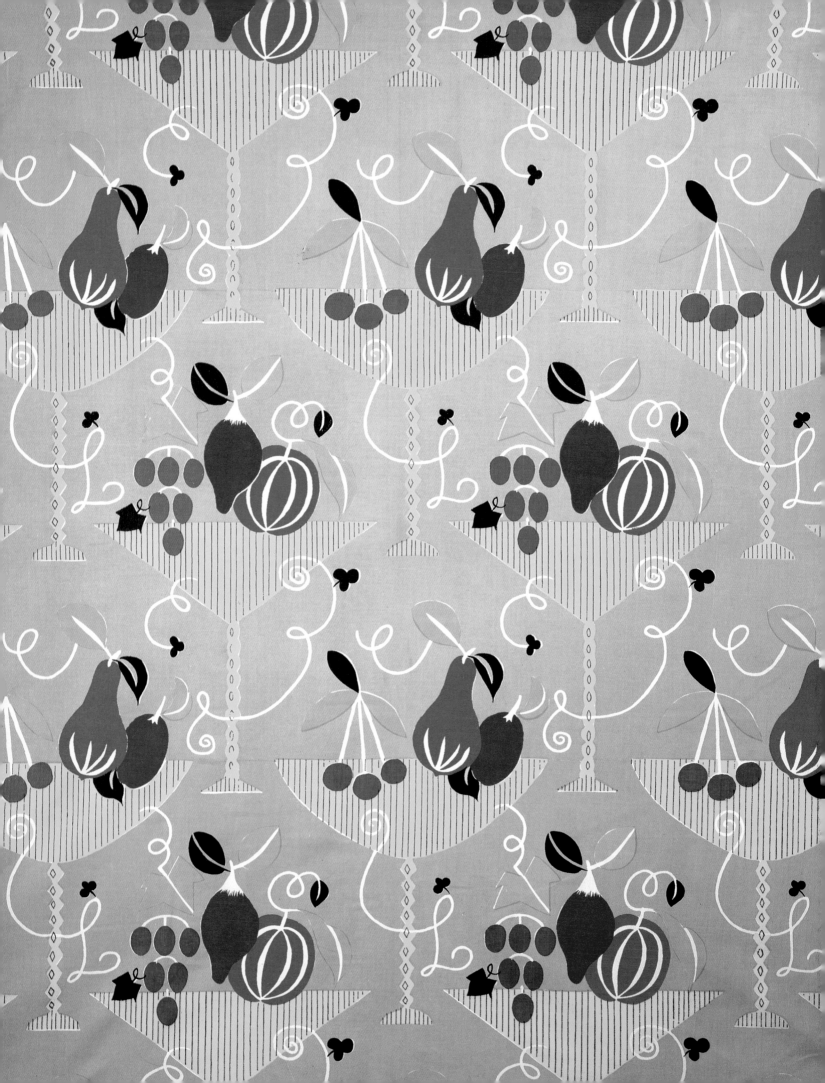

# CHAPTER SIX

# FANTASIES

## *(1915–1960)*

'EVERY EPOCH finds its expression in a style. It is interesting to distinguish in the multitude of contemporary manifestations, the more or less temporary movements of those who set the trend and create the style. It is not a reflection of the major part of present production – quite the contrary: it is that of a minority, who manage to model the taste of the public.' (Sonia Delaunay, in *Tapis et Tissus*.)[1]

It is tempting, when discussing French textiles after the First World War, to jump straight to the exhibition held in Paris in 1925, the *Exposition Internationale des Arts Décoratifs et Industriels Modernes*. That is because this exhibition celebrated a style whose name eventually became a household word: Art Deco. There is good reason for its fame among the general public, for the exhibition 'was heralded and acclaimed as none had ever been before'. These words were written in 1928, begrudgingly, by an American, C. Adolph Glassgold, who much preferred German modern design. His further remarks, however, help to explain why – aside from the quality of the decorative arts on show – the 1925 exhibition also remained the most acclaimed of this century. Surveying French modernity from the end of World War I, he begins, 'Süe et Mare began doing creditable things in the modern style, and at the *Salon d'Automne* of 1919, Jallot had refined his furniture, Ruhlmann had struck his stride, and Dufet et Bureau had made the closest approach to what we recognize as the modern French style. In a comparatively short time, considering the frightful financial and social state of France during the years following the establishment of peace, she was able to hold an exhibition [in Marseilles] which was prophetic, though weak in arrangement, poor in quality, and incoherent in effect. This was 1922. Three years later came the *Exposition*. . . .'[2] The brilliant success of this 1925 exhibition was, therefore, to many people, a complete surprise.

The Exposition was not a surprise stylistically, for many of the furniture forms – the rounded ample shape of chairs, for instance – had been developed before the First World War. Nor did all the textiles have new patterns. The fabrics on the walls of Jacques Ruhlmann's *Pavillon d'un Collectionneur* – sporting giant urns of stylized flowers – had been designed by Stéphany, made by Cornille Frères and exhibited in Lyons in 1918. Many of the boldly delineated flowers (especially the rose motif which could be found carved into wood, worked into carpets, printed on cloth or posters or bulging from the surface of vases) could have been seen twenty or more years earlier, in the work of the Silver Studio in England or of Charles Rennie Mackintosh in Scotland[3] and ten or so years before the exhibition on artist-designed French textiles.

*Designed by the Libert studio in 1952, this hand-screen-printed cotton satin was produced for Warners in the following year.*

What was new, and striking, was the unity within so many of the pavilions, and the predominance of modern architecture, seen to advantage in buildings given ample space, at least in comparison to previous exhibitions. (The Eiffel Tower, when it was built for the 1889 Exposition, had its base almost completely concealed by closely packed surrounding pavilions.) Another innovation was the exclusion of displays other than decorative arts; there was no agriculture, no scientific or mechanical marvels. Moreover, the 1925 pavilions were set amid gardens that were themselves innovative, making extended use, for the first time, of artificial lighting and of concrete. Modern lighting was also a feature within the French displays, both in its appearance within room-sets and its use in dramatizing the displays. The French pavilions had internal and external light fixtures installed for use only after dark, presenting the night-time visitors to the Exposition with a theatre of shape, colour and mass.

All this emerged from a nation which many thought had been crippled by the war; indeed, the Exposition could be interpreted as a message from France that, on the contrary, it was alive and kicking. The French government – on this occasion helped by regional authorities, chambers of commerce and other local agencies – renewed its role as patron of the decorative arts, making substantial grants to the national factories, the schools of fine art and groups of artists and designers. A collective effort on a massive scale, the Exposition reasserted France's traditional role as the arbiter of style.

To understand how this came about, and why a successful exhibition was so crucial to the large luxury sector of France's economy, one must return to the Great War, which began in August 1914. After reaching within striking distance of Paris (having come from the north by way of Belgium), the Central Powers – Germany and Austria-Hungary – were driven back slightly and at the end of the year were in trenches which stretched from Ostend through northern France to Switzerland. Behind this line were many of France's textile centres, including

Lille, Roubaix and Rheims. Some of France's richest wheat fields were also occupied; there were serious food shortages, and by 1918 the cities were on rations, having three meatless days a week. The economic struggle necessary to continue the war relied in great measure on the old and on women, who kept farms going and worked in the factories, and on inflationary policies, such as the printing of more money. By the time the war had ended in November 1918 and Europe had time to take stock, it could see only devastation. In total there were nearly 20 million dead, including soldiers, civilians and the 6 million who died that winter of influenza, plus another 21 million wounded, many mutilated for life. Ten per cent of the French male population had been killed, leaving behind a population that did not increase in size, but instead, as the years passed, contained a disproportionate number of widows and old people. The economy had little opportunity to expand, for there were restrictions on internal consumption; the value of the franc was kept high (to prevent wages and prices from rising too quickly), and this made exports difficult. In addition, France lost virtually all its trade with Germany, Austria and Russia, except for an increased export of printed fabrics to Germany, largely as a result of the return of Alsace to France.

Clearly, there were serious difficulties facing the textile industry; between 1916 and 1918 the cost of wool had risen by 250 per cent, that of raw cotton by 350 per cent. This, together with other rising costs, meant that printed cottons that before the war had been valued for export at just over 5 francs per metre cost 25 francs by 1918. Linen, previously the cheapest fibre, became the most expensive, having increased its price nearly six times over. Only silk prices were less than twice their previous cost. Printed and Jacquard-woven silks were scarce, because the continued manufacture of patterned silks was dependent on a constant demand from the fashion industry, and even in the early 1920s, it was calculated that 80 per cent of Paris was still dressed in black. The fine cotton, tulle, lace and embroidery centres bore the brunt of the war, and production ceased in Caudry and St-Quentin. In northern France alone, an estimated 250,000 buildings had been destroyed. The cotton and woollen industries in this area had to be rebuilt, and this was not yet complete in 1921.[4] Even those factories and workshops that were physically untouched by the war had lost workers, and they continued to do so. (With bricklayers' wages higher than those of weavers, many of the latter left their occupation to earn more money in the reconstruction of devastated areas.)

*Below: These three cloths, handwoven by Tassinari & Chatel, recreate something of the impact of the displays at the Paris Exposition of 1925. The centre fabric of silk and rayon, depicting a tropical Garden of Eden, was by Jean Georges Beaumont, who also designed for Sèvres porcelain and Aubusson carpets and tapestries. On its left is* Spires, *similar in style to some of the batiks by Marguerite Pagnon, and on its right, a design in the style of Stéphany.*

*Below right: This dining room, illustrated in* Intérieurs executés dans le goût moderne *in about 1920, was designed by Francis Jourdain, who had founded the Atelier Moderne in 1912 and opened his Paris shop, Chez Francis Jourdain, shortly after the end of the First World War. It shows the rectilinear motifs often associated with German and Austrian* Jugendstil *interiors. The curtain treatments are simple, with a reserved but striking use made of appliqué and fringe.*

By 1922, when F. Schumacher's representative Mr. Pozier made a European tour, visiting mills in France, England, Germany and Czechoslovakia, Schumacher could only report to their customers that 'while we feel that there are unmistakable signs of improvement, it would not be true to state that business in Europe is brisk. Germany is probably the only exception among the countries manufacturing upholstery fabrics, and even there, while they have orders for many months ahead on certain kinds of goods, other looms are idle with no demand for their products.' Several factors were cited in explanation: wholesalers still had large stocks, 'contracted for at high prices, often delivered to them by manufacturers long after the need for these goods was past; consequently they are placing no new orders . . . the house and apartment shortage, and the rent laws, prolonging leases after the war, have practically stopped all new work and re-decoration.'[5] It is little wonder, then, that eight months earlier, the writer of an article on the results of a collaboration between the architect and *décorateur* Pierre Chareau and the painter Jean Lurçat began by admitting that 'I know it would be difficult, even in our day, to extricate among the jumble of opposing tendencies, among the diverse influences, the principle of the decorative arts movement. Such chaos, which engenders a fantasy without apparent discipline, was not made to bring the young decorators towards a refined "style", nor to arouse in them a desire to produce work of sanity [or] logic. . . .'[6]

References to 'fantasies', meaning both 'imagination' and 'whim', are often found in the literature of this period, and in this word one can catch the flavour of postwar France. These years, as recalled by a woman who was in Paris at the time, were characterized by a profusion of new ideas and new trends – from the mildly racy songs of Maurice Chevalier to the intriguing doctrines of Freudianism, and 'openly acknowledged' gay bars. The postwar Paris lifestyle embraced such diverse innovations as 'coloured photography, cocaine, silk stockings and chemises, safety razors . . . beauty salons, tennis, typewriters, painless divorces for American visitors, wireless, Citroën motor-cars, aeroplanes and cocktails'.[7] Paris itself was a 'cocktail' of all tastes and classes. It contained many Czechoslovaks, Hungarians, Russians and other refugees from the 1917 Revolution and the redivision of Eastern Europe in 1918; Brazilians made rich by coffee plantations; Argentinians, by beef; and, of course, Americans, for whom, with the introduction of Prohibition in 1919, Paris now had the added attraction of plentiful champagne.

Amid this *mélange* were the artists and designers who were renewing their lives and making new associations. For example, in 1919 Louis Süe and André Mare had joined together to form *La Compagnie des Arts Français*; René Joubert and Pierre Petit had founded *Décoration Intérieure Moderne* (DIM). Both firms were regarded as traditionalists (deriving their furniture forms from the Louis-Philippe style and, in the case of DIM, also occasionally from the period of Louis XVI), but the furniture each produced differed greatly, as did their use of textiles. DIM was particularly well known for sparse furniture placed on bold, often cubist-inspired carpets, while Süe and Mare themselves believed 'that our dwellings are made essentially for human beings and not for automatons. Therefore we strive for warmth and harmony, supple lines and reposeful forms, in order that the home be restful and in contrast with an ever more exacting and harassing type of existence.'[8] Their fabrics were both inviting and luxurious – velvets, figured silks, plain satins and tapestry. Although some they designed

On succeeding Paul Follot as artistic director of Pomone in 1928, René Prou replaced traditionalism with a rationalist approach, exemplified by this common room. It was designed in collaboration with Albert Guénot and exhibited at the annual salon of the Societé des Artistes et Decorateurs in 1929. All the furnishings, including the boldly-patterned textiles, were available from the Bon Marché in which the studio Pomone was located.

Above right: This photograph shows one of the barges which Paul Poiret exhibited at the Paris Exposition of 1925. This work was criticized for its riotous colour, which was perceived as overwhelming the discipline of his design. He remained most famous for the pattern-on-pattern combinations represented by this interior.

themselves, others were by André Saglio (known as Dresa), Gustave-Louis Jaulmes, Charles Martin, Paul Vera and Charles Dufresne. Poiret's decorating firm, Martine, also continued to operate, but never re-established the leadership it had enjoyed prior to the war. Such small ateliers (and there were many) worked principally for an elite clientele and used the most expensive materials.

Soon the department stores were providing modern interiors for a different market. At Au Printemps, Primavera had begun to do so, as did Maurice Dufrène, who in 1921 created the atelier La Maîtrise, in Les Galeries Lafayette. Le Louvre had its Studium Louvre. These workshops had far wider impact than the exclusive Paris ateliers. In 1926 it was said of their rival Pomone (directed by Paul Follot from its inception in the store Au Bon Marché three years earlier) that it 'fills up apartments all over France and wins over to modern art the provinces, conquered by the comfort and practical seduction of its works, discarding both affected and uncouth styles . . . enabling French people of moderate means to live in smart homes'.[9] 'Modern' here must be read with care, for Follot was the champion of traditionalism. Although distinctly of its time, Follot's work retained the rich effects and sense of luxury that suggested the elegance of the past. He used pattern in abundance, unlike his former colleague (at La Maison Moderne from 1901 to 1903), Maurice Dufrène, who designed plainly upholstered furniture for both the inexpensive machine-made furniture and the artisan-made pieces sold by La Maîtrise. Both men were prolific designers, concerning themselves with all aspects of the decorative arts, including textiles; and both men's work was prominently displayed at the 1925 exhibition.

The Exposition Internationale included displays from twenty-two countries. Germany, Norway and the United States were absent, and only Japan and China represented those non-European countries that were not territories or protectorates of a European state. The criteria for display were that articles should show modern inspiration and real originality (either in the development of existing art forms or in the invention of the entirely new). The impact of the French section was assured from the start, for it occupied about two-thirds of the area – mainly along the Left Bank of the Seine near Les Invalides – that was given over to the exhibition. On the Right Bank the Grand Palais was devoted entirely to French textiles, which were also part of the displays created by the Paris stores and ateliers, as well as those in the regional pavilions. Here, too, there was great contrast, even contradiction. From Alsace and Rouen came printed textiles which had 'an interesting space', but, according to the official report of the Exposition, 'scarcely in accordance with the importance of their role in current furnishings'. Far more prominently displayed were the hand-made fabrics, and these naturally received more acclaim. Aside from the cloths that displayed patterns by artist-designers (among which handwoven silks were the most numerous) there were other fine cloths from Lyons which did not display their designers' names, as well as carpets, tapestries, batiks, and large-scale filet crochet and macramé panels. Rodier, who had recently added upholstery cloths to his dress fabric range and had a collection of designs of 'rare variety' – numbering nearly 20,000 – used a variety of techniques, including piece dyeing, printing and *dévoré* (the technique of removing parts of a cloth's surface to create a pattern), but was best known for his distinctively coloured mixed-fibre cloths, produced by cottage weavers in Picardy.[10]

Among this profusion of exhibits three currents could be discerned. Each one itself contained diverse elements, and each also affected the course of textile design and manufacture. The first was the French tradition of hand-crafted elegance, embodying the belief that the modern rested firmly on the past. The second was the desire for modernity itself, whether expressed in machine-made goods or abstract forms. And the third was the upsurge of collaborative efforts, whether in the small ateliers, between freelance designers and manufacturers, or in the department store studios (which employed designers who also retained the right to work for private clients). The result was a microcosm of Paris itself: variety, individuality, debate and competition. This was the stuff of which great exhibitions are made; this was the environment from which came designers who were acclaimed far beyond the borders of France.

Although the modern movement in design was new to many outside the immediate circles of avant-garde design, those who orchestrated it, or who rose to prominence as a result of their textile designs, were not themselves young. In the year of the Paris Exposition, Süe was fifty and Mare was thirty-eight. Follot was forty-eight, Dufrène forty-nine, Jaulmes fifty-two, and Martin sixty-seven. Sonia Delaunay, whose 'simultaneous' fashions and fabrics drew much attention at the exhibition, was forty. Apart from Mare, there were only a handful of others who were under forty; they included Hélène Henry (thirty-four), a handweaver who later had her designs manufactured by other weaving establishments, and Eric Bagge (thirty-five), who was among those who designed for Rodier. These were men and women whose creative lives had been interrupted at their peak; there was lost time to be made up, and this sense of urgency is apparent in their work. Their impatience manifested itself most clearly in the fact that they often bypassed the traditional structure of production. Among the modern furniture designers, only Mercier Frères (who also used illustrations by Bagge) were representative of the enduring ateliers of cabinetmakers, and none of the avant-garde textiles were produced by machine. On the whole the block-printed fabrics were designed and/or made by those skilled in other related fields, whether paper printing (as had been the case with Dufy) or wallpaper printing (as was the case with Follot, the son of Felix Follot, whose family had founded a wallpaper manufactory in 1859). Some production was gradually being transferred to established textile manufacturers in the Paris area, such as Gros Roman and P. A. Dumas, who still did block printing. Within the handweaving trade, much of the innovation came from firms originally associated with fashion (such as Bianchini-Férier or Rodier). The exceptions were few: a small group of high-quality silk-weaving firms in Lyons, and a handful of carpet and upholstery cloth weavers in the

*A cotton velvet designed by Paul Follot in about 1926 and block-printed by hand. Follot was a prolific designer of textiles, furnishings and interiors. He did not design for machine production, preferring to promote the manufacture of exclusive fabrics such as this.*

Leaves *by Follot (above) and*
Doves *by Stéphany (top) were two
of the four fabrics, shown in the
Paris Exposition of 1925, which
were subsequently exhibited in
Schumacher's New York
showroom, and which were
exclusive to the firm's American
range.*

Roubaix-Tourcoing area, such as Vanoutryve, Ferdinand Leborgne and La Manufacture Française de Tapis & Couvertures. Even in these cases many of the modern pieces were commissioned by a decorator or made especially for the exhibition, and were not part of normal production.

It is little wonder, then, that the Paris exhibition was both a success and a surprise. Mature designers, some having started their careers working in the art nouveau style (and having anticipated the exhibition previously, for it was planned first for 1907, then 1922 and again for 1924), were at last given a vehicle in which to demonstrate their skills and express their ideas. It was the visual equivalent of an animated conversation, and one which echoed, if not around the world, then certainly over Britain and the United States. It did so in part because of a growing awareness that such events had a publicity value which could be used by others to promote their own enterprise. This was quickly appreciated by the Americans, who in the three years following the Paris showing not only had the chance to see a sample of it (loaned by the French government) in Boston and New York, but also mounted their own displays of modern interiors at Wanamaker's and Macy's and in Schumacher's showroom – the last of these containing fabrics by Follot, Stéphany and Séguy. The *Toiles de Rambouillet* collections had already been in Schumacher's range since 1923, the same year in which Dufy's *Toiles de Tournon* and silks were made available in the United States by the opening of a New York branch of Bianchini-Férier (which also produced designs by Charles Martin and Robert Bonfils). Fabrics by other French designers including Dresa, Rodier, Vera, and Bénédictus were also imported by American firms. In Boston, Jordan, Marsh G. displayed a girl's room by Mercier Frères. Part of the impact of the Art Deco exhibition derived from the striking way in which items were displayed; and the new controlled manner of arranging products was to be seen in the windows of Sak's Fifth Avenue and, soon, elsewhere. There were many other exhibitions in this period, and not all were of French decorative arts, but each owed a debt to the Paris exhibition, which more than any other established the modern style in America as, in the words of Glassgold, 'a force to be reckoned with. Manufacturers evidenced a desire to experiment with it, department stores to display it, and designers to create it.'[11]

The 1925 exhibition generated volumes: official publications, reports, enquiries and articles, some long after the event was over. These, too, helped to spread the taste for French textiles, and it was thought by at least one American journalist that 'there is no doubt but that it is through fabrics that the art of to-day can most readily become known to the great public and influence its taste'.[12] Although it may have established a taste for the modern French style, the exhibition did little to increase American imports of French furnishing fabrics. Imports of tapestries and other Jacquard-figured upholstery fabrics, made of cotton or other vegetable fibres (such as linen or jute), did rise dramatically between 1923 and 1927, but these were supplied principally by the Belgians, Germans and British. At the beginning of the 1920s the American consumption of silks for all uses (of which France was an important source) remained the same as it had been prior to the war. The demand for silks was, however, increasing, but to the benefit of American, not French, manufacturers. By about 1926 the American consumption of raw silk was nearly four and one-half times what it had been in 1910.[13] While the French were finding it difficult to increase exports of their own fabrics to the United States, many of the silks (and fabrics from other fibres) that were made in America carried designs created in Paris and Lyons. Cheney Silks, for example, used designs by Holzach (rue Beauregard) and also mantained a studio in Paris, run by Henry Créange. The firm kept a close eye on the fabrics being produced by Bianchini-Férier and other French manufacturers and used the works of French artists in their advertisements. They were not alone in this practice; Stehli Silks, which was already becoming known for its range of modern fabrics designed (mainly for dresses) by Americans, nevertheless had a 1928 advertisement illustrated by Bernard Boutet de Monvel. The practice of obtaining designs from foreign sources still carried no stigma. In 1917, in a description of an apartment planned for an October bride, it was revealed that 'at the casement windows hang [sic] an American cretonne which is frankly copied from a well-known French design – yellow birds posed on green urns of fruit against a grey background barred off in narrow black and white lines'.[14] And the Cheneys, certainly, made no secret of their use of French designers and artists as an inspiration; speaking in 1925, Charles Cheney told a Chicago audience: 'Three weeks ago I had to make a speech in Paris and I had to tell the people [there] that the American silk industry needed their help, that we were in a certain measure dependent upon them for art, for guidance in the creation of our products on the one hand as we were upon Japan for the source of our raw material on the other.'[15]

Several French designers, such as Bénédictus, Séguy and Georges Valmier, assisted foreigners in their search for French patterns by producing pattern books, particularly between 1924 and the early 1930s. These and other designers also contributed to the many series of pattern books – containing single motifs or

Nouvelle Variations, *one of several books containing patterns by the influential and innovative designer Bénédictus, was published in 1927. Plate 15, shown here, includes (upper right) a pattern typical of those he supplied to the Lyons firm of Brunet-Menuié.*

fully-worked patterns – that were issued by Paris publishers such as Charles Massin & Cie. and Armand Guérinet. Some were the work of single designers and others were compilations.[16] These found their way into many manufacturers' libraries; several Bénédictus and Séguy albums were, for example, purchased by Templeton, carpet-makers based in Glasgow, and were subsequently used as source material. Among the libraries that may be taken as an indication of the level of interest in books and catalogues of French furnishing textiles is the New York Public Library, located in the heart of New York's fashion and textile district and mandated to serve the city's industries. With the books and periodicals on the subject at New York's Fashion Institute of Technology, the collection represents the best source outside France of contemporary information on French designers of this period.

As a *tour de force* in the emerging field of marketing and promotions, the Art Deco exhibition also gave rise to what can be called a 'listing' syndrome, of which the main symptom was the incantation of names, given with relish in the sure knowledge that they would be recognized throughout the civilized world. In 1932 Gaston Derys, the honorary *conservateur* of the Musées de la Ville de Paris, demonstrated in *L'Art vivant* that he suffered from this ailment. He began with the works of Bénédictus (who had died in 1930), describing them as 'cloths so iridescent, so well studied, with their trim and precise geometry'. He then went on to praise 'the ingenuity of Jean Beaumont; the studied elegance of Robert Bonfils, the enticing and new creations of Brunet-Meunié; the renowned symphonies in *gris* [probably here meaning unbleached cotton, as in greycloth], wool and silk, the softness of feather and of mother-of-pearl of Rodier and Georges Hoffmann, and Jean Fressinet, and Séguy, and Garceion, and Lamorinière, and Stéphany, and Maurice Dufrène, and Paul Follot, and Louis Sognot, and Sonia Delaunay, and Deschelmaker, and Desseroit . . . and those cloths of such noble ornament that constitute Michel Dubost'.[17] The designer, having been all but anonymous for over a century, now became a selling point. This feature appealed strongly to the British, even if the modern French style itself was not appreciated by British craftsmen-designers – wedded as they were to more 'homespun' styles. By the late 1920s British manufacturers had turned to the practice of naming names, an exercise that became more widespread in the 1930s when, as the French had done immediately after the war, they used the promotion of artist-designers as an aid to an ailing industry.[18]

Although some English manufacturers produced their own designs in 'French' style, there were many others who purchased the authentic article from French studios. These were professional studios, in which a number of designers worked together, being salaried by the studio's owner, who was a designer himself. Some had a long history of supplying designs to British manufacturers. The Libert studio – which was one of the largest in Paris and still employed between sixty and eighty designers in the 1950s – was selling designs to Alexander Morton at the beginning of the century. But the most fruitful years for French designers with British contacts were those between 1920 and 1960. Both wars depleted manufacturers' studios of their staff, and both were followed by periods when many, and varied, designs were needed – in order to discover, after the wartime hiatus, which style or styles the public would prefer. The designers who supplied these were seldom mentioned by name. Of necessity, they had to be both versatile and prolific, able to accommodate a wide range of manufacturing methods and markets. They often

The creation of minutely rendered floral patterns was a skill for which many French studios remained known well into the twentieth century. This design, purchased in Paris from the Libert studio in 1938, shows the light, free manner with which this period treated the Empire style.

produced alternative colourways from selected designs, or reworked patterns in a matter of days to meet their customers' requirements. Some studios, such as Libert's, produced both modern and traditional design, while others, such as Wolfsperger's, specialized in classic French patterns. Many of the studios were family run. Léon Kittler founded a studio in 1897 which was maintained by three generations. Eugène Wolfsperger, active in the 1920s and '30s (inheriting the Wilheim & Wolfsperger studio) passed his studio to his son, Marcel, who maintained the atelier until his death in 1960, after which the remaining designs and collections were dispersed. Atelier Pollet, similarly, was run first by father and then by son. Others were established by descendants of textile manufactures; one such was the Giraud studio, started in 1953 by Jean Marie Giraud, the son of a silk manufacturer in central France who specialized in velvets. Part of the backbone of the industry, such studios have left evidence of their work in the archives of most of the major furnishing fabric firms of the day – not only in Britain, but in France, the United States, Sweden and elsewhere.[19]

By far the largest concentration of studios was in Paris, but there were also a number in Lyons. Mulhouse, however, no longer retained its reputation for freelance designers. Foreign manufacturers, it has been said, enjoyed visiting Paris not only because a massive choice of designs was on offer, but also because of the attractions of the city itself.[20] These included not only good food, wine and entertainment, but also the plentiful and inexpensive supply of old textiles, which could be found with ease in the markets. Often a good piece of *toile de Jouy* could be purchased for much less than a new design. In the United States the colonial revival of the 1920s brought with it a taste for French provincial furniture – said, in a Schumacher promotion, to have 'a quality of simplicity, sincerity and closeness to the people, that forms a bond between these two'.[21] There was a corresponding interest in old textiles which suited rustic furniture. In an article of

1930 devoted to this subject, it was noted that 'with the expansion of our interest in furniture from French villages and country sections, there comes an increasing demand for variety in fabric.' Paris alone could not meet this demand, 'which has been anticipated by diligent importers, those restless seekers who have wandered, and are still wandering hungrily, up and down the countryside around Angers, Bordeaux, Lyons, Marseilles, Avignon and through Alsace, Normandy and Brittany, peering into little farmhouses and the homes of simple merchants. . . .' The author goes on to describe in detail the 'delectable fabrics' – of every conceivable type – which were bought by American decorators and, of course, textile designers, 'who are ever in quest of documents for study and reproduction'.[22] It was during this period that British as well as American manufacturers' archives were greatly enhanced by such purchases, which included, after 1927, record books and samples from the dispersed Jouy estate (some of which, for example, were purchased by the Morton family for their firm's use). Other textile firms still active shed old sample blocks and designs as economic pressures increased in the 1930s. Private collectors in France, some among them also manufacturers (such as Lauer) or designers (such as Wolfsperger), amassed large numbers of excellent pieces. Many museums' collections of eighteenth- and early nineteenth-century French textiles were also being formed during these years – encouraged, no doubt, by Henri Clouzot, whose extensive studies resulted in articles, books and a fine collection, particularly strong in French prints of the late eighteenth and early nineteenth centuries, which was eventually divided between the Philadelphia Museum of Art and the Bibliothèque Forney in Paris, where he was director from 1908 to 1920, subsequently becoming curator of the Musée Gallièra.

The use of old fabrics such as tapestries, brocades, embroideries and canvasworks, or needlepoint, was, as we have seen, not a new idea; and firms specializing in their sale already existed. In 1919 one such firm, Benguiat & Vitall, published their third *Catalogue of the entire stock of rare and beautiful antique textiles and embroidery of the widely known connoisseurs and experts . . . now discontinuing their Paris and New York establishments*. However, the taste for simpler textiles, including scenic and small-patterned prints as well as ginghams, was new. Many forged 'antique' fabrics were also produced to meet the demand, particularly scenic designs, which were still plate-printed in France from zinc plates, as well as produced by roller-printing machines. (The plates were necessary where large designs were desired.)[23] The popularity of traditional scenic designs coexisted with the French artist-designers' production of textiles with jagged-edged, stylized scenes, but the traditional patterns outlived their modern counterparts, remaining standard offering in many French department stores' and manufacturers' ranges into the 1960s. Contrary to expectations, the modern *toiles* seem to have had little appeal for the young; at least Henri Clouzot thought not, for in 1926 he reported that there was 'nothing young about the homes of the youngest people in the world. Guillaume Janeau lately quoted from an American architectural review this praise of the New York Gladstone [Hotel]: '"Homelike atmosphere is obtained in the foyer by use of antique furniture and decorations." . . . On the other side of the Atlantic Ocean [i.e. New York] they compose decorations with old tapestry, old Jouy cloths, and even old paper hangings . . . . Nothing in accordance with the rhythm of . . . the most intense modern life in the world.'[24] Although the production of simpler cloths – ginghams

*Les Olivades is the only textile company in Marseilles to continue the* provençale *tradition of fabric production. The company archives date from 1818 and represent the collected resources of many small Marseilles ateliers that did not survive the Second World War. The example shown here, called* Coucareu *and designed in the 1930s, typifies the traditional patterns which they have made available since the 1950s.*

and the small floral patterns now commonly called *Provençale* prints (although owing much to the small dress patterns originally made by Oberkampf) — were given a boost by this trend, it was the scenic *toiles* that most captured the imagination of the 1920s. They were illustrated extensively, whether in books and articles about their history, as part of rooms depicted in magazines such as *Vogue* (which then included features on decorating), or in advertisements for the manufacturers, wholesalers or department stores that made new versions available. By 1927 this trend had been labelled 'romanticism' and was described by *Harper's Bazaar* as having started with young designers first, especially illustrators, then fabric designers. It was, they concluded, 'a small cloud at the moment, a reaction to cubism and *art nègre*'.[25]

Like the taste for scenic patterns, the development of abstract designs also occurred throughout this period. Many were inspired by artefacts from the French colonies. The 1922 exhibition in Marseilles — described by Glassgold as 'prophetic, though weak in arrangement, poor in quality, and incoherent in effect' — was indeed, a prediction of things to come. The *Exposition Nationale Coloniale de Marseille* was also an indication of the interest that already existed in the indigenous arts of the French Empire. With 52 million inhabitants in 1914, this was the second largest empire after Britain's and encompassed French Indo-China (Cambodia, Laos and Vietnam), the major part of the northwestern third of the African continent (Tunisia, Morocco, Algeria and what was then called French West Africa and French Equatorial Africa), Madagascar, some Pacific islands including Tahiti, and a small foothold in South America, in French Guiana. Most of this colonization had taken place since 1880; Morocco came under French control in 1912, and Syria and the Lebanon had been handed to the French when the German and Turkish empires were distributed among the Allies in 1918. A key figure in the influence of northwest Africa on French arts was Louis Lyautey, a cavalry officer who was in Algeria from 1904 to 1910 and in 1912 was made President-General of Morocco. There he integrated local leaders into his government and encouraged the arts by inviting French painters and writers to work in Morocco. Many of the other French colonies were also emerging at the same time as important sources of materials for cabinetmakers, whose lavish use of rosewood, teak, mahogany, amaranth, amboyana, ebony, ivory, bone, snakeskin and other colonial imports was a hallmark of French Art Deco furniture.

The influence of colonial artefacts on textiles manifested itself in crudely delineated forms, in entirely geometric patterns and in the use of the ikat (warp-dyed) technique or its imitation. The interest in such patterns was equally widespread among designers, manufacturers and *éditeurs* (who sub-contracted their production). Some had specific interests. For example, Georges le Manach, an *éditeur* who specialized in silks for interiors, had both traditional and modern designs in his range; of the latter it was said that they were 'inspired – but very freely – by Moroccan cloths'.[26] Rodier, on the other hand, had a collection of Cambodian *sampots* (ikats) which were shown at the Marseilles exposition, but he also explored the potential of other exotic or colonial styles. He did this with such success that when Henri Clouzot reported on the 1926 *Exposition de la Croisière Noire* (showing the trophies of the expedition into French Equatorial Africa, Sudan and Nigeria) he described the 'huge surfaces [with] designs both harmonious and complicated' and commented that 'there are in these decorations certain parts which are worthy of inspiring our manufacturers and we shall no doubt one day see them in some of Rodier's most beautiful stuff'.[27] The peak of general enthusiasm for the 'darkest Africa' style was probably reached in 1931, when *Harper's Bazaar* illustrated hair styles and jewellery inspired by the French colonial exhibition of that year,[28] but there were plenty of other events to keep the textile industry interested, ranging from the *Exposition du Sahara* in 1934 to the excavations (brought to a halt in 1940) of early textiles in Palmyra, an ancient Syrian desert city which lay on the east–west trading route during the second and third centuries A.D. Archaeological finds provided a natural corollary to colonial imagery; particularly important was the work of Henri Breuil, an outstanding draughtsman who was professor at the Collège de France from 1929 to 1947, published more than 600 books and articles and was best known for his copies of cave paintings found in Europe, North and South Africa and China. The bison and stick-figures from Altamira, which he first studied in 1901, were a favourite source of textile imagery in the 1950s. Also, there were sections of the industry, most notably printers, who depended on the export of their cloths to the colonies. All these factors (and there were others) contributed to the presence of 'native'-style textiles in French interiors until 1960 and even beyond.

Painters, too, had responded to *art nègre*, to such an extent that the modern movement in painting is often given sole credit for the abstract patterns so often used in textiles of this period. There is little doubt, certainly, that many painters – among them Léger and Picasso – contributed to this trend; however, many of the textile designers working in this style drew their inspiration not from modern painting but directly from African artefacts. Nor was all abstract textile design inspired by *art nègre*. The painter Sonia Delaunay, for example, designed textiles based on pure abstraction – as opposed to the abstracted *art nègre* forms of cubism.[29] Many other artists who designed textiles did not embrace abstraction; among these were Dufy and Dufrèsne, who have already been mentioned. Both of these artists also designed tapestries, and it was in this arena that the long-established link between art and textiles was most strongly supported. When the Golden Gate International Exposition was held in San Francisco in 1939, an impressive group of French tapestries were borrowed from a single Parisian collector, Marie Cuttoli, who lent pieces by Georges Braque, Le Corbusier, André Derain, Ferdinand Léger, Jean Lurçat, Man Ray, Henri Matisse, Joan Miró, Picasso and Georges Rouault.[30]

The work of French artists also inspired designers elsewhere. During the 1920s in the United States Cheney Brothers used the work of Kees van Dongen, Marie Laurencin, Jean Dupas and Gabriel Moiselet as inspirations for designs, together with the stained glass of Maumejean frères and the metalwork of Edgar Brandt.[31] This practice continued among American textile manufacturers until after the Second World War; in 1957, for example, *American Fabrics* suggested Matisse's 'Jazz' series as a fruitful source of patterns.[32] French artist-designed tapestries also had a profound effect on French fabric design, particularly in the decade after the end of the war, during which time a number of tapestry exhibitions were mounted, some of which were subsequently shown in the United States and Britain.

The active participation of artists in textile design also had an effect on technology. Many of them found that existing technical processes often did not give the freedom they needed to express their ideas. The interference of textile technology was particularly marked in Jacquard weaving – so much so that Michel Dubost, who was responsible for the designs made by Francis Ducharne

*Above left: Rodier's hand-woven dress cloths were already well known in Europe when he added furnishing fabrics to his range in about 1925. Limiting himself initially to cotton and linen cloths, chiefly used as tablecloths and curtains, by 1927 he had begun to make wall-hangings and to experiment with upholstery fabrics of mixed fibres – including jute, silk, cotton and wool. In the same year he supplied some of the curtains for the liner, the Ile de France. This example was exclusive to Schumacher in New York.*

*Above: A Rodier fabric, designed by Pablo Picasso and handwoven in cotton and linen in about 1928. Between 1927 and 1939 Picasso produced a number of screens and fabric designs for the interior designer Jean Michel Frank, whose austere interiors were popular with some of America's richest and most prominent families, among them the Rockefellers and the Crockers.*

(founded in 1920 and producing woven and printed silks and velvets in Lyons and Paris), openly acknowledged the contribution of Louis Tronchon, Ducharne's technician, who translated each design on a *mise en carte*, from which the Jacquard cards were cut.[33] The desire for a more direct method of producing patterns on textiles was expressed in the renewed use of block printing by artists, such as Dufy, who were skilled in linocuts or woodcuts. It can also be seen in the popularity of batik, a wax-resist process which was, in its European form, nearly always used for freehand 'painted' designs (rather than the elaborately detailed block-printed designs which characterize Javanese batiks). Batiks were a prominent feature of the 1925 Paris Exposition, and in France Madame Marguerite Pangon was their foremost exponent. Of all the printing techniques, however, it was screen printing that offered the best combination of faithful translation to cloth with the needs of bulk production. The search for this combination had begun several decades earlier. As early as 1873, a French textile trade journal had reported that 'without specifying the mode of application, Bellingard and Giraud reserve the right to use photography for themselves in the decoration of all kinds of fabrics of all sizes. The advantage of photography is that it reproduces artwork very accurately and what's more, photography on fabrics withstands washing very well.'[34] This method of printing did not become established, but the photographic engraving of rollers was introduced at the beginning of the twentieth century. Meawhile, others in France had been developing a variation of *pouchoir* printing (a stencil-like process that was used to produce coloured illustrations) which utilized a zinc plate in place of stencil-board and dyes applied from a compressed air chamber (spray-gun) instead of a brush. Pouchoir-printed textiles designed by Alphonse Mucha and others were available in 1901, and possibly earlier. This method of printing was well established by 1925, and gradually gave way to the use of a silk screen and a squeegee.[35]

Innovation was also taking place in the use of fibres, including metallic yarns and paper yarns.[36] Of these the most important was the increasing use of artificial silk (later called rayon or acetate). The most influential designer in support of its use was Bénédictus, who in 1924 was credited by *Art et Décoration* with the observation, 'I am aware that [artificial silk] has found a use in furnishings. But it has been considered as a shameful substitute, a simple counterfeit of real silk, and to make the public buy, we asked [artificial silk] to supply at a cheaper rate the same sumptuous effects as real silk. This was a fundamental error and it has caused a lot of misunderstanding, an error analogous to that of an architect who tries to make cement look like stone.' Bénédictus recognized that this new fibre had become associated with cloths with 'an aggressive shine, vulgar colours, [and] a glassy look' and understood that 'a new material needed a new aesthetic'.[37] In 1925 he therefore began a close collaboration with Brunet-Meunié, a Parisian firm of *éditeurs* founded in 1815 which now specialized in artificial fibres. Two of their fabrics were shown at the 1925 Paris Exposition, and Bénédictus also collaborated with Tassinari & Chatel in the making of cotton and *fibranne* (viscose) damasks.

It was fortunate that France had a designer who, as *Art et Décoration* also explained, believed that 'modern art should not be just for the fortunate few. It is relatively easy to make beautiful things in silk at 200–300 francs a metre but there is a whole middle class clientele which cannot pay such prices.' For although the enthusiasm for French style was good for Paris and its designers, and for the

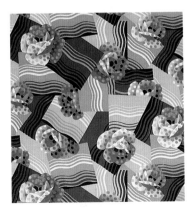

*Printed in France in the 1920s, this cotton is an example of the use of screen or pouchoir printing. The shaded areas of pink have been applied by air-brush while the rest of the pattern was shielded.*

makers of luxury textiles, these, whether hand block printed or handwoven, were made only in very small amounts. With the arrival of the effects of the 1929 Wall Street Crash, the luxury trades of France were hard hit. The work Bénédictus had undertaken, to encourage shorter repeats (which were less costly to prepare for weaving and less wasteful in use) and many effects from fewer colours, now became of greater importance. The use of silk declined rapidly in Lyons until, in 1938, over 72 per cent of the fibres used there were acetate.[38] Single silk strands, extruded as a continuous fibre, had to be carefully twisted together – or 'thrown' – to create usable yarn. Acetate rayon was easier to spin and therefore did not require skilled workers; and this, together with improved machinery, meant that a female weaver who once made 3–4 yards or metres could in the same time, and on the same machine, make at least ten. The markets for cloth, however, were shrinking. Prices of all cloths began to rise; a printed percale that cost 13.50 francs in 1927 was likely to cost 16–19 francs per metre in 1935. The silk that had been 200 francs per metre in 1924 was about 360 fifteen years later, and a good acetate damask was 100 francs per metre.[39] By the late 1930s, surface detail had replaced elaborate pattern; quilting, tweeds, and repoussé effects were more typical than colourful chintzes, which were rapidly becoming luxury cloths.

The outbreak of war in 1939 brought into focus the strain under which the French textile industry had been operating for some years. The decision, by the French government in 1934, not to pin the new exchange rate to the pound sterling was later seen as responsible for 'a paralysis of our exportation, an increase in foreign imports, a slow-down in our economic activity, a lowering of salaries which inevitably provoked the reaction of 1936'.[40] In fact, the social unrest of 1936 preceded the worst year of the inter-war period for foreign imports (1937). Although there was a brief respite for the next two years (when the franc was devalued, production rose – by 14 per cent in the case of Lyons fabrics – and many countries began to withdraw orders from Germany and Austria as a result of Nazi policies), this benefited mainly dress-fabric manufacturers. The price of furnishing fabrics continued to rise, and sales slumped.

The end of the decade brought more political unrest, war and then, in 1940, occupation of northern and northwestern France by the German army and the collapse of the Third Republic. France's cotton centres were more badly damaged than they had been in the First World War; Lyons, effectively cut off from Paris, turned its looms to the production of parachutes, barrage balloons and other war materials. Less affected by the war than other centres, Lyons nevertheless lacked labour in its rayon industry (silk was less hard hit because it relied principally on female labour), and as the naval war accelerated, it lost orders in America and the French colonies. Fuel and oil for machines ran out, by 1942 silk supplies were gone, and in 1943, when fibranne also disappeared, M. Brochier, the president of the Syndicat des Fabricants de Soieries de Tissus de Lyon, declared, 'We find ourselves in a shipwrecked economy.' All they could do, he concluded, was to 'keep intact the life-force of our industry'.[41] This they did, and by the early 1950s Lyons was exporting silks to ninety different countries; Great Britain was its largest customer.[42]

Aided by the Marshall Plan (introduced in 1947), France's textile industries were renewed, and by 1951 cloth represented 21 per cent of the total value of French exported products and, as such, was the most important.[43] However, progress was much slower in the manufacture of furnishing fabrics than in those

*Above: Between 1940 and 1944, a number of French artists and designers created prototypes in the anticipation of renewed textile production when the war ended. This hand-screen-printed rayon, following the French tradition of scenic prints, was designed by Friesz in 1943. The scarcity of dyestuffs during the period is reflected in the restricted number and the pale shades of the colours.*

*Above right: Celebrating the drama of the New York skyline, this design for a five-colour roller print was produced by Atelier Pollet in 1956. It typifies an increased awareness of American tastes.*

for dress. While French textiles regained their reputation for infinite variety, and Parisian designs and colours met with great favour in America, French manufacturers nevertheless had increasing difficulty exporting to the United States, which had introduced new import regulations and tariffs in 1951. Studios and freelance designers, of course, had a good decade; this was the time when some foreign manufacturers were prepared to buy twenty designs, print five to ten and be happy with two or three successful ones. Others foreign firms continued, as a manufacturer in Lyons commented, 'to copy exactly the fabrics which have obtained the favour of the public'.[44]

In stylistic terms each decade of this period has been roughly assigned its own character: bright stylized flowers and exotic motifs in the 1920s, neutral-toned 'cubist' patterns and textures in the '30s, dusky neo-realism in the '40s, (arising from the study of medieval tapestries undertaken by some of the French artists who organized exhibitions during and just after the war) and clear crisp abstract patterns in the '50s. However convenient these divisions may be, they overlook the unity of the period. The 1950s were – in terms of production methods and the structure of the industry – far more like the 1920s than the 1980s; and the 'Paris-fever' of the 1950s was an echo of post-World War I days. But dramatic changes lay ahead; the late 1950s witnessed rampant inflation, and although French industry in general grew rapidly, employment in the textile trades declined by nearly 30 per cent, eliminating much of the specialist work, especially in silk weaving and block printing.[45] The United States had developed a much more efficient – and self sufficient – industry, and the threat of Third World production was soon to unite both countries with Britain and the rest of Europe in the defence of their textile industries.

In the mid-1950s, fresh, impressionistic flowers became a feature of many screen-printed fabrics. Some, such as this print from Pierre Frey, became representative of a new classic French style and remained in production for several decades.

The fashion for lacquered surfaces and brilliant colours is echoed in this cotton satin, surface-roller-printed in France in the early 1920s. Such fabrics were produced for a middle-class clientele.

Three printed cottons, all designed in France between 1928 and 1934, showing the range of treatments given to floral patterns which were intended to be neither overtly modern nor rigidly traditional. The shadow design in the background of the main fabric, produced by Vanoutryve, shows the influence of etched glass.

The design of this gouache, prepared by Max Forrer's Paris studio for a printed textile, shows a compromise between angular forms and floral patterns that is charactertistic of much of the studio work produced in the early 1930s.

Dubbed 'the château of the Atlantic', the SS France made her maiden voyage to New York in April 1912. The First-Class reception rooms were in the style of Louis XIV and helped to promote and to perpetuate the reprospective fashion for this period into the 1920s. Similarly, the Moroccan Room, where coffee was served by appropriately dressed waiters, illustrates a form of colonial style that would also reappear in the 1920s. French liners were to become famous for their modern interiors with the launch of the Ile de France in 1927.

A silk designed by Michel Dubost and based on a geometric scheme by Monod-Herzen. It was used during the mid-1920s as a wallcovering in the entrance hall of François Ducharne's Paris house, and designed after Dubost became associated with the Société des Soieries Ducharne in Paris in 1922.

This silk, called L'Alhambra, was designed in 1921 by Michel Dubost. Originally a student of the Ecole des Beaux-Arts in Lyons, he returned in 1917, some years after his graduation, to teach both there and at the Ecole de Tissage. Students of the latter school wove this piece.

A figured silk crêpe designed in the Moorish style by Madeleine Legrange and woven in about 1920 by Courdurier, Fructus & Descher. The crêpe surface was created by juxtaposing threads twisted in opposing directions; metal threads have also been incorporated.

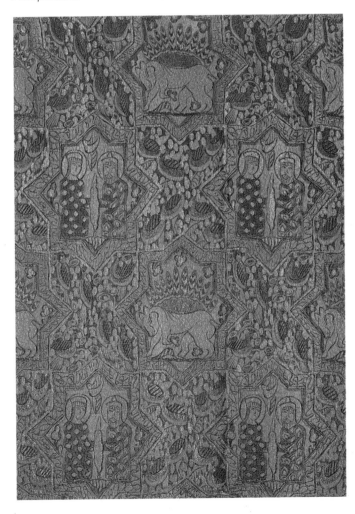

189

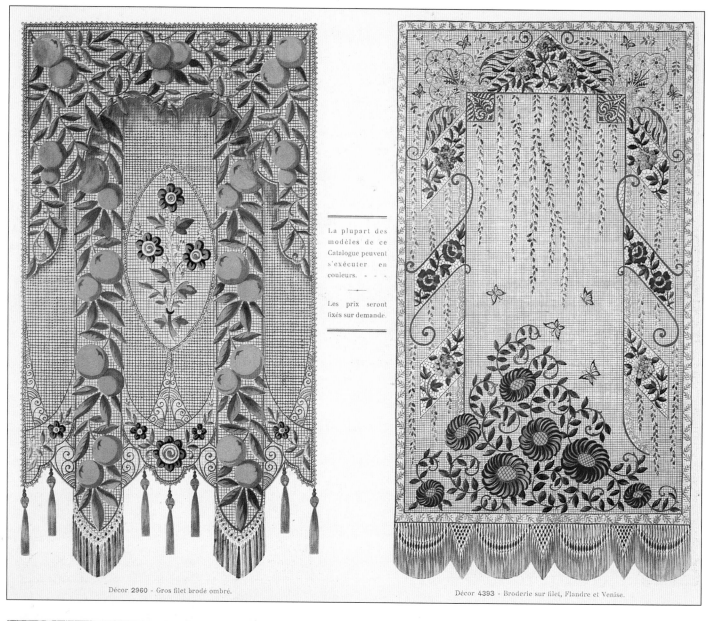

La plupart des modèles de ce Catalogue peuvent s'exécuter en couleurs. - - -

Les prix seront fixés sur demande.

Décor 2960 - Gros filet brodé ombré.

Décor 4393 - Broderie sur filet, Flandre et Venise.

These two stores, or flat window curtains, were illustrated by Maison Gaston Didier of Paris in their catalogue, Stores, rideaux, couvre-lits, linge de table: dentelles et tissus, published in about 1935. Hand-assembled and often finished with hand embroidery, filet-lace panels such as these could be made in any dimension and in many colours, as could all the other goods advertised.

The deliberately uneven areas of sky blue in this printed cotton of 1926 characterize many of the surface roller prints of the period. It was produced from a French design for Warner & Sons, London.

Created by René Herbst, this room was exhibited in the Salon d'Automne – the prestigious annual Paris exhibition of the work of cabinetmakers and interior decorators – in 1921. A total of five patterns, including one on the ceiling, are used in a very controlled, architectural manner, demonstrating the debt owed by the style of the 1920s to the late Empire period. After about 1926 Herbst became a major exponent of metal furniture, and in 1929 he co-founded the U.A.M. (Union des Artists Modernes).

A beech 'gondola' chair, veneered with white shagreen, designed by André Groult and exhibited in the Pavilion de l'Ambassade Française at the Paris Exposition of 1925. It is upholstered in a cut velvet made for Groult by Delaroière & Leclerq which shows the energetic abstract floral style now most closely associated with art deco.

The influential patron and socialite Charles de Beistegui created this dining room just after the Second World War, at his villa at Groussay, west of Paris. The combination of a striking provençale print with a bold eighteenth-century-style check was subsequently widely imitated. For the main salon at Groussay, Beistegui – a millionaire with eclectic tastes – also commissioned Prelle to weave the same brocaded lampas as would later be used in the restoration of Marie Antoinette's bedchamber at Versailles (p. 35).

Modern scenic patterns, although usually associated with the decorative artist Raoul Dufy, were produced by many other textile designers. The damask shown here was designed by A. Lorenzi and manufactured by Bianchini-Férier in 1921.

K 711. **PERCALE** glacée "*Les Roses*". Existe en fond vert, blanc, jaune. Largeur 0m78,0m80. *Le mètre* . . . . . **13.50**

K 712. **TOILE** métis, belle qualité, "*Le Meunier, son Fils et l'Âne*". Se fait en bleu et en rouge. Largeur 0m80. *Le mètre* . . . . . **16.50**

K 713. **IMBERLINE** de coton, double face. Existe en rouge et vert, rose et or, bleu et or, jaune et bleu. Largeur 1m28/1m30. **Exceptionnel.** *Le mètre.* **16.50**

K 714. **TOILE** pur fil, "*Les Oiseaux*". Se fait en fond bis, blanc, jaune, rose, bleu. Largeur 0m80. *Le mètre* . . . . . **25 fr.**

K 715. **CRETONNE** forte, "*Les Corbeilles*". Existe en fond or, bis, blanc. Largeur 0m78,0m80. *Le mètre* . . . . . **14.50**

*Illustrated on the cover of the catalogue of 1927, for the department store Au Gagne-Petit, are five cloths, including a cotton imberline (centre, priced at 16.50 francs per metre), a glazed percale (left, 13.50 francs) and a cretonne (right, 14.50 francs). The most expensive fabric was the full-colour toile, priced at 25 francs per metre. The single colour scenic print was 16.50 francs. The latter reproduced Huet's 'Le Meunier, son fils et l'âne', the original of which had been copperplate-printed at Jouy in 1806.*

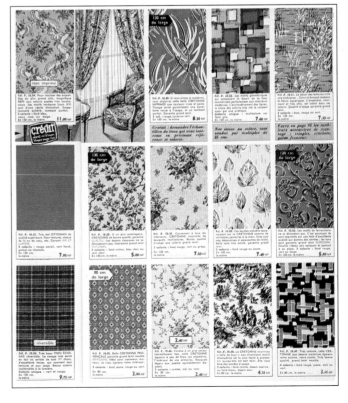

*This selection from Les Trois Suisse's catalogue of 1961/62 shows the perennial use of established French patterns alongside modern geometric designs. The cretonne provençale (lower left) is proposed for use in wall panels. In the same row is a toile de Jouy taken from a copperplate-printed cotton, Les Délices des Quatre Saisons, designed by Jean Baptiste Huet and first printed by Oberkampf in about 1785.*

*Opposite:* The revival of interest in modern tapestry after the Second World War led to the production of screen-printed panels which could fulfil the same function at considerably lower cost. This example of 1957, one of several decorative panels designed for the Parisian éditeur Victor Coates, was by Cecchini.

*Opposite below:* The Cortège of Orpheus, a silk damask designed by Raoul Dufy, was woven by Bianchini-Férier in 1921. In 1920, Dufy had noted in his chapter in Amour de l'art that modern painters, particularly the Fauves, had contributed their use of pure colour and freely curving lines to textile design. The name given to this fabric may be a pun on Orphism, a branch of the cubist movement that was developed by Guillaume Apollinaire in 1912, and was based on the use of colour in nonrepresentational forms.

*Above right:* The architect and designer Pierre Chareau was an ardent supporter of modern design who often incorporated metal, wrought iron and glass blocks into his interiors. Although he usually used textiles handwoven by the prominent textile artist Hélène Henry, this example, which he designed himself, is a block-printed linen. It was shown used as chair upholstery in a bedroom exhibited at the influential Lord & Taylor exhibition in New York in 1928. Chareau worked in America from early in the Second World War until his death in 1950; the house that he designed for the artist Robert Motherwell in East Hampton is still intact.

*Right:* The post-war spirit of fun and frivolity is vividly expressed in this screen-printed cotton, manufactured to a design of 1956 by the artist Ferdinand Léger.

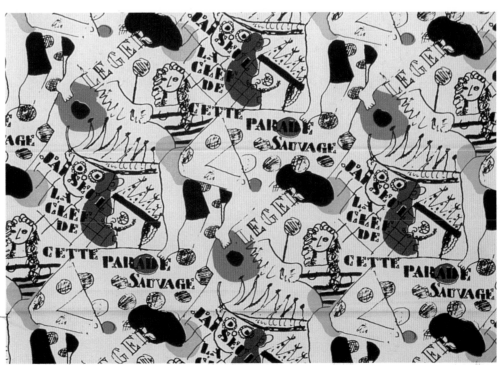

These two interiors show the endurance of certain French textile and furnishing styles throughout this period. Above is a bedroom design by V. Ricci, illustrated in Intérieurs en couleurs, 1922. A number of similar features – the type of textile design, the colour scheme, the bed inset into a shallow alcove and even a similar use of trimmings – can be seen in Pierre Frey's country house, shown on the right as it was illustrated in Connaissances des arts in 1956, more than thirty years later.

*A number of English firms enjoyed great success with designs bought in from French studios. Shown here are three cloths produced by G. P. & J. Baker, who purchased the design, Ruban, from the Paris studio, Reupp, in 1899. The block-printed linen with dark ground was produced in 1915, and the glazed cotton with light-green ground in 1935. New versions in different colours were created in 1940 and in 1967; the third sample shown is one of several current colourways now produced as a screen-print.*

*In the eyes of the rest of the world, modernism was firmly associated with French furnishing fabrics of the 1920s and '30s. Nevertheless, the room depicted by G. Paris for the January issue of La Rire in 1931 retains many features typical of some fifty years earlier. Such conservatism was an important characteristic of the decoration of French interiors.*

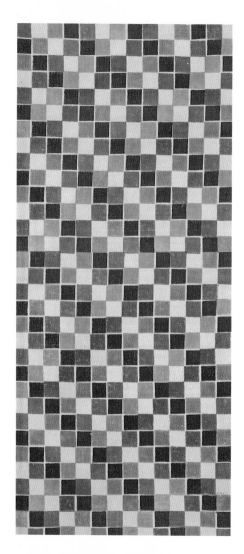

*Above:* The pop and op art fabrics of the 1960s had precursors in a number of designs produced by French artists in the 1950s. This example, screen-printed in black and white, was one of several textiles designed by Louis le Brocquy. They were produced in 1956 and 1957 by David Whitehead Ltd, an English firm well known for its avant-garde designs.

*Left:* This cotton velvet was block-printed in 1927. The design is by Sonia Delaunay who, with her husband, the painter Robert Delaunay, explored the visual interplay of adjacent colours, an approach, which they christened 'simultaneous contrasts'.

*Below:* Carnival, designed by Suzanne Fontan, was hand-screen-printed on heavy cotton duck for Greeff Fabrics of New York in about 1947. Five years later, Fontan founded a furnishing textiles company in collaboration with the established Paris wallpaper manufacturers Nobilis, founded in 1925.

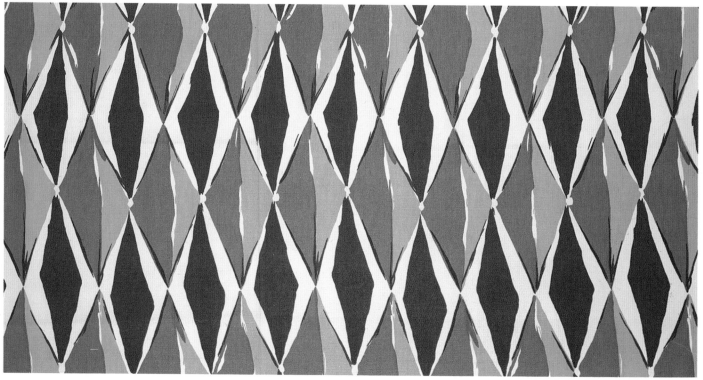

The French design of this
hand-block-printed linen reflects
a Viennese influence in its
chequerboard motif. The design
was purchased by Warners and
manufactured at their Dartford
printworks, near London, in 1928.

A design for a two-colour
hand-screen-printed cotton,
purchased by Warner & Sons from
Hélène Gallet in 1947. Gallet ran
her own Paris studio, the Société
de Dessins pour l'Ameublement.

The studio of Paul Pollet, produced a wide variety of designs for printed and woven textiles, and for wallpapers. The design shown here dates from about 1935 and was intended for a cloth woven with a variegated warp.

Left: During the 1930s both floral and abstract motifs were often produced using the pre-printed warp technique. This example dates from about 1933 or 1934.

Opposite: A hand-screen-printed linen produced in 1929, this French-made furnishing fabric reproduced the free, abstract forms of contemporary constructivist art.

*During the decade after the Second World War, French, and, particularly, Parisian themes were prominent in many American fabrics; these two examples were both available from Greeff Fabrics, New York. The caricature of the Paris Opera (above) was designed for a fabric with matching wallpaper by the American artist Saul Steinberg in 1953, while* Festival *(right), scattered with fans, was printed in 1951 and included the words 'Designed in Paris by Andrew Shunney' on its selvedge.*

*Right: Although the decoration of this bedroom by Suzanne Guiguichon seems to place it in the 1950s, it was designed prior to 1939, when it appeared in* The Studio Yearbook of Decorative Arts. *Between 1921 and 1929, Guiguichon worked for La Maîtrise, the modern atelier of the Paris department store, Galeries Lafayette. Thereafter she worked for private clients.*

*Below: Illustrated in the* Répertoire du goût moderne *of 1929, these chairs show the way in which an exaggerated wood grain was usually complemented by woven upholstery cloths with a small pattern or tweed-like effect. The chairs were designed by Francis Jourdain, who campaigned throughout his working life (he died in 1958) for the production of well-designed, reasonably priced furniture.*

*Opposite:* Ships, a wooden-roller-printed jute produced in 1928 by G. P. & J. Baker of London, is thought to employ the design purchased from Seguy on 15 December 1926. During 1926 and 1927 Bakers bought several designs from Seguy, paying between £5 and £9 for each one.

*Left:* Lisieres Fleuries produced this fifteen-colour block print in 1930. It typifies many contemporary designs with a colonial theme, and derives its imagery from the landscape and animals of French northwest Africa.

*Below:* The American economic crisis of 1929 forced Paul Poiret onto shaky financial ground, and by 1933 he had closed both the Atelier Martine and his couture house. Between the crisis and the closures he had begun to produce designs for other companies. This block-printed cotton, Pineapples, of about 1930, was exclusive to Schumacher's range.

# POSTSCRIPT

*Opposite: A richness, both of colour and of imagery, characterizes many of today's French textiles. Here, the screen-printed cotton curtains (made from Percheron's Damas du Lac, taken from an eighteenth-century document and manufactured by Lauer for the 1991 collection) suggest the luxury of a silk damask. Machine-made tapestry cloth, from Nobilis-Fontan's own mill, evokes the splendour of centuries gone by, while Pierre Frey's Jacquard-woven viscose and cotton cloth, Majorelle, evokes France's long-held love of Moorish patterns.*

*A number of English firms continue to commission new designs from French studios, artists and freelance designers. Shown here is* Floral Splash, *by Agathe Charlot for the Warner range for autumn 1990.*

'THE BEST image of France rests on its traditional products.' (Patrick Turbot, in *L'Entrepreneur Français à la découverte du marché des Etats-Unis*.)[1]

To tell the story of the industry behind today's French textiles would require another volume. Since 1960 so many firms have expanded, regrouped, divested and diversified that the pattern of current French textile production is barely recognizable as related to that of the 1950s. Lyons no longer remains the centre of the raw silk trade, as it was after the Second World War; between 1969 and 1974 alone, the spinning of new synthetic fibres doubled, while the production of most natural-fibre yarns fell by nearly 40 per cent. During the same period two firms, D.M.C. (Dolfus Mieg & Cie.), and Agache Willot (formed in 1967 by the fusion of Ets Agache and M. J. Willot & Cie.) became dominant, by acquisition extending their interests into all areas of textile production and virtually every textile-producing region in the world.[2]

During the same time, the areas of interior and furniture design also underwent radical change. As the housing shortage of the 1950s abated, the 'building boom' of the 1960s gave impetus to the campaign to promote industrial design in France, a campaign that owed much to a decade of effort by Jacques Viénot, founder in 1951 of both the Institut Français d'Esthétique Industrielle and the magazine *Esthétique industrielle*. Another organization, the Union des Artistes Modernes bequeathed to postwar France its championship of tubular steel furniture, perpetuated through its affiliate Formes Utiles, founded in 1949. Their rationale never replaced the ideas of more conventional interior designers – much to the regret of avant-garde French design pundits – but by the early 1960s, fashion, too, had abandoned its once-exclusive use of the finest, most supple fabrics; Courréges turned to vinyls, Paco Rabanne to metal plates, Pierre Cardin to heat-formed fabrics. Out of these tendencies came a dozen or so years of metal-and-plastics mania, during which time thermoplastic resins, inflatable polyvinyl chloride, fibreglass, polystyrene, polyurethane foam over steel tubing and brightly coloured vinyls were the principal vehicles of avant-garde furniture, leaving little need for upholstery fabric in the most modern interiors, apart from solid-coloured stretch nylon jersey and textured weaves, such as those designed on a hand loom by Bernard Jolier (who had founded Tissu Placide Joliet in 1947). Lighting and colour became the dramatic elements of modern French interiors.

Despite the rejection of traditionally made fabrics for avant-garde settings, classic French décor continued to be a source of inspiration for many interiors of the 1960s. The 'classic' room was not necessarily retrospective in style, but it drew on the French tradition of combined patterns and skilfully juxtaposed colours. Such interiors incorporated both woven and printed fabrics, although weaves remained the dominant upholstery fabric in the modern-classic rooms of the decade. Initially, the 'Op'- or 'Pop'-inspired printed textiles of the '60s – whether following the geometric lead of Victor Vasarely or using large-scale floral designs and striking colours – were generally to be found in use as curtains, and emanated from the high-priced, high-quality ranges such as those of Noblis, Frey, Chotard, Deschemaker or the small boutique in Paris's rue St-Roch where Manuel Canovas first sold textiles of his own design in 1963.

By the mid-1960s this internationally adopted style was made affordable by Prisunic, a French chain of department stores which issued its first mail-order catalogue in 1966 and stocked mass-produced furniture designed by Marc Berthier, who headed the Prisunic design studio, and by Olivier Mourgue, Marc

*The continued association of French designers with specialized fabrics, often reinterpreted using modern images and colours, is demonstrated by this collection of textiles. The moiré plaid was produced by the Tal factory near Lyons for Designers' Guild. To its left is a chiné damask by D.M.C. (Dollfus Mieg & Cie.). Manuel Canovas's screen-printed cotton, with its bright array of exotic flowers and animals, is reminiscent of a traditional* pekin, *while the cotton velours, Samoa, by Lalièvre is printed with an abstract pattern of dark, mottled colours. All the fabrics were launched in autumn 1990.*

*The Paramount Hotel, situated off Broadway in New York, re-opened in 1990, having undergone a complete refurbishment masterminded by Philippe Starck, perhaps the most influential designer of the last ten years. The public areas of the Paramount represent a dramatic departure from the institutional look characteristic of many hotels. Both the lobby and the mezzanine floor above it, shown in this picture, are scattered with a large number of chairs and sofas. The work of various contemporary designers, each is upholstered in either one or two colours of plain velvet. The effect is rich, original and rather theatrical – typical of Starck's interiors.*

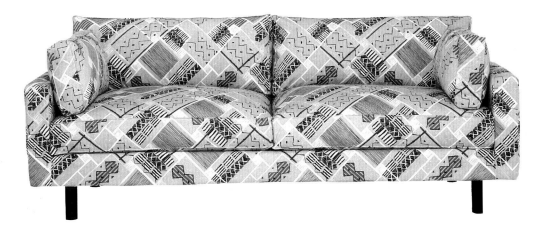

*Kovenchina is part of Les Noires, a collection designed and produced by the French éditeur Etamine. The cotton upholstery fabric is printed in a variety of colourways, including pink, blue and yellow, as well as in black and white, as shown on this Etamine sofa. The collection was launched in January 1985.*

*Opposite below:  Fabrics included in the January edition of Maison Française in 1989. The screen-printed cotton upholstery fabric on the chair, employing freely interpreted rococo motifs, was designed by the partnership Robert Le Héros for Nobilis-Fontan. Founded in Paris in 1986 by four graduates of the Ecole des Arts Décoratifs, Robert Le Héros uses raw textures such as wild linen and pure cotton, on which they print mythological and classical designs. The other fabrics shown are, hanging left to right, a printed cotton satin by Jacques Grange for Romanex; a moiré fabric of cotton and viscose mix by Pierre Frey; a printed cotton toile by Burger Borderieux; and, draped top to bottom, a silk and polyester taffeta by Jean Deschemaker; a cotton and polyester Jacquard by La Filandière; and a cotton Jacquard tapestry by Lauer.*

Held and others. (All of these were exponents of 'high style' metal and plastics furniture – Mourgue, for example, is best known for the jersey-covered polyurethane foam 'Djinn' furniture used in Stanley Kubrick's film *2001: A Space Odyssey*; Held also designed for Knoll International.) This move towards good design at a reasonable price was paralleled by the work of Primrose Bordier, who, together with her five associates, specialized in the design of medium-priced furnishing textiles, household linen and wallpapers. The democratization of 'high style' received a setback in the late 1960s and early '70s, when increased petroleum prices made plastics more expensive. The growing importance of a 'return to nature' subculture diverted attention along ethnic lines, towards bamboo, rattan and wood, North African and Indian textiles and flea market finds. During the 1970s, mainstream interiors adapted some of these trends; full, well-padded furniture was often upholstered in printed fabric employing large-scale ethnic patterns or giant leaf and flower motifs, their size a legacy from 'Pop'-influenced designs of the 1960s.

During the same period distribution networks gradually expanded, so that by the mid-1980s France's major furnishing fabric firms, particularly those of the *éditeurs*, were well represented in all the main markets of the world. Les Tissus Manuel Canovas, for example, built on the early initial word-of-mouth success of what is now known as its *Candide* collection – with boldly drawn, imaginatively coloured florals – and now has subsidiaries in Italy, France, Switzerland, Spain, the United States and England, the latter two opened in the mid-1980s. Likewise, *éditeurs* often themselves represented ranges from other countries. Etamine also began life as a boutique, opening in 1974. Established by Francine Royneau, Françoise Dorget and Marilyn Gaucher, Etamine were, by 1977, the French distributor of the British firms Osborne & Little and Designers Guild. In the early 1980s they also became the distributors for Colefax & Fowler and designed their first range of furnishing fabrics, which they began to export; by 1984 exports represented nearly one-third of its sales. Thus the structure of manufacturing, attitudes towards interiors and the methods of marketing were all subjected to major modifications.

Yet, as the writer of the introductory passage was at pains to point out, little had changed in terms of France's image as a manufacturing nation. A Gallup poll of 1982 found that when Americans were asked to name the area in which France led the world, their answer was, first, fashion (55 per cent) and, second, wine (52 per cent). Culture – meaning books, music, art and films – followed at 28 per

cent. In truth, helicopters, aircraft and their engines top the list of French exports to the United States; wine accounts for less than 3 per cent, and both fashion and textiles for less than 2 per cent of total exports, below refined petrol products and bottled water.[3] Similarly, when 200 company directors in 16 countries were asked in 1984 to name the leading country in terms of technology, only 4 per cent named France, which placed it ahead of Italy, but behind Sweden, the UK, Germany and, overwhelmingly (named by 72 per cent), Japan.[4] Although France has become a leader in certain technological spheres – for example, in aviation and nuclear power technology – the world persists in seeing it as a country that epitomizes the good life. And although the overall export figures for French textiles is small, among the three or four dozen leading French furnishing textile houses, exports often account for 30–40 per cent of their turnover.

In matters of style, then, the French still have a great deal of influence. With regard to furnishing fabrics this may well be due – at least in part – to the fact that despite the radical restructuring of the industry, most of the well-known firms are far from being newcomers to the field. Paule Marrot Editions, Georges Le Manach, Souléiado, Lauer, Nobilis-Fontan, J. Brochier-Chotard, Broussac, Pierre Frey, Deschemaker, Lelièvre, Vanoutryve, Manufacture d'Impression sur Etoffes (anciens établissements Ch. Steiner), Prelle, Tassinari & Chatal, and others, all descend from foundations laid between fifty and two hundred and fifty years ago. Many of them also maintain a family interest. The relatively young firm Pierre Frey, founded in 1935, currently operates as both *éditeur* and manufacturer under the guidance of Pierre's son Patrick; the managing directors of the 130-year-old weaving establishment Vanoutryve, come, alternately, from one of the two founding families, Vanoutryve and Rasson. Even some firms that are no longer run by the same family have at their head those who themselves maintain a textile tradition; at Prelle, for example, the managing directors, Philippe and François Verzier, come from a family that descends from one of the founders and, except for one generation, has always maintained itself through textiles. Such firms provide a stable backdrop against which new, young designers have emerged.

*The architect François Catroux created this bedroom for his apartment in the Quai de Bethune, Paris, in about 1966. The design is a modern interpretation of the age-old baldequin, with yellow and white diagonal strips of skai (plastic leather) lining the whole of the room. Experimentation with alternative materials marginalized the role of textiles in avant-garde interiors of this period.*

*This corner of a Paris apartment epitomizes the casual yet elegant style for which the French were known in the 1960s. Its arrangement owes much to the interiors of the Empire period and of the early twentieth century, when the French love of Turkish informality brought banquettes and pattern-on-pattern room decoration into favour.*

When, in 1986, the company Robert Le Héros was set up independently by four graduates of the Ecole des Arts Décoratifs, to produce their own designs, they soon found a niche offered to them in the Nobilis-Fontan range, through which their whimsical, painterly fabrics are now marketed.

The massive archives of many French firms have also contributed to the strong sense of continuity that persisted throughout the postwar years. During the 1980s these became of greater interest, as the renewed production of 'document' fabrics grew. Among printed furnishing fabrics, which in 1987 represented about 35 per cent of sales by French *éditeurs* (the remainder being weaves), about half carried 'document' designs.[5] The interest in both French-made textiles and their patterns is evidenced in Mulhouse and the surrounding area, where nearly 40 per cent of all French textile-printing takes place. Between 1983 and 1988 the Alsatian firms' production increased by over one-third, and over half of this is exported. 'Document' styles are well provided for there, due both to the wide variety of production techniques that are still used, ranging from hand block printing to transfer printing, and to the design service offered by the Musée de l'Impression sur Etoffes. Both French and foreign manufacturers use this service, irrespective of whether or not they have their own archive. Elsewhere are other major sources of French 'documents', not the least of which are the archives amassed by American and British firms since the 1920s. Because of the value now placed on old designs, dispersed archives continue to be part of the exports of France; only relatively recently the contents of the Kittler Studio, for example, were purchased by the Design Loft in New York, which specializes in the provision of French designs and samples to textile and wallpaper manufacturers. The international structure of the furnishing fabric industry means that today one may well be purchasing a textile with a French design, but made in Britain, Switzerland or Belgium for a firm in the United States, Britain or elsewhere.

The style associated with France, whether modern or traditional, naturally draws upon that nation's past; the French are the masters of pattern-on-pattern, of grand gestures such as tented rooms, and, of course, of the classical textile designs and interiors based on those of the eighteenth and early nineteenth centuries. They also retain the love of colour, a touch of fantasy, a taste for the exotic, a facility for luxury and an eye for novelty which characterized the best of the Art Deco style. From this wide range of possibilities, the French textile industry is able to supply the world market with something that still *is* a luxury product, whether the high-quality ranges available from French manufacturers and *éditeurs*, or the limited-edition fabrics such as the printed cloths designed by the architect Philippe Starck for his clients, the avant-garde handwoven creations of Geneviève Dupeux (who created the Atelier National d'Art Textile at the Gobelins in 1976, and who maintains her own workshop), and the handwoven silks still produced by Prelle and Tassinari & Chatel for costly restoration projects. Although French textile designers and manufacturers have been gently chided on occasion over the last thirty years for their classic – rather than overtly modern – tastes, they have continued, nevertheless, taking a phrase coined by Guillaume Jeaneau in 1930, to combine 'the imagination of a modiste with the precision of an engineer'.[6] In today's post-modernist world it no longer seems unfortunate that French style expresses itself neither entirely in modern mass production, nor exclusively in artisan-made textiles, but instead retains its assured stance as the grande dame of the elegant interior.

# NOTES

## Preface

**P.01** J. Beavington Atkinson, *Blackwood's Magazine*, xci, April 1862, p. 476, cited by Stephen Wildman, *Royal Society of Arts Journal*, Sept. 1989: p. 660 and note 1.

## CHAPTER ONE

**1.01** Andrew Ure, *The Philosophy of Manufactures: or, an exposition of the scientific, moral, and commercial economy of the factory system of Great Britain*, H. G. Bohn, London, 3rd ed., 1861: p. v.
**1.02** See Ministère de la Culture, *La Manufacture du Dijonval et la draperie Sedanaise: 1650–1850*: pp. 6–15.
**1.03** J.B., *An Account of the French Usurpation upon the Trade of England, and what great damage the English do yearly sustain by their Commerces, and how the same may be retrenched, and England improved in Riches & Interest*, London, 1679: pp. 2, 5–7.
**1.04** Chobaut, 1939: p. 3.

## CHAPTER TWO

**2.01** 'On vit alors sur les étoffes, ce qui étonna, des fleurs & des fruits imitant parfaitement la nature, des pêches avec leur velouté, des raisins avec leur transparent [sic], des oiseaux avec toute la richesse & la pompe de leur coloris, des paysages charmants ou les lointains habilement placés, faisoient l'illusion le plus ravissante.' Abbé Bertholon, *Du Commerce et des manufacteures de la ville de Lyon*, Montpellier, 1789: pp. 195–6. The Abbé was describing the work of the textile designer Philippe de Lasalle.
**2.02** Joubert, p. 86. He lists Barbier, Bourjol, Laurozat, Nau, Despeignes, de Courcy, David, le Roux, Doré, Mercier, Buffault, Martin, Doucet, le Boucher, Greguelu and le Sourd.
**2.03** Duhamel 1765, p.A. There were other centres specializing in woollens for servants' livery and military uniforms. Specialization was usually more beneficial to the merchants than to the weavers, who had to bear the heaviest consequences if their work fell from fashion. Red and black cloths retained their associations with power long after the Revolution, e.g. Stendhal's *Le Rouge et le noir*, 1830.
**2.04** Rodier, pp. 273–9, recounts a revealing story of the merchant Nau, (listed fourth by Joubert, see note 2.02), who in 1757 placed an order for 352 aunes of *chiné* taffetas with the Lyons weavers Thevillon and Vingtain. They made 500 aunes more, in hopes that Nau might start a fashion for this pattern, but found instead that three years later Nau used their sample as the basis for a new design for the Queen's furnishings at Versailles. This he had woven by a different Lyons weaver, St Michel, who amended the design further. The ensuing battle between the two weaving firms over the right to the design reveals much about the perils of a weaver, for St Michel, although allowed eventually to finish his order for Versailles, had also woven extra aunes, which were confiscated by the five judges – all merchants. Half were distributed among the merchant-manufacturers of Lyons; St Michel was also fined 1,000 livres. A sample of *taffeta chiné* from Nau is preserved in the Schweizerisches Museum für Volkskunde, Basle.
**2.05** Bertholon, p. 193. '. . . nous aurons toujours un respect imbecile pour des usages ridicules.'
**2.06** Wyndham Beawes, *Lex Mercatoria Rediviva . . .* , J. Rivington & Sons et al., London, 1783: p. 734. Holland was also a route through which English machines and cloths were smuggled into France. Until 1785, when a complete ban was implemented for about a year, there was a 25 per cent duty on imported printed cottons and a 15 per cent duty on white cottons. The French East India Company paid 15 per cent and 5 per cent respectively.
**2.07** P. Dardel, *Navires et marchandises dans les ports de Rouen et du Havre au XVIIIe siècle*, S.E.V.P.E.N., Paris, 1963: pp. 212–3; and Bimont, p. 6. The use of linen was not new to Abbeville; the Mocassi manuscript of 1736 contains samples of coarse Abbeville linen and jute checked and diapered cloths.
**2.08** See Bimont, p. 9, who describes these cloths as suitable for all furnishing uses except fixed upholstery.
**2.09** Roubo, p. 463; 'ne laissoient pas d'aimer la magnificence'.
**2.10** Tuchscherer, 'Woven Textiles', in Carlano and Salmon, p. 36.
**2.11** Bimont, pp. 5–9. *Les Camelots* could be striped or plain, and were also suitable for bed and wall-hangings and curtains; the silk or silk-blend *moires* were not recommended for bed or window curtains, since they wrinkled when handled. An illustrated volume of Bimont's manual, dated 1766, is in the Musée des Arts Décoratifs.
**2.12** Bimont, p. 13. The changed tastes of the period can be charted by comparing his recommendations with those of the architect Germain Boffrand (1745, *Livre d'architecture*) and Jacques François Blondel (1752, *Architecture françoise*).
**2.13** The Barbier Manuscripts, Vol. h14, 19 Dec. 1782. These letters, now in the V&A Library, are discussed in Mary Schoeser, *Textile History*, 1981, Vol. 12, pp. 37–58. The signature is difficult to read, but the name suggests an Englishman; the red was *cramoisi*, meaning dyed with cochineal.
**2.14** Prices from Barbier. Vol. f13 (91), 6 Sept. 1760 and Vol. h37(141), 9 Nov. 1788, in a letter from the 'president du parlement de Bretagne'; and Bimont (his price lists of 1766 and 1770 were identical). Bimont, p. 7, described *velours d'Utrecht* as made of linen and goat-hair. Havard's *Dictionaire* cites numerous cases of taffeta's use among the nobility, adding that an unspecified 'machine', introduced by Louis Millet in Lyons in 1753, caused the sharp decline in its price. The relative stability of prices is indicated by Rouen's *siamoises*, which were listed in the *Journal de Commerce*, July 1759, as about 27–35 sous for ¾–⅞ aune wide cloth, and by Bimont in 1766 and 1770 as 34–40.
**2.15** Arthur Young, p. 83.
**2.16** Bertholon, p. 155, noting that 'C'est sur-tout à présent qu'il faut profiter de la liberté & de l'indépendance accordée aux Etats-Unis de l'Amérique. . . . Au lieu de leur porter notre or, donnons-leurs plusieurs de nos ouvrages manufactures. . . .'
**2.17** *Londres, la cour et les provinces d'Angleterre, d'Écosse et d'Irlande*, Chez Briand, Paris 1813, p. 15, referring to the armed vessels that patrolled the coasts of Kent and Sussex after the mid-1760s, and the law that gave customs officials the right to enter houses where contraband was thought to be stored.
**2.18** Fowler & Cornforth, *English Decoration in the Eighteenth Century*, Barrie & Jenkins, London, 2nd ed. pp. 43–4.
**2.19** John Gwyn, *An Essay on Design*, London, 1749, p. 71.
**2.20** La Combe, p. 53. '. . . trente années de conduite irréprochable ne sont pas un titre ni une garantie pour obtenir de l'Anglaise sa confidance.' He noted that since about 1765 numerous foreign artisans had settled in London because of the misery and despotism in Germany and France, producing an effervescence useful to commerce ('a produit une éfervescence utile au commerce').
**2.21** Joubert, *op. cit.*, p. 86, 'qui levent au papier verni, tous les beaux dessins qui paroissent, & que l'on a la facilité d'acheter'; for information on Lasalle's technical achievements see Daryl M. Hafter, pp. 139–64. An excellent study of the designer in Lyons is given in Lesley Miller, *Designers in the Lyon Silk Industry 1712–87*, Ph.D. thesis, Brighton Polytechnic, 1988.
**2.22** Hafter, p. 144, citing Lasalle, writing in Jan. 1760; and Bimont, pp. 12–13 and 33.
**2.23** Bimont, p. 34, 'En mettant deux différentes sortes d'Indiennes ou d'autre étoffe, ou bien deux dessins differents; le dedans du lit est d'une coleur et le dehors d'une autre, ainsi que les rideaux, et on fait les coutures ouvertes'; also pp. 20–40. For *duchesse* beds, he also noted (p. 120) protective cases of serge, needing 42 aunes, and (p. 7) that *velours* serving for women's gowns and men's clothes were also used for 'des Bergères, Fauteuils à la Reine, Cabriollets, ou même pour une Duchesse'.
**2.24** Bimont pp. 78, 7 and 48: 'Il peut servir de sopha dans le besoin'; and Sheraton 1792, pl. 45.
**2.25** Roland de la Platière, *L'Art du fabricant de velours de coton. . . .* , p. ii; see also Florence Montgomery, 'John Holker's Mid-Eighteenth-Century *Livre d'échantillons*', *Studies in Textile History in Memory of Harold B. Burnham*, Veronika Gervers, ed., pp. 214–31; The French did not just accept British technology, they often

adapted and improved it; Rupied, pp. 23–5, for example, noted in 1786 that the Alsatians got the hand-burnishing technique from the English, but that Gavaudan, from Lyons, had just perfected a machine for this purpose.

**2.26** Central to this movement were the writings of François Marie Arouet de Voltaire (who lived in Switzerland from 1754 until his death in 1778), the Swiss-born Jean Jacques Rousseau and the Baron de Montesquieu, whose 1748 comparative study of ideas on law and government, *Esprit des lois*, is considered one of the most important books produced in eighteenth-century France.

**2.27** Edited by Denis Diderot with the collaboration of Jean le Rond d'Alembert, the *Encyclopédie ou Dictionnaire raisonné des Sciences, des Arts et des Métiers* began as a translation of Ephraim Chamber's Cyclopaedia (1727) but was greatly extended; it complemented the 1723–30 *Dictionnaire universel de commerce* of Jacques Savary des Bruslons, which was published for the sixth time in five volumes between 1750 and 1765 and translated into English by Malachy Postlethwayt (who added several sections) in 1751–5.

**2.28** Ure, *op. cit.*, p. v.

**2.29** D. G. C. Allan, 'The Laudable Association of Antigallicans' in *RSA Journal*, Sept. 1989, p. 626, referring to a previous article in the same journal (CV11, 1959, p. 217). (The Laudable Association of Antigallicans was a short-lived London dining club.)

**2.30** Hellot, *L'art de la teinture des laines, et des étoffes de laine, en grand et petit teint, avec une instruction sur les debouilles*, Paris, 1750 (in English 1789 and 1901); Macquer, *Art de la teinture en soie*, France, 1763 (part in English 1789 and 1901); d'Aplinhy, *L'art de la teinture des fils et étoffes des ventables causes de la fixité des couleurs de bon teint et suivi des cultures du pastel, de la gaude et de la garance*, Paris, 1776 (in English as above); also of great importance was C. L. Bertollet, *Eléments de l'art de teinture*, Paris, 1791, based on principles developed prior to the Revolution.

**2.31** *La Combe*, p. 233.

**2.32** Naomi Tarrant 'The Turkey Red Dyeing Industry in the Vale of Leven' in *Scottish Textile History*, 1987, pp. 38–9, see also CIBA Review Vol. 12, no. 135, Dec. 1959, pp. 21–6. Adrianople was the former name for Edirne, Turkey.

**2.33** Rupied, pp. 8–9.

**2.34** Bimont, 1770, p. 97, for example, notes *damas de Gênes* [Genoa] *cramoisi* at 16–17 livres and other colours 2 livres less; cheaper reds were *damas de Lyon cramoisi* 14–15 livres, *damas de Tours* 11–14 livres and a very common (not cochineal-based) red 9–10 (for each type other colours cost less).

**2.35** Albrecht-Mathey, p. 12, citing an account of sales for a month in 1749, and p. 16, citing correspondence to Abbé Terray, Minister of the Treasury, from Mon. d'Aigrefeuille, Inspector of Manufactories in Alsace. Rupied, p. 23, said that the women who coloured printed cloths by hand received 2–4 livres per week in 1786.

**2.36** Madder from different areas, for example,

gave different tones to the resulting red; smokey or rosy reds came from Smyrna or Cyprus madder, whereas madder from Provence, an increasingly important area for its cultivation, gave a warmer red. Rouen dyers increased the 'warm' tones of their reds by including treatments in tin compounds.

**2.37** La Combe, p. 223. As late as 1860, a report lists rich velvety cherry red as Alsace's speciality, a yellowish poppy red as Switzerland's and a red of slightly brownish cast as England's, while Rouen is credited with a red possessing the greatest intensity and coming closest to the genuine Turkey red shade (see CIBA 135, p. 26).

**2.38** La Combe, p. 224; Rupied, p. 8.

**2.39** See Josette Brédif, *Toiles de Jouy*, pp. 66–67. Later Oberkampf was to return to using French cottons, including those from Bourges and St-Quentin. In 1807 he set up his own spinning mill at Chartemerle, Essonne.

**2.40** Canvas wallcoverings depicting the Wetter factory, painted in a private house in Orange, show copperplate engraving. The work of Joseph Gabriel Rosetti, they are thought to date from 1764–5, although they include the figure of Pignet, who did not become a partner until 1774. Copper plates were also used as early as 1775 for printing wool and plush in Amiens. See CIBA 31, pp. 1099–1103 and 1111.

**2.41** Rupied noted its usefulness, pp. 9–10: 'pour des genres qui ne varient point ou peu, comme meubles . . .', referring in this case to engraved copper cylinders. Joubert, p. 76, said copper plates, with which he tried to print on mohair, would have cost 100 livres. Five engraved copper plates in the Musée Lambinet in Versailles appear, from their design, to have once belonged to the Petitpierre firm in Nantes, but have small additions; this is evidence that copper plates were sold on to other textile printers, a practice that was certainly widespread among paper printers, who originated the use of engraved plates, and handkerchief printers, who maintained the use of copper plates into the 1840s.

**2.42** Alsace was perfectly placed to become an important textile centre, being on established trade routes that ran from France towards Germany and Switzerland, as well as northwards from Italy. Furthermore, the trade in printed textiles had never been banned in Mulhouse, so that whereas prior to 1759 this free city had played an important part in smuggling these cloths into France, it afterwards exploited the same networks to sell its own products legally to France. The history of this region's printworks is well documented.

**2.43** After Alsace, Rouen was, by 1786, the largest printing centre, with twelve firms plus another fifteen or so outside the city; Nantes followed closely with nine major firms and about as many short-lived enterprises at the same date. Similar concentrations of firms were to be found in and around Paris and Lyons; Bordeaux, although having fewer printworks, was also active in the trade of printed goods. In addition, many small printworks were scattered over the country.

**2.44** See Pierre Caspard, 'Manufacture and Trade in Calico Printing at Neuchâtel: The Example of Cortaillod (1752–1854)', *Textile History*, Vol. 8, Pasold, London, 1977, pp. 150–62.

**2.45** In 1790 Oberkampf was producing English-designed fabrics for English consumption, a practice that was no doubt encouraged by the Treaty of Eden. In 1923, however, Maciver Percival in *The Chintz Book*, p. 68, recorded that in 1783 Jouy dispatched its goods to ten houses in London, and to Amsterdam, Antwerp, Basle, Berlin, Brussels, Constantinople, Frankfort, Hamburg, Lisbon, Luxembourg, Madrid, Salonica and Trieste. He does not give his source of information, but it may have been the de Maraise records, or other accounts which remained at the Chateau of Montcel until shortly before 1927, when they were dispersed among the Oberkampf descendants.

**2.46** Fowler and Cornforth, p. 47; see also *George IV and the Arts of France*, 1966.

# CHAPTER THREE

**3.01** Anon., *Londres, la cour et les Provinces d'Angleterre, d'Écosse et d'Irlande, ou Esprit, Moeurs, Coutumes . . .*, Paris, 1813: pp. 105–6. 'La société en France est plus générale qu'en Angleterre; le luxe des Français doit donc être plus brillant, plus frivole, plus remarquable, plus agréable que celui des Anglais, qui, plus concentré, est plus frappant, plus étonnant et plus solide. Il est plus orgueilleux que vain; en France il est plus vain qu'orgueilleux.'

**3.02** A.N. 41 AQ 82, Letter to Soleillet, 12 September, 1791; and André Maurois, Charles Brisson and Jean Clarenson: *Les Draps d'Elbeuf et de Louviers*; Syndicat Patronal de L'Industrie: p. 27.

**3.03** There were conflicting opinions regarding protectionism; in favour was Monsieur Boislandry, deputy for Versailles and a muslin manufacturer, while Monsieur Goudard, deputy for Lyons and a silk manufacturer, was for free trade. See Félix Pouteil: 'La contrabande sur le Rhin au temps du premier empire' in *Revue Historique*, March–April 1935, pp. 257–86.

**3.04** For example, in *Les Indiennes de la Manufacture Oberkampf de Jouy-en-Josas*, 1982, Josette Brédif notes the high demand for *perses* from Belgium and Holland in 1796.

**3.05** *Maghien Dictionnaire des produits de la nature et de l'art qui font l'objet du commerce de la France*, Paris, 1809, recorded (p. 223) that 1,683,000 lbs. *pesant* of cotton yarns had been exported to the Levant alone in 1789, while by 1807 all exports of cotton yarns had fallen to 64,824 lbs. *pesant*; the latter cost 335,000 francs raw and was re-exported spun for 665,000 francs.

**3.06** Brédif, *Toiles de Jouy*, p. 33; the tent described survives in the Mobilier Nationale, Paris, GMT 2462.

**3.07** Clouzot, in *Histoire de la Manufacture de Jouy*, 1928, gives a summary of the life-span of many printing factories in France. (Also published in English; see Bibliography.) Although more recent studies have shown some of his information to be incomplete, his outline of the French printing industry up to the end of the Empire remains the most comprehensive.

**3.08** See Serge Chassagne, *Oberkampf un entrepreneur*, pp. 305–22; and *Londres, la cour et les Provences d'Angleterre . . .* , *op. cit.*, Vol. 2, p. 4, 'Les Anglais n'ont presque pas besoin de lois prohibitives contre les marchandises françaises, c'est l'opinion publique qui les proscrit.'

**3.09** Rapport de Bardel, 12 Sept. 1808 AN 02622. 'Depuis la Révolution beaucoup d'anciens teinturiers ont quitté leur état, ils ont été remplacés par des jeunes gens à qui la teinture des Soies pour meubles était peu familière . . . On peut encore ajouter que depuis la suppression des maîtrises toute personne prenant patente, ayant le droit de fabrique, sans justifier d'aucun apprentissage, il s'est élevé beaucoup d'ateliers, dont les chefs manquent de capacité.'

**3.10** W. O. Henderson, *The Industrial Revolution on the Continent*, Frank Cass & Co. Ltd., London 1967, p. 87; Brédif, *Toiles de Jouy*, p. 32, notes that one of Oberkampf's difficulties was competing with the increased number of factories producing inferior, cheaper goods. Clouzot (*1760–1815* Part I, pp. 63–5) lists the names of thirty-eight manufacturers or printers in Paris, only six of which are known to have survived to the Restoration.

**3.11** See Brédif, *Toiles de Jouy*, pp. 80–5 and pp. 96–7.

**3.12** For example, 'Les Arts', 1780; 'Le Marchand d'orviétan', 'La Chasse au Sanglier' and 'La Foire du Caire', c. 1785; and 'Les Tableaux', c. 1795. The list was published in Henri Clouzot's 'Les toiles imprimées de Nantes', *La Renaissance de l'art français*, XI, 1924: p. 167.

**3.13** 646 plate designs, as opposed to 30,000 block designs, are known to have been produced at the Jouy factory.

**3.14** See, for example, inv. 836/3002 Musée des Tissus, Lyons.

**3.15** There were 14,777 working in 1788.

**3.16** Le Bourhis, p. 152.

**3.17** For example, the catalogue for the *Exposition publique des produits de L'industrie française au Palais du Louvre*, Paris, 1819, p. 4, lists one Marchault, rue de Faubourg St Martin, as a 'Manufacture pour la restauration des vieux draps'.

**3.18** Anon., *Memorandums of a Residence in France in the Winter of 1815–16*, Longman, Hurst, Rees, Orme & Brown, London, 1816, p. 233–5.

**3.19** Musée du Louvre.

**3.20** Watercolour by A. Garneray in 1811; in the Olivier le Fuel Collection, Paris.

**3.21** These are analyzed in great detail in Coural *et al.*, hereafter referred to as *Soieries Empire*, Mobilier National, Paris, 1980.

**3.22** Catalogue from the 1983 Fashion Institute of Technology (New York) exhibition, *Silks from the Palaces of Napoleon*, p. 6; the catalogue, edited by Chantal Gastinel-Coural, provides a

good brief summary of *Soieries Empire*.

**3.23** *Soieries Empire*, p. 134, brocades, pp. 38–88.

**3.24** i.e. 1804 for St-Cloud, *ibid.*, p. 97.

**3.25** i.e. the *velours chiné* ordered for Versailles and illustrated in the next chapter was 168 francs per metre, 129.42 metres were delivered in 1813 for wall-hangings, see *ibid.*, pp. 104–5.

**3.26** *Ibid.*, pp. 102, 134–5.

**3.27** *Ibid.*, p. 41, the fabric used had been ordered in 1802 for St-Cloud; the budget for the Empress's rooms in 1805 was 80,000 francs.

**3.28** AN 02499, dr. 11, p. 7. Pernon to Desmazis, 20 March 1807, 'C'est un secret qui a valut de tous temps la préférence de son achat a ma manufacture.'

**3.29** See *Soieries Empire*, p. 388.

**3.30** Napoleon also suggested that all vessels returning to America be required to take French silks back in part payment of the value of their off-loaded goods. A similar plan had already been proposed; see *Mémoire de la Chambre du Commerce de Paris*, 1804, Chambre du Commerce library 452.789, p. 23.

**3.31** Jean Louis Prevost's plates, published in 12 *livraisons*, contained roses, lilac, narcissis, pansies, jonquils, auriculis, iris, peach blossoms and jasmine, mainly in bouquets. In 1802 Redouté had already issued plates showing lilacs, which occur on several of the fabrics for Versailles. The Malmaison gardens had been stocked between 1809 and 1811 with plants and seeds which Joséphine had purchased in England for 19,515 francs; see *George IV and the Arts of France*, op. cit., p. 5.

**3.32** 'Il faut des choses très solides, telles que ce soit une dépense faite pour cent ans.' See p. 22, *Soieries Empire*.

**3.33** Not all dyes immediately came up to standard; in 1812–3 the Mobilier Impérial still found cause for complaint (e.g. see *Soieries Empire*, p. 341).

**3.34** Both the first and second editions of the latter, *L'Art de la teinture*, were translated into English; in the second edition, the translator noted (p. xxiv, *Elements of the Art of Dyeing*) that 'The various essays on dyeing, and dye-stuffs, which have within these few years been multiplied in our Encyclopedias, & c. are, in a great measure, extracts from Berthollet.'

**3.35** These are listed in *Histoire documentaire de l'industrie de Mulhouse* (HDIM) 1902, pp. 397–401, and in Jean-Michel Tuchscherer, *The Fabrics of Mulhouse and Alsace 1801–50*, pp. 17–20.

**3.36** In 1818 Pelletier and Caventou isolated the acid 'carminique', the principal colourant of cochineal; and eight years later the same was accomplished for madder, when Robiquet and Colin isolated alizarin. Their work was based on foundations laid by J. A. Chaptal, who published *Traité de la Teinture du Coton en Rouge* in 1805 and who established the first chemical factory in France.

**3.37** M. L. Costaz *Rapport du jury central sur les produits de l'industries françaises*: Paris, de l'Imprimerie Royale, 1819, p. 4 and nos. 103, 223, 310, 608 and 609.

**3.38** See Thornton, 1984, p. 210 and note 11

p. 394, giving, as an example, the publication of Percier and Fontaine's *Recueil* in Venice in 1843.

**3.39** P. Leuilliot, *L'Alsace au début du XIX^e siècle*, Paris, 1959, Vol. II, p. 389. Prelle & Cie., silk weavers founded in Lyons in 1749, have a group of silks that were probably produced for Turkey between 1814 and 1830; these were discussed by Guy Evans in 'From West to East', *Hali*, No. 38, pp. 28–31. On prints, Liebach-Hartmann & Cie., for example, printed small, delicate floral patterns in a 'Genre spéciale pour la Turque et la Syrie', MISE book 6, p. 93, 1825–30.

**3.40** See F. and M. Kimball, 'Jefferson's Curtains at Monticello' in *The Art of the Weaver*, Universe Books, N.Y., 1978, pp. 54–6, in which his sketches are published. The curtains mentioned were derived from two small prints in the House of Representatives. All of Jefferson's Paris purchases were thought to have been taken to Monticello when he first retired there in 1793. He began remodelling three years later, adopting French styles.

**3.41** See 'Of Muslins and Merveilleuses', *Winterthur Portfolio* 9, 1974, University Press of Virginia, Charlottesville, pp. 43–66.

**3.42** See, for example, Jane Nylander, 'Bed and Window Hangings in New England', *Upholstery in America & Europe from the Seventeenth Century to World War I*, W. W. Norton & Co., New York, 1987, pp. 179–81, including 1825 sale notice of the contents of the Marshall B. Spring house in Boston: 'Drawing room curtains and drapery, of blue French Damask, lined with Yellow silk, laced and fringed, with muslin curtains, draperies supported with rich ornaments. . . .'

**3.43** There were also emigrés in London who may have contributed to the provision of some furnishings such as copperplate-printed silks, illustrated by Sheraton in Pl.32 of the 1792 *Drawing Book* on chair backs and seats, since there was certainly at least one French copperplate printer, a Madame Bové, working in London by the late 1790s. Many emigrées made straw hats.

**3.44** Maison Grand order nos. 1664, 1805–6, 1605 and 1640; and Warner Archive, letter from Thomas Smith to Wilson & Co, 3 Aug., 1820, notes that he saw a working Jacquard loom 'in one of the largest manufactories in the environs of Paris'. The first Jacquard attachment was put into use by Pernon in 1806 but had to be removed; it was improved in 1811–2 by Dutillieu's regulator, which ensured that repeat lengths were more uniform. The ban on French fabrics seems to have been easily transcended; aside from the evidence of the Grand orders, Daniel Koechlin-Schouch, in 'Notice necrologique sur M. James Thomson', *Bulletin de la Société Industrielle de Mulhouse (BSIM)* 23 (1850–1), p. 183, for example, recorded that James Thomson, the Lancashire calico printer, had made, in 1815, an exclusive arrangement with Nicolas Koechlin et Frères to import their Turkey-red fabrics.

**3.45** Vermont and Darnley, *London and Paris, or Comparative Sketches*, Longman, Hurst, Rees,

Orme, Brown & Green, London 1823, p. 289.

**3.46** See William M. Reddy, *The Rise of Market Culture*, Cambridge University Press 1984, pp. 89–93; Maurois, p. 27; and Penot, pp. 332–3.

**3.47** See Margaret A. Fikioris, 'Neoclassicism in Textile Designs by Jean Baptiste Huet, *Winterthur Portfolio* 6, University Press of Virginia, Charlottesville, 1970: pp. 75–110.

**3.48** See M. André Brandt, pp. 27–41 and Jean Marie Schmitt, pp. 181–192.

**3.49** Pouteil, *op. cit.*, p. 277, citing the prefect of Strasbourg: 'Il est reçu dans cette ville de marchands que l'on peut être en même temps contrebandier et honnête homme.'

**3.50** The absence of internal tariffs meant that once goods were inside France they could be freely moved; as early as 1804 the Paris Chamber of Commerce was against banning imports, especially of muslins, since they were embroidered in Paris and resold (even in London) at six times their cost; the duty on India muslins, they said, was putting girls out of work. See *Memoire*, note 30.

# CHAPTER FOUR

**4.01** Jean François Persoz, *Traité Théorique et pratique de l'impression des tissus*, 4 vols., Victor Masson, Paris, 1846, preface.

**4.02** France had the largest population in Europe, but until about 1850 half of the workers were constantly employed in agriculture – more than twice the proportion of agricultural workers in England. See J. C. Toutain, 'La population de la France de 1700 a 1958', *Histoire quantitative* Vol. III, Paris 1963, pp. 54–5 and 160–1.

**4.03** T. A. B. Corley, *Democratic Despot: A Life of Napoleon III*, 1961, p. 297. The aggregate income during the Second Empire rose by 73 per cent.

**4.04** Mark Girouard, *Cities & People*, Yale University Press, New Haven and London, 1985, p. 286.

**4.05** Gustave Claudin, *Paris*, Faure, Paris, 1867, p. 146.

**4.06** *Memorandums of a Residence in France in the Winter of 1815–16, op. cit.*, p. 333, and *Abeilles Parisiennes*, 'Tablettes Mensuelles de l'industrie et du commerce'; Mme Constance Aubert, No. V, 25 February, 1850, Paris and London, p. 3: 'ne ressemble plus aujourd'hui à l'antique salle, nue et dégarnie, à laquelle on accordait autrefois, comme par nécessité, des rideaux de percale et des chaises de crin.'

**4.07** *Harper's Weekly*, June 6, 1857, p. 359.

**4.08** Persoz, *op. cit.*, vol. 2, 1847, p. 299: 'qui a donné au fabricant le pouvoir d'imprimer les dessins les plus difficiles avec toute la précision et l'économie possibles'. The perrotine was invented in 1834.

**4.09** Le Normand, p. 135–7: 'la taffetas, la lévantine, le tricat et le velours, sont les étoffes de soie dont on se sert pour cette sorte d'impression.'

**4.10** *The Foreign Quarterly Review*, Vol. 3, Sept. 1828–Jan. 1829, p. 379 and *passim*;

BSIM 1862, p. 449: 'les articles riches et destinés à la consommation des classes aisées . . . piqués, jaconnas, tissus légers de toute espèce . . . l'indienne proprement dit'.

**4.11** HDIM, 1902 gives a complete account of Alsatian firms.

**4.12** Henry Danzer, *Les industries textiles à l'Exposition Universelle de 1889*, Vol. 1, p. 121.

**4.13** MISE book 1054, 1857–8, p. 41: 'C'est sans doute une belle rayure, mais elle est loin de valoir ses f21. . . .'

**4.14** HDIM, p. 639: 'L'un des plus grands ateliers de dessin travaillant pour le monde entier.'

**4.15** MISE 1061, 1867–9, pp. 168–9. The same book also contains a sample of chintz known to have been used by Queen Victoria; and MISE book 137, pp. 254–261.

**4.16** Letter, 4 April 1862, from McDowall to Stead McAlpine; correspondence 1862, John Lewis Partnership archive.

**4.17** Quoted in MISE cat. on C. Steiner, introduction by Paul R. Schwartz, 1964, p. 2, courtesy of Jacqueline Jacqué; 'Frédéric Steiner ayant poussé jusqu'aux dernières limites la perfection de ses produits, [mais] il n'y a de comparable que ceux de Charles Steiner de Ribeauvillé, qui travaille d'après les procédés de son oncle.'

**4.18** HDIM pp. 636–7, 641.

**4.19** See David Greysmith, 'Patterns, Piracy and Protection in the Textile Printing Industry 1787–1850', *Textile History*, 14(2), 1983, pp. 170–4; in 1869 the salary of a Rouen designer was 4,000–12,000 livres (a chemist got 2–3,000 more and a printer got 5 francs a day); see *Exposé de la situation des industries du coton et des produits chimiques dans la Seine Inférieure et l'Eure 1859–69*, Rouen, 1869; p. 33.

**4.20** HDIM p. 637. He later returned to Paris to open a studio with Paul Tournier 1863–8.

**4.21** See A. Alphand, *Les Promenades de Paris*, Rothschild, 1867–73.

**4.22** For further information see BSIM nos. 811–2, 4/1988 and 1/1989, especially pp. 81–4.

**4.23** Prelle order book 1, 22 May, 1866.

**4.24** Marie Bouzard-Tricou, 'Analyse et catalogue raisonné de la production des Frères Grand, fabricants de soierie à Lyon, de 1808 à 1871, d'après les archives de la Maison Tassinari et Chatel, leurs successeurs, 11, place Croix Paquet', Mémoire de maîtrise, Université de Lyon, Nov. 1985, p. 68.

**4.25** Isabella L. Bishop, *The Englishwoman in America*, John Murray, London, 1856: p. 340.

**4.26** *Exposition de l'industrie française de 1849*, in *Judicateur Annuaire . . .*, Lyons, V. E. Ayné, 2nd ed. 1849–50, p. 133: 'tres beaux satins unis, blancs, noire et autre couleurs'; 'Ses produits ont puissamment contribué a conserver à la fabrique lyonnaise sa supériorité pour les articles qui, malgré la concurrence, ont une si grande part dans le chiffre de nos exportations.'

**4.27** Marius Morand, *Le Commerce de Soies de Lyon*, A. Rey & Cie, Lyons, 1906: pp. 20–23.

**4.28** Tassinari & Chatel order no. 2096.

**4.29** AN BB[18] 1420 8133. Letter dated Lyons, 21 March, 1844.

**4.30** *Indicateur Annuaire*, p. 4; 'Il est à remarquer que jamais, dans une période aussi rapprochée que celle de la première publications a celle-ci, les mutations ne furent plus considérables', the second edition was needed to accommodate so many changes.

**4.31** *L'Echo de la fabrique*, 1831–2, p. 5; and *Women and the Making of the Working Class: Lyons 1830–70*, Laura S. Strumingher, Eden Press Women's Publications, Inc., Vermont and Montreal, 1979.

**4.32** Gay L. Gullickson, *Spinners and Weavers of Auffray*, Cambridge University Press, Cambridge, 1986, pp. 108–13; and Claude Fohlen, *L'Industrie Textile au Temps du Second Empire*, Librairie Plon, Paris, 1956: pp. 200–5.

**4.33** *Exposé, op. cit.*, p. 28.

**4.34** *A Frenchman Sees the English in the 'Fifties; adapted from the French of Francis Wey by Valerie Pirie*, Sidgwick & Jackson Ltd., London 1935, p. 260.

**4.35** Florence Baptiste, 'Paterson et ses Français', *Le Monde alpin et rhodanien*, 3e–4e trimestres 1989, pp. 33–45.

**4.36** Richard Redgrave, *Report on the Present State of Design applied to Manufacturers, as shown in the Paris Universal Exhibition*, 1855, Vol. III, p. 398.

**4.37** Le Normand, pp. 128–9; 'imprimé en noir avec des dessins appropriés au dessus des fauteuils, bergères, sophas, chaises, etc.', adding that 'on substitue, dans toutes ces circonstances, ces draps, ainsi imprimés, au velours d'Utrecht, et ils font beaucoup d'usage.'

**4.38** *Abeilles Parisiennes*, p. 4 and p. 57; 'L'ameublement doit etre en préférence de couleur foncée ou bigarrée. La moquette est fort bien pour les rideaux et les meubles.' Falcot, in *Traité Encyclopédique*, 1844, was not of the same view – presumably because he was familiar with the finest silk velvets – and described moquettes as 'naturellement grossier' – naturally vulgar', see p. 101.

**4.39** *Harper's Weekly*, 25 Dec., 1858, p. 818, letter from their European correspondent on a chateau in the country.

**4.40** Henry Danzer, *op. cit.*, Vol. 2, p. 375, and MISE book 1062, 1870, *passim*.

**4.41** See *Le Moniteur*, nos. 2, 4, 5, and 9, July, August, September and November 1368 on trade; and *Peterson's Magazine*, Vol. XXXVI, Dec. 1859 No. 6, p. 44, 'Before our American women can dress perfectly, they must have the taste of the French, especially in colour.'

**4.42** Kenneth L. Ames, 'Designed in France: noted on the transmission of French style to America', *Winterthur Portfolio* 12, 1977, pp. 103–14; the author demonstrated the dependence of the Philadelphian furniture maker George Henkels on Guilmard's publications, and the fabrics represented are also faithful to those shown by Guilmard.

**4.43** See Falcot, p. 85 and *passim*, for explanations of the variety and method of manufacture of velvets.

**4.44** *Progress of Manufactures since 1836*, London, 1861, p. 653, quoting Dufour.

**4.45** Prominent among these men was Henry Cole, who organized an exhibition, in 1852, intended to show articles designed according to 'False Principles', and thereby improve British taste and design: included among the British textiles were two with designs from Mulhouse.

**4.46** Redgrave, *op. cit.*, pp. 320, 398.

**4.47** See Prelle pattern 4576, a brocatelle ordered in brilliant blue by 'Walter & Son de Londres, 4 Mars 1867'.

**4.48** Ure, *op. cit.*, p. 600.

**4.49** An excellent recent review of this topic is to be found in the *Royal Society of Arts Journal*, September 1989, pp. 652–664.

**4.50** David Greysmith, *op. cit.*, p. 173 note 63.

**4.51** MISE book 137, p. 262.

**4.52** *Godey's Lady's Book*, Vol. 21, Dec. 1839, p. 45, Vol. 22, Jan. 1840, p.2, and Vol. 6, July 1833, p. 17.

**4.53** *American Silk Journal*, Jan. 1887, pp. 4–5. Person always resided in Paris, and was, between c.1848 and 1858, travelling to the United States as a respresentative of the (then) large importing firm Francis Cottenet & Co.; *Harper's Weekly*, 12 Sept., 1857, p. 583.

**4.54** Anon., *Wagons composant le train impérial*, Paris, 1856.

**4.55** *Harper's Weekly*, 6 June, 1857, p. 359. With the potential for display of horse-drawn and railway carriages and the period's love of ostentation, it is hardly surprising to find that some mechants in Lyons, such as Boirivent aîné, specialized in supplying the growing market for silks for *voitures*. *Indicateur Annuaire*, *op. cit.*, p. 47.

**4.56** Claudin, *op. cit.*, p. 142. A total of 630 million francs was invested in the French railways between 1840 and 1847 alone.

**4.57** Eugène Delacroix, *Journal*, Plon, Nourrit, Paris, 1893 and 1895, III, pp. 371–3.

**4.58** See Eugène Muller, *La Boutique du marchand de nouveautés*, Paris, 1868, pp. 16–17, for the division of fabric departments into 'furniture' (including damask, *perses*, Utrecht velvet and moquette), 'indiennes' (now applied to all printed cottons, as well as organdy and other cotton fabrics), 'Fantaisie' (meaning merinos and other wool cloths), etc.

**4.59** The metre had been adopted as the legal unit of measurement in 1795 but private orders had continued to be measured in aunes.

# CHAPTER FIVE

**5.01** Natalis Rondot, *Moniteur des Fils, des Tissus, des Apprèts, de la Teinture*, 15 March, 1873, p. 165: 'La guerre, l'invasion, l'insurrection à Paris avaient appauvri notre pays; le luxe s'était évanoui; le deuil était général; la consommation intérieure était fort abaissée. Dans de telles conditions, avec le haut prix de l'argent, de la soie et des façons, avec le trouble et la désorganisation inséparables des dix mois de malheurs publics et de misères privées . . . il semblait que la fabrique de Lyon dût avoir fléchi. Au contraire, elle a été aussi vigoureuse que jamais.'

**5.02** *British Parliamentary Papers*, 1909, Vol. XCI (42), report on the cost of living among workers in France, p. 45 (hereafter referred to as 'PP 1909').

**5.03** HDIM, 1902, pp. 408–32; and e.g. MISE book p. 350.

**5.04** PP 1909, pp. 276–9 and 290.

**5.05** The 1879 Paris *Annuaire des Beaux-Arts et Des Art Décoratifs* listed only eight firms under the category of printed cottons for furnishings, including Besselièvre, but twenty-seven under wallpaper, including Follot, Dumas and Zuber & Cie.; Henry Danzer, *Les industries textiles à l'Exposition Universelle de 1889*, Paris, Vol. 1, p. 375; and Joseph Dépierre, *La Toile Peinte à l'Exposition de 1900*, 1902, p. 102. England in 1900 had 975 printing machines, 830 of them controlled by the Calico Printers' Association, who did not exhibit in the English section of the 1900 exhibition; those who did were Turnbull & Stockdale, Riley & Sons, and Steiner & Co.

**5.06** Edward Young, p. 31.

**5.07** Raimon, p. 278: 'A se livrer entièrement à la fabrication des soieries communes de grosse consommation, nous perdrions vite nos qualités naturelles et notre personnalité. Mais en nous confinant dans les articles de luxe, sans chercher a donner à notre industrie une base plus large, une activité plus constante, nous risquerions de ne plus être que des créateurs de modèles, des dessinateurs, que l'on copie, mais auxquels on n'achète pas'; see also Michel Laferrière, *Lyon, ville industrielle*, Presses Universitaires de France, Paris 1960.

**5.08** Florence Patricia Chapigny, *La Fabrique Lyonnaise de Soieries: Une Maison à Travers ses Archives; de Lamy et Giraud à Lamy et Gautier 1866–1919*, Mémoire de maîtrise, Université de Lyon, March 1981, p. 103.

**5.09** *American Silk Journal*, March 1887, p. 52; May 1887, p. 13 (hereafter referred to as 'ASJ').

**5.10** *Moniteur des Fils* . . . 5ème Année, No. 1, 1 Jan. 1873, p. 787; and *Un Siècle de commerce entre la France et le Royaume Uni*, Ministry of Commerce and Industry, London and Paris, 1908, pp. 48–9; the value of silks exported to Britain in 1907 was about 164 million francs.

**5.11** ASJ, Vol. 1, No. 2, Feb. 1882, p. 28; Young, *op. cit.*, p. 31; on the 1830s Connecticut silk growing, see *William E. Buckley, A New England Pattern: the history of Manchester, Connecticut*, Connecticut, 1973, p. 40.

**5.12** ASJ, July 1887, p. 106; Jan. 1887, p. 4.

**5.13** Cited in Raimon, p. 260.

**5.14** *Furniture and Decoration & The Furniture Gazette*, London, 15 May, 1895, p. 77.

**5.15** Cited in *Moniteur* . . . , 15 July, 1868, pp. 16–17; 'permettrait ainsi à nos manufacturiers de s'assimiler successivement les connaissances commerciales des Anglais'; *The Anglo-American Annual*, Part 2, 1896–7, (as note 18).

**5.16** The 1889 figures were published by Thomas G. Shearman in *The Forum*; on the British aristocratic taste see John Cornforth, *The Inspiration of the Past*, Penguin, New York and Middlesex, England, 1985: pp. 12–14 and *passim*.

**5.17** All three still hold major archives.

**5.18** *The Anglo-American Annual for British subjects and citizens of the United States in Paris*, Brentanos' & Neal's Library, Paris, 1896/7, 4th ed., Part I, pp. 107–37, 294–5, and Part II, p. 108; whether Altmans' the store and Altman the Lamy & Giraud agent were the same is not known.

**5.19** For further information see Pauline C. Metcalf, *Ogden Codman and the Decoration of Houses*, Boston Athenaeum, Boston, Mass., 1988, and Allen Tate and C. Ray Smith, *Interior Design in the Twentieth Century*, Harper & Row, N.Y., 1986.

**5.20** Raimon, p. 29; 'La valeur industrielle d'une nation ne se mesure pas toujours au chiffre de sa production. Elle est bien plutôt déterminée par la qualité de ses produits, par l'influence qu'ils exercent sur le marché, enfin, par le chiffre de ses exportations.'

**5.21** André de Fouquières, 'Du prestige de la mode aux États-Unis', *Gazette du Bon Ton*, No. 12, Oct. 1913, pp. 177–8: 'la mode est la seule industrie française qui soit prépondérante aux États-Unis. Et quelle source de fortune ne représente-t-elle pas? Nulle part, il n'est possible de voir une telle folie du luxe, une telle émulation dans la lutte pour l'élégance, *un tel respect*, des fantaisies de la mode. Jamais une américaine ne transforme au goût du jour une robe de l'autre saison, elle n'admet et ne porte que le *neuf*. Elle observe avec minutie les moindres transformations inventées par nos courturiers et l'originalité les effraie si peu que c'est à New-York que les "Maîtres" de la rue de la Paix adressent leurs plus audacieuses créations. Des sommes formidables sont réservées chaque année à la toilette féminine et nombreuses sont les maisons françaises qui doivent au faste yankee beaucoup de leur prospérité.'

**5.22** Henry, p. 968: 'Sans tenture, sans tapis de pied, sans couverture de meubles, il n'y aurait point, en effet, de mobiliers confortables, il n'y aurait non plus d'intérieurcoquet, douillet. Tout dans nos habitations paraîtrait froid, étriqué, nu.'

**5.23** H. Havard, *L'Art dans la maison*, 1887: p. 188, 192, 207 and *passim*; the first edition was published in 1884.

**5.24** *The Ladies' Treasury for 1878*, ed. Mrs. Warren, Bemrose & Sons, London, p. 402.

**5.25** Quoted in Peter Thornton, *Authentic Decor*, citing Tove Clemmensen's work of 1942; see note 1, p. 396.

**5.26** Havard, *L'Arts de l'ameublement: les styles*, 1897, pp. 184–5.

**5.27** *The Anglo-American Annual*, *op. cit.*, p. 294; Raymond Cox, p. 45, explained that at the 1878 Paris exhibition, unadulterated Japanese art had been shown, whereupon Paris department stores began bringing in shiploads of inferior goods which eventually caused the enthusiasm for *le japonisme* to abate.

**5.28** Charles Rearick, *Pleasures of the Belle Epoque*, Yale University Press, New Haven and London, 1985, p. 139, citing the report of the exhibition by Emile Monod. He also notes that belly dancing became a craze.

**5.29** HDIM 1902, p. 455: 'Meubles riches à la plance de 50 à 60 couleurs, renaissance (composition: *La Danse et le Chant*, panneaux avec personnages de 1 mètre de hauteur, 700 planches gravées, se vendent 30 fr. le mètre.)'; Havard, *op. cit.*, 1887, p. 215.

**5.30** Henry, pp. 970–1: 'Ces admirables panneaux défilant sous nos yeux semblent répéter le traditionnel Morituri te salutant. L'art de la tapisserie est en effet condamné a périr; . . . les conditions de production de la tapisserie ne répondent plus aux exigeances modernes. De tous les tissus d'ameublement, c'est le seul qui soit entièrement fabriqué à la main et sa confection est d'autant plus lente que sa trame est plus fine et son point plus serré.'

**5.31** Maple & Co. Ltd., *Blinds, Linens, Draperies and Curtain Fabrics*, V&A Library, undated but probably 1905–15, p. 30 and BF RES 5889: 'toiles écrues pour peinture en imitation de tapisseries et d'étoffes anciennes.'

**5.32** Havard, 1887, p. 204; 'aux habitudes vagabondes de notre temps'. He also notes that wool moquette, woven on wide looms, cost 60 francs per square metre, while tapestries cost at least four times as much.

**5.33** *Furniture and Decoration & The Furniture Gazette*, *op. cit.*, referring to eclecticism as a 'fashionable medley'.

**5.34** Anna Vera Eisenstadt, *Questions Franco-Italiennes dans l'industrie du meuble de luxe en Lombardie et le régime douanier français*, Milan, 1917, pp. 4–7: 'du Louis XIV, du Louis XV et surtout de Louis XVI. Peu ou presque point d'Empire. Point d'art moderne', and 'Nos filles naissent fileuses et nos fils ont le gout de la sculpture dans le sang.'

**5.35** PP 1909, p. 235.

**5.36** Eisenstadt, *op. cit.*, p. 5, 'trop "parvenu", trop allemand'; and C. Adolph Glassgold, 'The Modern Note in Decorative Arts' Part I, *The Arts*, Vol. 13, p. 160, citing Verneuil.

**5.37** Raimon, p. 82; 'En dépit de certaines exagérations, souvent voulues, l'art nouveau, le *modern-style*, comme on l'appelle, qui a ses fanatiques et aussi ses détracteurs systématiques, marque une recherche des tonalités claires qui n'est past sans charme et un honorable souci de se soustraire à la banalité conventionnelle. Ce n'est malheureusement pas suffisant pour faire oublier les siècles passés.'

**5.38** The writer most associated with such reforms in England and the United States was Charles Eastlake, whose London edition of *Hints on Household Tastes* (1868) was revised and published in the United States in 1872 and in France soon afterwards.

**5.39** Maple & Co. Ltd., *op. cit.*, pp. 98–9.

**5.40** The period had witnessed the publication of two important and influential historical works: Viollet le Duc's *Dictionnaire du mobilier français* (4 Vols., Vve. A. Morel & Co., Paris, 1872–4) and Henry Havard's *Dictionnaire de l'ameublement et la décoration depuis le XIIIe siècle jusqu'à nos jours* (4 Vols., Maison Quantin, Paris). Work on the latter began in 1878, and it was published in 1888–90. It is illustrated and the entries include many citations of extracts from inventories, but his lack of enthusiasm for the Empire period is evident. Havard's introduction is a remarkable

treatise on the need to study the past with regard to its material culture.

**5.41** Claude Roger-Marx, 'Du Choix d'un Papier Peint', *Gazette du Bon Ton*, Tome I, Jan.–June 1914, pp. 217–8: 'Depuis quelques années le despotisme des propriétaires inflige d'autres supplices. La plupart des appartements modernes rappellent uniformément un XVIIIe siècle de cocotte. Les murs sont d'un gris aveuglant; les trumeaux lamentables dominent nos glaces; c'est une profusion de noeuds Louis XVI, de perles, de frises, de rosaces, toute une patisserie d'un beurre douteux. Des panneaux pleins, entourés de moulures, interdisent à notre fantaisie de choisir le tone ou le dessin approprié à chaque pièce et aux objets qu'elle est appelée a contenir.'

**5.42** See for example MISE box 997/1 and /2, 1906, with samples from Charles Besselièvre, Charles Steiner and Marie Lévy; Havard in 1887 (p. 215) also noted that some people soaked velvet and satin in the lees of wine to make it seem old.

**5.43** See Werner J. Schwiger, *Wiener Werkstätte – Design in Vienna 1903–32*, Thames & Hudson, London, 1984 (from the original in German, published by Christian Brandstätter, Verlag und Edition, Vienna).

**5.44** Roger-Marx, *op. cit.*, p. 218; '. . . la prédeliction s'affirme aujourd'hui pour les ors somptueux, les violets brûlants, les bleus foncés, les orangees et les riches accords empruntés à l'Orient . . . enfin nos décorateurs osent jeter, avec une apparent irrégularité, sur nos murs ces fleurs indisciplinées, presque irréelles, dont les pétales resplendissent d'un éclat étrange. Aus calmes rayures succèdent des stries compliquées, de sort que, s'harmonisant avec les étoffes des sièges, la richesse des tapis, la hardiesse des robes . . . comme s'ils voulaient participer d'un siècle où la volupté, l'amour de la vitesse, et le besoin d'étonner mènent le monde.'; '. . . multiple la lumière et la vie, par l'enchevêtrement des couleurs et des lignes, comme nous le voyons dans les intérieurs adorables d'un Vuillard ou d'un Bonnard'.

**5.45** The Bon Marché had a policy of buying French goods: silks from Lyons, woollens from Roubaix and Rheims, worsted from Elbeuf and Sedan, laces from Calais, and fine *toiles* and table linen from Armentières, Cambrai and the Vosges. They delivered by rail to customers throughout France at no charge, provided the purchase was over 25 francs. See Henry Danzer, *Les industries textiles à l'Exposition Universelle de 1889*, Vol. III: p. 234. (This exhibition was the first to include aspects of social work in factories, and Danzer's report gives detailed information on wages, costs of food and housing, noting, for example, that a terraced house ['contigus'] cost 5,600 francs in 1888.)

**5.46** See M. A. Fleury, *Annuaire de L'Union des Syndicats Patronaux des Industries Textiles de France*, Société General d'Impression, Paris, 1910. 3ème Année, pp. 95–105. The silk industry in Lyons remained busy through the lean years of 1908–11, but it did so by dropping

prices to a point where scarcely any profits were made. Not all sections of the trade suffered, however, for the *ASJ* (No. 5, May 1910, p. 23) noted that Richard Frères, which made silk finishing machines (i.e. to print, moiré, etc.) was very busy with orders from the 1,283 silk mills in the United States.

# CHAPTER SIX

**6.01** Sonia Delaunay, introducing *Tapis et Tissus*; Editions d'Art Charles Moreau, Paris, 1929, p. i; 'Chaque époque trouve son expression dans un style. Il est intéressant de distinguer dans une multitude de manifestations contemporaines les mouvements plus ou moins temporaires de ceux qui forment les éléments directeurs et qui créent le style. Ce n'est pas le reflet de la majorité de la production actuelle, au contraire, celui d'une minorité, qui parvient à modeler le goût du grand public.'

**6.02** C. Adolph Glassgold, 'The Modern Note in Decorative Arts', Part II, *The Arts*, Vol. 13, 1928: p. 221.

**6.03** For a fuller discussion of this point, see Mary Schoeser, *Fabrics and Wallpapers: Twentieth Century Design*, Unwin Hyman, London, 1986, pp. 46–55.

**6.04** *ASJ*, Vol. XL, No. 7, July 1921, p. 44; Albert Aftalion, *L'Industrie textile en France pendant la guerre*, Université de France, Paris, and Yale, New Haven, *La Dotation Carnegie pour la paix internationale*, c. 1921, pp. 28, 123.

**6.05** 'European Conditions Affecting The Upholstery Trade', F. Schumacher & Co., No. 4, May 1922.

**6.06** 'Deux Décorateurs Modernes', *The Living Arts*, No. 1, October 1921, pp. 39–40: 'Je comprends qu'il soit malaisé, de nos jours encore, de dégager, parmi le fatras des tendances opposées, parmi les influences diverses, les principes du mouvement décoratif moderne. Un tel chaos, qu'engendre une fantaisie sans apparente discipline n'est pas fait pour attirer les jeunes décorateurs vers un "style" épuré, ni pour susciter en eux le désir de produire des oeuvres saines [ou] logiques. . . .'

**6.07** Sisley Huddleston, *Paris Salons, Cafés, Studios*, J. B. Lippincott Co., Philadelphia and London, 1928, p. 19. The production of fabrics for the interiors of cars, trains and airplanes remained an important source of business for many French upholstery fabric manufacturers.

**6.08** Lord & Taylor catalogue of French furniture, 1928.

**6.09** Gaston Derys, 'Pomone et l'art Moderne', *La Renaissance*, 9, Année No. 1, Jan. 1926, p. 73, quoted from the English text.

**6.10** Office central, Vol. 6, p. 43.

**6.11** Glassgold, *op. cit.*, pp. 225–8.

**6.12** Marcel Valotaire, 'New Textiles from France', *Creative Art*, Vol. 3, No. 6. Dec. 1928, p. 385.

**6.13** U.S. Tariff Commission, Washington, *Textile Imports and Exports 1891–1927*, U.S. Government Printing Office, Washington, 1929, pp. 29, 239 and *passim*.

**6.14** Virginia Robie, 'With the new printed

fabrics', *The Art World*, Sept. 1917, p. 564; this journal absorbed *The Craftsman*.

**6.15** Information on Cheney from David Cohen, J. Paul Getty Museum, and Charles Cheney, *Silk: an industry and an art*, Chicago, 1925, p. 7; Stelhi Silks advertisement, BF 5538; the advertisement, however, refers to 'world famous designers', which suggests that they also used French designs.

**6.16** These were published by his wife from 1928. Examples can be seen in the Bibliothèque Forney, e.g. *Le Journal de la Décoration*, 1927, which includes the work of several designers for both textiles and wallpapers, and *Studio des arts décoratifs*, 1928, 4e série, with motifs by Hennequin-Rêveur.

**6.17** Gaston Derys, 'La Soie Moderne dans la Mode et l'Ameublement', *L'Art Vivant*, Feb. 1932, p. 96; 'tissus si chatoyants, si bien étudiés, avec leurs géométries accortes et précises, louons l'ingéniosité de Jean Beaumont, les recherches de Robert Bonfils, les séduisantes et neuves créations de Brunet-Meunié, les prestigieuses symphonies en gris, laine et soie, les douceurs de plumage et de nacre de Rodier et Georges Hoffmann, et Jean Fressinet, et Séguy, et Garceion, et Lamorinière, et Stéphany, et Maurice Dufrène, et Paul Follot, et Louis Sognot, et Sonia Delaunay, et Deschelmaker, et Desseroit . . . et ces tissus d'une si noble arabesque que compose Michel Dubost'.

**6.18** This was not the whole story; there was a great deal of difference between the addition of artists' designs to a conservative range by, for example, Tootal Broadhurst & Lee Co. Ltd. in 1928 and Allan Walton in the 1930s, for Walton himself was an artist.

**6.19** The Warner Archive, for example, contains designs from this period which were purchased from at least thirty identified French studios (many others did not sign their work, but used monograms or initials only). The Morton archive is now owned by Courtauld Fabric Group, London. Although their woven designs were very progressive, in 1930 Swedish printers still relied almost entirely on foreign designs; see Nils G. Woolin, *Swedish Textiles*, Utställning sförlaget, Almqvist & Wiksells Boktrychkeri A. B., 1930, p. 72.

**6.20** I am grateful to M. Giraud for this and other insights into the work of Parisian design studios.

**6.21** *The French Provincial Spirit in Fabrics for Present-Day Use*, F. Schumacher & Co., advertisement page issued c. 1922. I am indebted to Richard Slavin for a copy of this and other Schumacher advertisements.

**6.22** Florence Brobeck, 'Fabrics for French Provincial Interiors', *Good Furniture & Decoration*, Dec. 1930, pp. 283–8; aside from the textiles *per se*, she also mentions and illustrates painted 'tapestry' panels. Two months earlier the same magazine had an article (pp. 181–8) illustrating twenty-one scenic prints, in which it was noted that the 'reviving interest in the eighteenth century has brought the cottons of Jouy and the other textile centers of France of that period into their proper recognition as authentic works of art.'

**6.23** Office central, *op. cit.*, p. 43.

**6.24** Henri Clouzot, 'Une Oeuvre d'Edgar Brandt à New York', *La Renaissance de l'art Française et des Industries de Luxe*, 9eme Année, No. 1, Jan. 1926, p. 2, quoted from the English text.

**6.25** *Harper's Bazaar*, Sept. 1927, p. 67; for *Vogue* illustrations see, for example, the covers of the Dec. 1922 and Oct. 1928 issues.

**6.26** 'Les Tissus de Georges le Manach', *Mobilier et Décoration*, 13eme Année, 4 April, 1933, p. 150: 'son souvent inspirés – mais très librement – des tissus marocains'.

**6.27** Henri Clouzot, 'Au Musée des Art Décoratifs exposition de la Croisière Noire', *La Renaissance . . .* No. 10, Oct. 1926, p. 572. The expedition was led by Haardt, Audoin and Dubreuil. The quoted section did not appear in the parallel French text.

**6.28** *Harpers' Bazaar*, Aug. 1931, pp. 50–1; this was not a new phenomenon, in the *Gazette du Bon Ton*, (Jan.–Feb. 1920, p. 5) Pierre Mac-orlan, in 'L'ethnographie Source d'Elégance', described hair styles that had been developed by 'some curious spirits having searched among various peoples of Central Africa for elements of the naive yet mannered attitude which we admire in the Bambara statuettes'; 'Quelques esprits curieux ayant recherché chez divers peuples de l'Afrique central les éléments de cette sensibilité à la fois candid et maniérée que l'on admire dans les statuettes du pays Bambara. . . .'

**6.29** Delaunay, p. 2.

**6.30** Department of Fine Arts, Division of Decorative Arts, *Decorative Arts*, Official Catalogue of the Golden Gate International Exposition, 1939.

**6.31** See Cheney Brothers' advertisement in *Harpers' Bazaar*, April 1927, p. 139; Aug. 1926, inside front cover; March 1926, back cover; Feb. 1927, inside front cover. The designs after Brandt came about because he designed the iron work for their new building in New York, constructed in 1925; the fabric was used for automobile interiors. The Cheney-Brandt project was described as a milestone in French-American friendship, 'marking the close relations in industrial arts between the two countries' (see note 24).

**6.32** *American Fabrics*, No. 40, Spring 1957, pp. 27–8.

**6.33** Luc-Benoist, 'Un Atelier Moderne de Décor Textile', *Art et Décoration*, Tome XLVII, Jan.–June 1925, pp. 23–38. Ducharne also had a New York showroom, opened in the early 1920s.

**6.34** *Moniteur des Fils, des Tissus, des Apprèts, de la Teinture . . .* , M. Michel Alcan (ed.), Paris, 5e Année, No. 3, 1 Feb., 1873, p. 71; 'Sans spécifier aucun mode d'application, MM. Bellingard et Giraud se réservent l'utilisation de la photographie à l'ornementation des tissus de toute nature et de toutes dimensions. La photographie a pour avantage de reproduire les oeuvres artistiques avec une grande finesse; de plus les épreuves sur étoffes présenteraient une grande solidité au lavage.'

**6.35** See M.-P. Verneuil, 'Le Pouchoir', *Art et Décoration*, Tome X, July-Dec. 1901, pp. 67–8; Jean Saudé *Traité d'unlu: minure d'art au pochoir*, Aux Editions de l'Ibis, Paris, 1925; and Office central, p. 43.

**6.36** See Warner, in Smith *et al.*, *Report 1925*, pp. 79–80, on paper-strip, wool and artificial silk wallcoverings that did not wear well; André Groult had also developed 'paper straw', which in 1930 he was using on walls and furniture; see Guillaume Jeanneau, 'Whither? the path of fashion at the Salon des Décorateurs', *Creative Art*, Aug. 1930, p. 92.

**6.37** 'Tissus et Tapis de Bénédictus', *Art et Décoration*, Tome XLV, Jan.–June 1924, pp. 97–8.

**6.38** Christian Roupioz, 'Programme de recherches en science humaines, dans la region Rhône-Alpes, conservation du patrimonie', *Restructurations et Crises dans la Soierie lyonnaise 1850–1940*, CHRS Centre Regional de Publication de Lyon, Paris, 1980: pp. 48–9.

**6.39** Prices taken from a series of catalogues from Au Gagne-Petit, Au Printemps and Aux Trois Quartiers, 1927–1935 (the latter 1929–1935); and Syndicat des fabricants de soieries et tissus de Lyon, 'Copie rendu des travaux, année 1938', Lyons, 1939; pp.3–7.

**6.40** Syndicat des fabricants . . . , *op. cit.*, p. 15; 'une paralysie de nos exportations, un accroissement des importations de l'étranger, un ralentissement de notre activité économique, un abaissement des salaires qui ont provoqué inévitablement la réaction survenue en 1936'.

**6.41** *Ibid.*, AGM 18 May, 1943, pp. 11–12: 'Nous nous trouvons dans une économie de naufragés'; 'de garder intacte la force vive de notre industrie. . . .'

**6.42** René Truchot, 'La Soierie Lyonnaise après la Guerre', *Les Études Americaines:*, Cahier XXV, 1951, p. 9.

**6.43** Roger Catin, 'L'Industrie Textile Française et la Marché Américain', *ibid.*, p. 1.

**6.44** Syndicat des fabricants, as note 39.

**6.45** See Jacques Michollin, *Problems of the Textile Industry in Europe*, Organisation for European Economic Co-Operation, Paris, 1957; pp. 33–5.

# CHAPTER SEVEN

**7.01** Patrick Turbot, *L'Entrepreneur Français a la Découverte du Marché des États-Unis*, 1987; p. 206.

**7.02** See Guirec Delanoë, *Étude sur l'évolution de la concentration dans l'industrie du textile en France*, Commission des Communautés Européennes, 1975.

**7.03** Patrick Turbot, *op. cit.*, pp. 206 and 219, citing a 1982 Gallup Poll and statistics provided by the French Embassy.

**7.04** *The Wall Street Journal*, 20 Feb., 1984, survey by Booz, Allen & Hamilton, p. 40.

**7.05** *Maison Française*, 'XIIe Biennale des Éditeurs de la Décoration', supplement, Jan. 1987, p. 13.

**7.06** Jeanneau, 'Whither? . . .' *op. cit.*, p. 91.

# SELECTED MUSEUMS

with collections of French furnishing textiles

**BOSTON**   Museum of Art, Society for the Preservation of New England Antiquities
**BRUSSELS**   Musée Royaux d'Art et d'Histoire
**DENVER**   Art Museum
**DETROIT**   Institute of Art
**CHICAGO**   Art Institute
**CLEVELAND**   Museum of Art
**HARTFORD**   Wadsworth Atheneum

**JOUY**   Musée Oberkampf
**KREFELD**   Deutsches Textilmuseum
**MULHOUSE**   Musée de l'Impression sur Etoffes
**LONDON**   Victoria & Albert Museum
**LOS ANGELES**   County Museum of Art
**LYONS**   Musée Historique des Tissus
**MONTBÉLIARD**   Musée du Chateau
**NANTES**   Musée des Salorges
**NEW YORK**   Cooper-Hewitt Museum, Fashion Institute of Technology, Metropolitan Museum of Art
**ONTARIO**   Royal Ontario Museum
**PARIS**   Archives National, Bibliothèque Forney, Bibliothèque National, Mobilier National, Musée de l'Homme, Musée des Arts Décoratifs
**PHILADELPHIA**   Museum of Art
**PROVIDENCE**   Museum of Art/Rhode Island School of Design
**STRASBOURG**   Musée des Arts Décoratifs
**TOURCOING**   Centre de Documentation des Fils et Tissus
**TOURS**   Musée des Beaux Arts
**VERSAILLES**   Musée National du Château
**WASHINGTON D.C.**   National Museum of History & Technology
**WINTERTHUR**   Henry Francis Dupont Museum

# PICTURE CREDITS

# SELECTED READING

*(see also footnotes)*

Achard, *Notice sur la création, les développements et la décadence des manufactures de soie a Avignon*, Apt, 1874.

Albrecht-Mathey, Elisabeth, *The Fabrics of Mulhouse and Alsace: 1750–1850*, F. Lewis, Leigh-on-Sea, 1968.

Allemagne, Henry René d', *La Toile imprimée et les Indiennes de traite*, Gründ, Paris, 2 vols., 1942.

Ariès, Philippe, *Histoire de la vie privée*, vol. 4: 'De la Révolution a la Grande Guerre', Georges Duby dir. Seuil, Paris, 1955 and 1987.

Audin, Marius and Vial, Eugène, *Dictionnaire des artistes et ouvriers d'art du Lyonnais*, Bibliothèque d'Art et d'Archéologie, Paris, 1918–19.

Baschet, Roger, *Rideaux et tentures . . . depuis le moyen age*, Baschet et Cie, Paris, n.d.

Bergeron, Louis, *Banquiers, négociants et manufacturiers parisiens du Directoire à l'Empire*, Paris, 1978.

Bertholon, Abbé, *Du commerce et des manufactures de la ville de Lyon*, Montpellier, 1789.

Bezon, M., *Dictionnaire général des tissus anciens et modernes* Th. Lepagnez, Lyons, 1856–7.

Bimont, M., *Principes de l'art du Tapissier: Ouvrage Utile aux Gens de la Profession & à ceux qui les emploient*, Lottin l'aîné, Paris, 1770.

Brandt, André, 'Apports anglais à l'industrialisation de l'Alsace au début du XIXe siècle', *Bulletin de la Société Industrielle de Mulhouse*, No. 1, 1967.

Brédif, Josette, 'Relations commerciales entre la manufacture Oberkampf de Jouy-en-Josas et la Provence', *CIETA Bulletin* 65, 1987.

Brédif, Josette, *Toiles de Jouy*, Editions Adam Biro, Paris, and Thames & Hudson, London, 1989.

Carlano, Marianne and Salmon, Larry (eds.), *French Textiles From the Middle Ages through the Second Empire*, Wadsworth Atheneum, Hartford, Connecticut, 1985.

Caron, François, *An Economic History of Modern France*, Methuen, London, 1979.

Centre Georges Pompidou, *Design Français 1960–1990*, A.P.C.I., Paris, 1988.

Chassagne, Serge, *La Manufacture de toiles imprimées de Tournemine les Angers 1752–1820*, Klinsksieck, Paris, 1971.

Chassagne, Serge, *Oberkampf: Un Entrepreneur capitaliste au siècle de lumières*, Aubin-Montaigne, Paris, 1980.

Chaubaud, Louis, *Marseille et ses industries, les tissus, la filature et la teinturerie*, Marseilles, 1883.

Chobaut, Hyacinthe, 'L'Industrie des indiennes à Avignon et à Orange (1677–1884)', *Mémoires de l'Academie du Vaucluse*, 1938.

Chobaut, Hyacinthe, *L'Industrie des indiennes a Marseilles avant 1680*, Institut Historique de Provence, Mémoire XVI, 1939.

CIETA, *Vocabulaire des termes techniques*, Lyons, n.d.

Clouzot, Henri, *Historie de la manufacture de Jouy et de la toile imprimée en France*, C. Van Oest, Paris and Brussels, 1928.

Clouzot, Henri, *La Toile peinte en France: La Manufacture de Jouy*, Versailles, 1912–14.

Clouzot, Henri and Morris, Francis, *Painted and Printed Fabrics: The History of the Manufactory at Jouy and Other Ateliers in France (1760–1815)*, Metropolitan Museum of Art, New York, 1927.

Colbert, Jean Baptiste, *Règlemens et statuts généraux pour les longeurs, largeurs, qualitez et teintures des draps, serges, et autres étoffes de laine et de fil . . .*, Paris, 1669.

Colbert, Jean Baptiste, *Instruction générale donnée aux commis envoyez dans toutes les provinces du royaume pour l'exécution des règlements généraux des manufactures et teintures . . . 1664*, Paris, 1670.

Corvisier, André, *Arts et sociétées dans l'Europe du XVIIIe siècle*, Presses Universitaires France, 1978.

Conseil de l'Europe, *Art sur soie: Bianchini-Férier, cent ans de création textile*, Paris, 1989.

Coural, Jean, Gastinel-Coural, Chantal, and Muntz de Raissac, Muriel, *Inventaire des collections publiques françaises: Paris, Mobilier National, Soieries Empire*, Réunion des Musées Nationaux, Paris, 1980.

Coural, Jean and Gastinel-Coural, Chantal, *Soieries de Lyon: commandes royales au XVIIIe s. (1730–1800)*, Musée Historique des Tissus, Lyons, 1988.

Cox, Raymond, *Musée rétrospectif de la classe 83. Soie et tissus de soie a l'exposition universelle internationale de 1900*, Belin Frères, St Cloud, 1900.

Dardel, Pierre, *Les Manufactures de toiles peintes et de serges imprimées à Rouen et à Bolbec aux XVIIéme et XVIIIème siècles*, Desvages, Rouen, 1940.

Dauphin, V., 'Les Manufactures de toile peintes en Anjour (1750–1840)', *Mémoire de la Société d'Agriculture, Sciences et Arts d'Angers*, 1923.

Deitlin, Evelyne, 'Une Fabrique de toiles imprimées en Aquitaine à Beautiran (1802–1832)', *Bulletin et Mémoires de la Société Archéologie de Bordeaux*, 1980.

Delanoe, Guirec, *Etude sur l'évolution de la concentration dans l'industrie du textile en France*, Commission des Communautes Européennes, November 1975.

Delaunay, Sonia, *Tapis et Tissus*, Editions d'Art Charles Moreau, Paris, 1929.

Delormois, *L'Art de faire l'indiennage a l'instar d'Angleterre et de composer toutes les couleurs bon teint propres à l'indienne*, Jombert, Paris, 1770.

Diderot, Denis and Alembert, Jean d', *Encyclopédie, ou dictionnaire raisonné des sciences, des arts et des métiers . . .*, Braisson, David, Le Breton, Durand, Paris, 1751–1777.

Dornsife, Samuel, 'Design Sources for Nineteenth-Century Window Hangings', *Winterthur Portfolio 10*, University Press of Virginia, Charlottesville, 1975.

Dreyfus, Michel, *Les sources de l'histoire ouvrière, sociale et industrielle en France au XIXe siècle*, Guide documentaire, Les Editions ouvrières, Paris, 1987.

Duhamel du Monceau, Henri Louis, 'L'Art de la draperie, principalement pour ce qui regarde les draps fins', H. L. Guerin & L. F. Delatour, Paris, 1765.

Duhamel du Monceau, Henri Louis, *Art de friser ou rationner les étoffes de laine*, L. F. Delatour, Paris, 1766.

Falcot, P., *Traité encyclopédique et méthodique de la fabrication des tissus . . .*, Bureau de la Publication, Elbeuf, 1844.

Fanelli, Giovanni and Rosalia, *Disegno moda architettura*, Vallecchi, Florence, 1976.

Feray, Jean, *Architecture Intérieure et Décoration en France: des origines à 1875*, Berger-Levrault, Paris, 1988.

Fohlen, Claude, *L'Industrie textile au temps du Second Empire*, Plon, Paris, 1956.

Garsonnin, Docteur, 'La Manufacture de toiles peintes d'Orléans', *Mémoires et Documents pour Servir a l'Histoire du Commerce et de l'Industrie en France*, 1913.

Gervers, Veronika (ed.), *Studies in Textile History in Memory of Harold B. Burnham*, Royal Ontario Museum, Toronto, 1977.

Gilonne, Georges, Bret, L., and Nicout, J., *Dictionnaire practique des tissus*, Bosc Frères & Riou, Paris, 1930.

Hafter, Daryl M., 'Philippe de Lasalle: from Mise-en-carte to Industrial Design', *Winterthur Portfolio 12*, University Press of Virginia, 1977.

Hardouin-Fugier, Elisabeth and Grafe, Etienne, *The Lyon School of Flower Painters*, F. Lewis, Leigh-on-Sea, 1978.

Havard, Henri, *Dictionnaire de l'ameublement et de la décoration depuis le XIIIe siècle jusqu'à nos jours*, Maison Quantin, Paris, 1887–90.

Havard, Henri, *L'Art dans la maison*, Edouard Rouveyre, Paris, 6th. ed., 1887.

Havard, Henri, *L'Arts de l'ameublement: les styles*, Charles Delagrave, Paris, 1897.

Henry, N. L. A., *Les merveilles de l'Exposition*, Plon, Lyons, 1891.

*Histoire documentaire de l'industrie de Mulhouse et de ses environs au XIXème siècle*, Société Industrielle Mulhouse, 1902.

Heutte, René, *Les Etoffes d'ameublement*, H. Vial, Paris, 1980.

*Impression sur étoffes XVIIéme-XVIIIème-XIXème: Prestiges, curiosités, anecdotes*, Banque de Paris et des Pays-Bas, Strasbourg, 1974.

Jacqué, Jacqueline and Sano, Takahiko, *Chefs-d'oeuvre du Musée de l'Impression sur*

*Etoffes de Mulhouse*, Gakken, Tokyo, 3 vols., 1978.

Japan Design Museum, *Etoffes imprimées françaises: Musée de l'Impression sur Etoffes*, Kyoto, 1981.

Joubert de l'Hiberderie, Nicolas, *Le Dessinateur pour les fabriques d'étoffes d'or, d'argent et de soie*, S. Jorry, Paris, 1765.

La Combe, François, *Observations sur Londre [sic] et ses environs, avec un précis de la constitution de l'Angleterre, et de sa decadence; par un atheronome de Berne*, La Combe, Paris, 1777.

Labouchère, Alfred, *Oberkampf (1738–1815)*, Hachette, Paris, 1866.

Le Bourhis, Katell (ed.), *The Age of Napoleon*, Abrams, New York, 1990.

*Le Centenaire de la Société Industrielle: son activité et ses créations 1826–1926*, Société Industrielle Mulhouse, 2 vols., Paris, 1926.

Lehmann, Colette, *Mobilier de Louis Philippe à Napoléon III*, Massin, Paris, 1983.

Le Normand, Louis Sébastien, *Nouveau Manuel complet du fabricant d'étoffes imprimées et du fabricant de papiers peints*, Roret, Paris, 1830.

Leprade, M. D. de, *French Textiles*, F. Lewis, Leigh-on-Sea, 1955.

*Lyon, Musée Historique des Tissus*, Graphic-sha Publishing Co. Ltd, Tokyo, Japan, 1985.

Mésangère, Pierre de la, *Meubles et objets de goût*, Paris, 1805–35.

Michel, Francisque, *Recherches sur la commerce, la fabrication et l'usage des étoffes de soie, d'or et d'argent*, Crapelet, Paris, 2 vols., 1852–54.

Ministère de la Culture, *La Manufacture du Dijonval et la draperie Sedanaise: 1650–1850*, Cahiers de l'inventaire 2, Inventaire Général des Monuments et des Richesses Artistiques de la France, Région des Monuments et des Richesses Artistiques de la France, Région de Champagne-Ardennes, 1984.

Montgomery, Florence, *Textiles in America, 1650–1870*, W. W. Norton & Co., New York, 1984.

Morin, Louis, *Recherches sur l'impression des toiles dites indiennes à Troyes (1766–1828)*, Troyes, 1913.

Musée de l'Impression sur Etoffes, *Toiles de Nantes des XVIIIème siècles*, Mulhouse, 1977.

Musée des Arts Décoratifs, *Des Dorelotiers aux passementiers*, Union Centrale des Arts Décoratifs, Paris, 1973.

Musée des Arts Décoratifs, *Cinquantenaire de l'exposition de 1925*, Paris, 1976.

Musée du Louvre, *Dessins français de 1750 à 1825: Le Néo-classicisme*, Paris, 1972.

Musée Historique des Tissus, *Le décor textile de la Salle du Trône des Tuileries 1818–1848*, Lyons, 1987.

Musée Historique des Tissus, *Les folles années de la soie – François Ducharne . . . avec la collaboration pour les dessins de Michel Dubost*, Sézanne, Lyons, 1975.

Musée Oberkampf, *Les Indiennes de la manufacture Oberkampf de Jouy-en-Josas*, Jouy-en-Josas, 1982.

Office central d'éditions et de librairie, *Encyclopédie des arts décoratifs et industriels modernes au XXème siècle*, Impr. National, Paris, 6 vols., 1926.

Pariset, Ernest, *Histoire de la fabrique lyonnaise*, A. Rey, Lyons, 1901.

Paulet, J., *L'Art du fabrique d'étoffes de soie*, L. F. Delatour, Paris, 1773–78.

Penot, Achille, *Statistiques générales du Haut Rhine*, Mulhouse, 1831.

Percier, Charles and Fontaine, Pierre, *Recueil des décorations intérieures comprenant tout ce qui à rapport à l'ameublement*, Paris, 1812.

Perez-Tibi, Dora, *Raoul Dufy*, Flammarion, Paris, 1989.

Persoz, Jean François, *Traité théorique et pratique de l'impression des tissus*, Victor Masson, Paris, 4 vols., 1846.

Peuchet, Jacques, *Dictionnaire universel de la géographie commercante . . .*, Blanchon, Paris, 1799–1800.

Peuchet, Jacques, *Vocabulaire des termes de commerce, banque, manufactures, navigation marchande, finance mercantile et statistique*, Testu, Paris, 1801.

Pitoiset, Gilles, *Toiles imprimées XVIIIème-XIXème siècles*, Société des Amis de la Bibliothèque Forney, Paris, 1982.

Poidebard, Alexandre and Chatel, Jacques, *Camille Pernon, fabricant de soieries à Lyon sous Louis XVI et Napoléon I*, L. Brun, Lyons, 1912.

Pommier, Henriette, *Inventaires de Archives textiles des maisons de soieries lyonnaise*, Centre National de la Recherce Scientifique, Paris, 1983.

Praz, Mario, *Psychologie et evolution de la décoration intérieure*, Tisné, Paris, 1964 (English edition, *An Illustrated History of Interior Decoration*, Thames & Hudson, London, 1987).

Raimon, Albert, *Exposition franco-britannique de 1908. Rapport du jury*, H. Bouillant, St Denis, 1909.

Ranson, Pierre, *Cahiers d'ameublement*, Campion Frères, Paris, 1773 and 1778.

Renouard, Alfred, *La Bibliographie Textile Française de 1820 à 1920*, Bosc Frères & Riou, Paris, 1924.

Reyniès, Nicole de (ed.), *Le Mobilier domestique*, Inventaire général, Ministère de la Culture, Paris, 1987.

Rodier, Paul, *The Romance of French Weaving*, Tudor Publishing Co., New York, new edition 1936 (first published 1931).

Roland de la Platière, Jean Marie, *L'Art du fabricant de velours de coton . . .* ; *L'Art de préparer et d'imprimer les étoffes en laines . . .* ; and *L'Art du fabricant d'étoffes en laines rases et sèches, unies, et croisées*, all Moutard, Paris, 1780.

Rothstein, Natalie, *Eighteenth Century Silk Designs*, Thames & Hudson, London, 1990.

Roubo, Jacques André, *L'art du Menuisier-Carrossier*, Saillant et Nyon, Paris, 3 vols., 1771.

Roy, Bernard, *Une Capitale de l'indiennage: Nantes*, Musée des Salorges, Nantes, 1948.

Rupied, *L'Art d'imprimer les Toiles en Alsace*, 1786 (MISE and AN Paris).

Rÿhiner, Jean, *Traité sur la fabrication et le commerce des toiles peintes*, 1766 (MISE).

Savary des Bruslons, Jacques, *Dictionnaire universel de commerce*, C. & A. Philbert, Copenhagen, 5 vols., 6th ed., 1756–66.

Schmitt, Jean Marie, 'Les relations entre l'Angleterre et l'industrie textile de Mulhouse au XIXe siècle: esquisse d'une mise au point', *Innovations et renouveaux techniques de l'antiquité à nos jours*, Association Interuniversitaire de l'Est, Tome XXIV.

Schmitter, M. T. and Focillon, Henri, *Exposition de soieries modernes d'ameublement*, Imprimerie Nouvelle Lyonnaise, Lyons, 1934.

Schoeser, Mary, 'The Barbier Manuscripts', *Textile History*, The Pasold Research Fund, Bath, Vol. 12, 1981.

Schoeser, Mary and Rufey, Celia, *English and American Textiles from 1790 to the present*, Thames & Hudson, London and New York, 1989.

Schwartz, Paul R. and Micheaux, R., *A Century of French Fabrics: 1850–1950*, F. Lewis, Leigh-on-Sea, 1964.

Smith, H. Llewellyn, et al. (eds.), *Reports on the Present Position and Tendencies of the Industrial Arts as indicated at the International Exhibition of Modern Decorative and Industrial Arts, Paris, 1925*, Department of Overseas Trade, London, c.1926.

Thillaye, L. J. S., *Manuel du fabricant d'indiennes*, de Fain, Paris, 1833.

Thornton, Peter, *Authentic Decor*, Weidenfeld & Nicolson, 1984.

Thornton, Peter, *Baroque and Rococo Silks*, Faber & Faber, London, 1965.

Tuchscherer, Jean Michel, *The Fabrics of Mulhouse and Alsace (1801–1850)*, F. Lewis, Leigh-on-Sea, 1972.

Tuchscherer, Jean Michel, Vial, Gabriel, Devoti, Donat, and Bernus-Taylor, Marthe, *Etoffes merveilleuses du Musée Historique des Tissus de Lyon*, Gakken, Tokyo, 3 vols., 1976.

Vaschalde, Jean, *Les Industries de la soierie*, Presses Universitaires de France, Paris, 'Que Sais-je?' series no. 975, 1961.

Verlet, Pierre, *Le Mobilier Royal Français*, Picard, Paris, 1990.

Young, Arthur, *Travels in France during the Years 1787, 1788, 1789*, Jeffry Kaplow (ed.), Anchor Books, Garden City, New York, 1969 (first published by W. Richardson, London, 1794).

Young, Edward, *Labour in Europe and America*, S. A. George & Co., Philadelphia, 1875.

# INDEX